ADVANCE PRAISE FOR
PRESSURED PARENTS, STRESSED-OUT KIDS

"*Pressured Parents, Stressed-Out Kids* is a useful guide for mothers and fathers who want to help their child succeed in school and on the playing field without driving themselves—or their youngster—crazy. The authors' advice is grounded in solid science and well worth heeding."

—Laurence Steinberg, Professor of Psychology, Temple University, and author of *The Ten Basic Principles of Good Parenting*

"*Pressured Parents, Stressed-Out Kids* can help you understand why society and our own natural instincts lead us to push our kids too hard, how we can deal with the competition we and our children face, and how we can ensure our kids are successful by giving them guidance rather than pressure. As mothers themselves, Wendy and Kathy understand all too well how we feel, and they combine that empathy with expert advice to make this an essential book for all parents raising kids in today's high-stress society.... There's no doubt the authors know what they're talking about, and with their help we'll all be raising successful and happy kids in no time."

—Stacy DeBroff, founder of MomCentral.com

"The pressure to succeed in an increasingly competitive society is taking a serious toll on the mental health of the nation's youth. Grolnick and Seal give realistic, research-based suggestions for helping your child negotiate this pressure and thrive."

—Deborah Stipek, Dean, Stanford School of Education

PRESSURED PARENTS, STRESSED-OUT KIDS

PRESSURED PARENTS, STRESSED-OUT KIDS

DEALING
WITH
COMPETITION
WHILE
RAISING A
SUCCESSFUL
CHILD

WENDY S. GROLNICK, PhD,
AND KATHY SEAL

Prometheus Books

59 John Glenn Drive
Amherst, New York 14228–2119

Note on Interviewees and Composites

All the stories and voices of families in this book are derived from our own experiences, from the research of Wendy Grolnick and her colleagues, and from interviews. To ensure the privacy of the parents and children interviewed and studied, and to protect their anonymity while staying faithful to their stories, their names as well as places and other details have been changed.

In several instances, the stories we tell and the characters in them are composites, derived from the experiences of more than one person. In the few instances when a parent or child is also a public figure, has given permission to use his or her name, or when that name is taken from a published work, we have used his or her real name. Beyond these instances, any similarity between the names and stories of people described in this book and those of individuals known to readers is inadvertent and purely coincidental.

Published 2008 by Prometheus Books

Inquiries should be addressed to
Prometheus Books
59 John Glenn Drive
Amherst, New York 14228–2119
VOICE: 716–691–0133, ext. 210
FAX: 716–691–0137
WWW.PROMETHEUSBOOKS.COM

12 11 10 09 08   5 4 3 2 1

Library of Congress Cataloging-in-Publication Data

Grolnick, Wendy S.
    Pressured parents, stressed-out kids : dealing with competition while raising a successful child / by Wendy S. Grolnick and Kathy Seal.
        p. cm.
    Includes bibliographical references and index.
    ISBN 978–1–59102–566–5
    1. Parenting—Handbooks, manuals, etc. 2. Parent and child—Handbooks, manuals, etc. I. Seal, Kathy. II. Titles.

HQ755.8.G752 2008
649'.1—dc22

2007051789

Printed in the United States of America on acid-free paper

CONTENTS

Authors' Note   7

Wendy's Preface   9

Kathy's Preface   17

Wendy's Acknowledgments   21

Kathy's Acknowledgments   23

Chapter 1. Parent Panic: It Takes You by Surprise   25

Chapter 2. Why Now? "Our Kids Are Competing All the Time"   41

Chapter 3. It's an Animal Thing:
            When Our Hardwiring Goes Haywire   71

Chapter 4. The Big Takeover: How Our Feelings Pull Us to Push   91

Chapter 5. Beyond the Carrot and the Stick:
            Fanning the Flames of Your Child's Inner Passion   107

Chapter 6. R_x for Intrinsic Motivation:
             Encouraging Your Child's Autonomy   129

Chapter 7.   The How-to of Autonomy   149

Chapter 8.   Stand by Me: Maximizing Your Involvement   175

Chapter 9.   "What Do You Expect?" Channeling Anxiety into Rules,
             Guidelines, and Information   203

Chapter 10. Calming Down: "That All Sounds Very Nice,
             But How Can I Use These Techniques
             When I'm Feeling So *Anxious*?"   219

             Endnotes   245

             Bibliography   265

             Index   275

AUTHORS' NOTE

To simplify our narrative, we have merged our children—Wendy's daughters, Allison and Rebecca, and Kathy's sons, Zach and Jeff—into one literary family. The "I" of the narrative is at times Wendy, the researcher and mother, and at other times Kathy, the writer and mother. We hope you'll find our combined voice a clear one.

When Wendy discusses her research, the "we" refers to her and her colleagues, most often the research team in her laboratory at Clark University.

WENDY'S PREFACE

Until I was twenty-three, I didn't wear glasses. Then suddenly my eyesight plunged from 20/20 to 20/200.

"You're not doing your eyes any favor," said my ophthalmologist when he learned that I was spending my first summer as a graduate student in a dark, narrow room, straining to watch grainy black-and-white videos of moms and their one-year-olds playing with toys. It was 1982, and video technology was almost as new as the babies. So for eight hours a day I stared at fuzzy, jumpy images, a stopwatch in one hand and a clicker in the other, running the tape forward and back. As I watched the mothers helping their babies work cobbler's benches and shape sorters, one question burned in my mind: how did mothers' different ways of helping affect their babies? Which worked better—guiding the kids with hints and nods, or jumping in full throttle, showing them exactly what to do?

This question was only one example of my fascination with parent-child interaction, which had begun when I studied infants' perception in Eleanor "Jackie" Gibson's lab at Cornell. Gibson—eventually one of only ten psychologists to win the National Medal of Science, and in those days one of the very few female university professors—had shown that even newborns are learning to distinguish among people, objects, and events in their surroundings. That corrected the idea of psychologist William James, who had said that infants see the world as a "blooming, buzzing confusion." Gibson had begun to question James's notion one summer when she and her husband, also a psychologist, visited the Grand Canyon with their two-year-old daughter. The Gibsons found themselves wondering whether she would see the drop-off and know to stop at the edge. Of course they didn't test their hypothesis right then and there, but later, back in her lab, Jackie Gibson designed the now-classic "visual cliff" experiment. To test the depth perception of babies, she put six- to fourteen-month-olds on a tabletop extended by a piece of Plexiglas and asked the mothers to coax them to crawl out on the clear plastic. Would the babies try to avoid the apparent danger of falling off? They did. Gibson found that crawling babies already perceive depth.[1] (Newborn kittens, day-old goats, and newly hatched chicks do, too.) Eventually Gibson showed that a great deal of human perception is inborn.

At Cornell I was also fascinated by new methods that enabled researchers to plumb the thinking of babies who couldn't yet talk. One of these methods was the "habituation paradigm." You used it to find out whether infants could tell the difference between two phenomena—say, between one video of a red ball moving toward them and another of the same ball moving away from them. You showed the first video repeatedly until the babies got bored and looked away. Then you'd show the second. If their attention perked up, that meant they noticed the difference between the two videos.

I used this method for my senior honors thesis. Under the supervision of then graduate student Arlene Walker-Andrews, I decided to figure out at what age children could distinguish emotions in others. I asked mothers to hold their two-month-olds on their laps while I showed their infants a slide of a neutral face on a screen and played audiotapes of a woman talking in a happy or sad tone. The woman on the video would say, "I'm really glad—I'm going to have a great day!" or "I'm so sad—I'm having such a hard time!"

I played the happy tape over and over, turning it off briefly each time the baby glanced away from the picture. The more familiar the infant became with the happy voice, the quicker she looked away. When the time of this gazing episode had dropped to half of the initial time, indicating familiarity, I played the sad tape. If the looking time jumped back up—as indeed it did for most of the babies—that showed they recognized the difference between the happy and sad tapes.[2]

This work fascinated me. But I soon realized that how the mothers and their children *related to each other* during the experiment fascinated me even more. Some mothers, apparently nervous, acted very protective. The minute their babies cried, they wanted to stop the experiment. (We did.) Others seemed much more at ease and casually tried to calm their babies when they fussed. The infants acted differently, too—some initially focused on the slides for a very long time, while others gave them a quick glance. Some got very excited when we showed them a new slide, while others stayed calm. Some babies wanted to stay closer to their moms than others did.

I'd reacted similarly to other researchers' findings about mothers and children. For example, in the visual cliff studies, what struck me most was that the babies were more likely to crawl out over the Plexiglas when their mothers said, "Go ahead, honey." Even at twelve months, they looked up to their moms for an opinion.[3]

Furthermore, since many of the same babies—children of students and professors and university employees—kept coming back to our lab for different experiments, I started to see how the kids changed as they grew. How did the different ways their mothers related to them, I wondered, affect their babies' emerging personalities? As I applied to graduate school, I realized that I wanted to study mother-baby relationships and infant development.

So off I went to the University of Rochester to work with Ann Frodi, who researched parent-child attachment. I liked attachment theory because it asserted that we're born with a basic need to connect to others. Parents don't have to learn how to love children, and vice versa. This idea similarly excited many psychologists and psychotherapists, especially because it meshed with their experience as parents. Mothers felt love flowing in with their milk, and fathers fell in love with their children at birth too. Yet attachment theory felt almost revolutionary to psychologists because it went beyond Freud, who had said that parent-child love developed over time. It also felt far more accurate than the behaviorist notion that, just as Pavlov conditioned his dogs to push levers for food, mothers condition children to love by "rewarding" them with milk.

No sooner did I arrive at the University of Rochester, however, than I met a group of psychologists whose ideas about motivation entranced me. Ed Deci and Rich Ryan chafed, as I did, at the behaviorists' narrow focus on rewards and punishments. They were developing a deeper explanation of why people do what they do; specifically, they were exploring intrinsic motivation: the energy that propels people to pursue activities purely for their own satisfaction and pleasure. Some of their counterintuitive findings particularly intrigued me. For example, Deci had found that if you pay undergraduates to play with enjoyable puzzles, they'll stop playing when you stop giving them money. But students who don't receive pay will keep on playing those same puzzles.[4] In other words, rewards are a form of control that can spoil your inner passion.

I also liked their belief that autonomy is both a basic human need and a prerequisite for intrinsic motivation. People are happiest and perform best, they said, when they feel that what they do comes from them. That struck a chord with me. I had always resisted control by my parents or teachers and enjoyed pursuing my own interests so much more than studying or doing what I *had* to do. I'd enjoyed college, where I chose my own courses, much more than high school, where I'd had to take the prescribed curriculum. Similarly, I found baking cookies at home a lot more fun than making baking powder biscuits at school to pass a home economics test.

While Deci and Ryan were studying intrinsic motivation among adults, I wanted to apply this theory to parents and children. I was curious about why some kids, when asked to take tennis lessons or a course at the science museum, shout, "Yes! I want to do that!" and others insist, "No way. I'm not going!" We all want our children to succeed in school and in life, but how, I wondered, do moms and dads affect a child's desire to learn?

That's the question that put me in front of those eye-damaging videos in the summer of 1982, trying to figure out how the mothers' different ways of helping affected their one-year-olds. My experiment took hours of coding, discussions, statistical analysis, and even some despair, but the results were definitive. Some moms had helped their babies only when they needed it—perhaps holding a toy still so they could play with it. Later, when these babies were left alone, they kept trying to work the new toys. But the kids whose moms had controlled their every move reacted very differently when left alone: they halfheartedly tried to work the toys and then gave up.[5] The correlation was clear, the differences striking. The more moms encouraged their babies' autonomy, the more motivated their kids felt to figure out the toys themselves. My two decades of studies on how parents can help kids learn and thrive had begun.

But a crucial twist in this theory was yet to come. It began with strong feelings I had during this initial experiment, which of course never entered into the study results. Still, I remember them sharply. Whenever I saw a mother grab her child's hand and put it on the toy, or even tell the child, "Do it like this" as she worked the toy for him, I felt very uneasy. "I'd *never* do that to my child!" I exclaimed to myself, although I wouldn't have children for many years.

Then I had my own children.

Allison was born in 1990 and Rebecca in 1992. Suddenly the parenting shoe was on the other foot. Real life assaulted academic theory. I saw myself doing what I swore I would never do: tying their shoes for them in a time crunch, saying too often, "Because I said so, that's why!"

I took control when I felt especially rushed. One day when Allison was three, for example, she wouldn't get dressed. My husband, Jay, and I had to leave for work and take her to daycare. But our daughter sat on her bedroom floor in her pajamas, hugging her stuffed panda bear, a stubborn expression on her face. I was beside myself. I felt like yanking her pajamas off and dressing her, even if she screamed bloody murder the entire time. A grown-up and a psychologist to boot, I couldn't believe I was yelling at my three-year-old. I hated this screaming and, for a moment, I hated myself for screaming.

Finally we let Allison put her clothes on over her pajamas, but I drove to work so angry that I was still shaking. We all lose our tempers and yell at our children from time to time, but I've always felt bad afterward and often apologized to them. As time went on, I wondered why I did it and if there was a way to stop or at least minimize both this irritation and my controlling behavior.

That wasn't all. As my daughters grew a bit older, I noticed that every now and then I felt an urge to take over—an impulse unrelated to the stresses of daily life. When Allison started school, I sometimes wanted to "fix" her homework before she handed it in, so that the teacher would think she was smart. Later, I wanted to insist that the girls not drop piano lessons, even though neither enjoyed playing the least bit, and getting them to practice was always a battle.

"*Wow*, is that *me*?" I thought as I saw myself wanting to violate their autonomy. Even if I didn't act on these impulses, it intrigued me that I *wanted* to.

That was not the last surprise. Soon I realized I had strong competitive feelings. At first it seemed like simple pride in my progeny. When Rebecca started walking at eight and a half months, I wanted to shout it to the world, even though I knew very well that it correlated with nothing whatsoever. "That's disgusting, wanting to brag like that," I scolded myself, struggling to rein in my smugness.

But that same struggle kept popping up. As time went on, I realized that I wanted my daughters to shine in many ways. When Allison started preschool, I found myself schmoozing with the other moms, trying to vault her into play date popularity and help her snare party invitations. "Why don't you put on the pink dress?" I'd plead with Rebecca before a birthday party, even though I knew she wanted to wear jeans. ("Why do I care so much about how she looks?" I'd ask myself—I who had vowed never to pressure my kids!)

My girls are teenagers now, and even though I've been studying this question for two decades, my pushy and competitive impulses still crop up now and then. For example, one of my daughters plays tennis competitively and the other plays varsity field hockey and lacrosse. I find myself looking at their rankings and team standings—not exactly obsessively, but more often than they do.

I know my closest friends feel competitive and want their kids to shine, too. When my friend Beth's daughter, who had taken ballet for six years, wanted to quit dancing so she could play team sports with her friends, Beth was distraught. "Jennifer loves being in the limelight at dance recitals!" she explained to me. "She always gets a solo—she's the best dancer in her class." After a great deal of discussion, Jennifer went out for soccer and softball. With her determined work ethic, she soon excelled in both sports. Beth bit her lip every time she felt herself about to ask Jennifer if she wanted to go back to ballet. (You'll read the end of this story in chapter 6.)

Noticing my own competitive feelings and those of my friends reminded me of a revealing sidelight to my early study of the babies and their moms. Even though I hadn't tested or rated the babies in any way, almost every mother asked me a version of this question: "How did my child do?" In fact, parents pose that question whenever they come into our Child and Family Development Laboratory at Clark University or when I meet them during field studies. Regardless of the topic—whether their children are writing poems, solving puzzles, or solving a hypothetical social dilemma—parents are very curious about how their children measure up. (No wonder *all* the children in Lake Wobegon are above average.)

Realizing that the overwhelming majority of parents share my anxious feelings and competitive thoughts, I have to conclude that parents who want to push and control their kids to excel aren't by definition "bad" people. In fact, they almost always have good intentions. They want the very best for their kids, and they don't want them to miss a single opportunity. Pushy impulses aren't the exclusive province of narcissistic status seekers, insensitive social climbers, stage mothers (or fathers), or even insecure human beings living vicariously through their children. They are, quite simply, normal and universal.

But when I arrived at Rochester to start my graduate work, nothing in the psychological literature addressed this question. Mother-blaming was still in vogue; psychologists tended to see mothers as the cause of children's problems. Anxiety about children's competitive status, if addressed at all, was considered part of mothers' smothering or overbearing behavior. There was little if any research about fathers. Angst about one's children was a cause for alarm, a problem to be treated, because it was assumed that "nice" parents didn't have such feelings. Psychologists and psychiatrists often chastised mothers for living through their children. Not long after my arrival, Alice Miller's book *The Drama of the Gifted Child* came out, targeting narcissistic mothers.[6] Miller described the damage done by extremely narcissistic parents who push or control their children, but she didn't address the feelings of worry and competition that are so common among *normal* parents. I kept in the back of my head that I might one day look into those feelings.

After graduate school I was thrilled to begin teaching at Clark, whose founding president, G. Stanley Hall, established the American Psychological Association and was the first psychologist to identify adolescence as a stage of human development.

Once I started at Clark, I realized this anxiety-pressure-control pattern operated when I taught too. Sometimes, if my students did poorly, I felt bad about myself and my teaching, and I felt good about myself if they did well. Those feelings, I realized, could make me pressure them. That insight increased my determination to research the anxiety that urges us to push our children. Where does it come from? How does this control affect children? And if this pressuring doesn't work, what should parents or teachers do instead?

I launched a research program, bringing kids and their parents into the lab at Clark to watch them work together, noticing especially their behavioral changes when I put them under competitive pressure. I also began field studies outside of the laboratory, looking there, too, for the differences between kids who were pressured by their parents and those who weren't.

The research I conducted over the next two decades has been so helpful in raising my own children—it explained so much of what we were going through together—that I want to share it with everyone.

The book you're about to read explains the source of the urge to pressure our kids. It shows how our evolutionary hardwiring and the escalating competition in our world conspire to make parents anxious. This anxiety in turn threatens to prevent us from being the parents we want to be. I will show you how to calm this anxiety, so you can avoid controlling and pushing your child. You'll learn how to turn your worry and fear into positive parenting. No longer will you have to choose between "hands on" and "hands off," between commanding and letting go. Instead you'll find out how to promote your child's motivation from within, energizing him to achieve and excel. You'll learn how to stay close to your child while nurturing her autonomy and to avoid conflict while promoting her growth into a competent adult.

KATHY'S PREFACE

My grandparents immigrated to Philadelphia from Russia, Lithuania, and Hungary, and when I was growing up my family still treasured learning in an Eastern European way. In our basement den, bookshelves ran floor to ceiling, filled with my father's medical school texts and my mother's collection of Tolstoy, Dumas, and Iris Murdoch novels. My parents filled our house with magazines and newspapers, gave us music lessons, and took us to the theater. Every summer we went to the Jersey shore where we swam, visited the Bookmobile, and played all day long. My parents did all they could to give us opportunities to discover who we were and what we loved.

Along with my parents' respect for learning came an unspoken expectation that we would excel. The Old World tradition of reverence for the scholar mixed with the insecurity of our immigrant past produced a striving not only to belong but also to be the best. Every night at dinner my parents talked about current events and whether my brother would get into Harvard. I swallowed whole my parents' love of learning while resenting the pressure that came with it.

Then, to borrow a phrase from Wendy's preface, I had my own children. Zach was born in 1976 and Jeff four years later. I felt the same mix of intense love and protection that my parents must have felt. As they'd done for me, I gave my children every opportunity I could, from Saturday classes at the science museum to tennis lessons, from YMCA sleep-away camp to summer school courses in video production. As so many of the parents I interviewed for this book said to me, "When they were happy, I was happy."

Just like my parents, I wanted my sons to love learning but also to strive and achieve. I sent them to a laboratory elementary school that didn't give grades, but I was thrilled when a teacher read aloud Zach's composition on parents' night. In middle and high school I wanted them to earn As, even if I never said so out loud.

At the same time I often felt like one of the mothers I interviewed for this book, who said, "As a parent I don't think you're ever 100 percent sure you're doing the right thing." I saw so much potential in my children and wondered, "How much should I push them?" But I shrunk away from the father on Zach's Little League team who offered the kids $5 for every home run they hit.

And Jeff didn't seem to be reading for pleasure—what about pushing him with a point for every book he read, I thought, with a promise to take him to a theme park when he got ten points?

There was another phenomenon, too, one that I rarely let on to anyone. I couldn't stand the anxiety that took over my mind and body when, for example, I watched my sons pitch in Little League. What if Zach kept chalking up walks? What if Jeff beaned a batter? What if one pitch *lost the game?* My heart pounded, my mouth dried up—you would've thought they were playing for their lives.

In the same way, I panicked at first if they flunked a test in school or weren't getting along well with other children.

Sometimes my anxiety erupted into yelling. "You have to read more, so you'll do well on your SATs!" I shouted at Zach one afternoon when I was stressed out and he lay on the couch watching TV reruns. Afterward I felt awful. I didn't want to browbeat him!

Not only did I hate pressuring my kids, but I also knew deep down that it would only make them feel guilty and distance them from me. It felt unpleasant, and knowing that I was "overreacting" didn't help one bit. Wasn't I pressuring them for their own good?

When it came time for my children to apply to college, I wanted them to go to the place that was right for *them,* but at the same time I had to battle an urge to push them to apply to places I could brag about—colleges, as my father would say, with "cachet."

Soon after my children were born, I began working as a freelance writer so that I could be home in the afternoons when they returned from child care or school. Assignments for parenting and women's magazines gave me the opportunity to ask my favorite parenting questions to psychologists and therapists. That's how I met Wendy. As I interviewed her in a San Francisco hotel for an article I was writing, she explained an idea I hadn't heard before. Children need structure, she said, although within that structure they need choice, which promotes their autonomy. She explained Self-Determination Theory, which says that children are born with intrinsic motivation to learn and that parents need to nurture this inner passion to explore the world and build their competence.

Yes! I thought. This theory felt so right—it provided a way to guide my children without yelling, a way to encourage their sense of self while staying close and guiding them. Wendy's ideas seemed to cover all the parenting bases that we deal with in real life, and I thought this completeness must have come from the way she connected research to her own experience as a parent. I liked very much her combination of hard research and theory with the practice of everyday life.

When Wendy and I began working together on *Pressured Parents, Stressed-Out Kids*, I was excited to see in addition how well her research explained all those emotions swirling around inside me, tangled in that undifferentiated mass we call love. It pulled apart the skeins of affiliation, tenderness, and high expectations on the one hand and my anxious response to the pressures of competition on the other. It showed me that instead of pressuring my kids I could encourage their autonomy, but that didn't mean pushing them out in the world alone, to sink or swim. Parents need to stay highly involved, at the same time focusing on their children's intrinsic motivation, the passion within them that would make all the difference in their success and self-fulfillment in life.

And so this book was born. Writing it has helped me understand my parents and myself, and it has given me answers to questions that puzzled me for a long time. I hope that it will do the same for you.

WENDY'S ACKNOWLEDGMENTS

What a pleasure it has been taking the journey of this book along with coauthor Kathy Seal. Over the years during which we worked on the book, I marveled at her amazing writing ability, her insight and wit, and her patience as I tried to convey my ideas. I'm grateful to have had the opportunity to work with Kathy and have grown as a result of our collaboration.

Several people contributed to the book, either directly or indirectly. I am grateful for the support of my colleagues at Clark University, especially Michael Addis, Esteban Cardemil, James Cordova, and Abbie Goldberg, who were enthusiastic and supportive throughout and understood when I needed space to complete the book. I'm particularly grateful to the parents and professionals who agreed to be interviewed for the book and who contributed their own experiences. Their stories bring the book alive. Several friends and family members were kind enough to share their experiences and listen to my ideas: Maxine Grolnick, Deborah Godwin, Judy Tullie, Elizabeth Mirro, Scott Kimmel, Candy Weiner, Laurie Skole, Maria Markenson, Cathy Dorison, Susan Merrell, and Janine Idelson each contributed in various ways.

I am grateful for the support of our agent, Barbara Lowenstein, who provided helpful advice and feedback as we conceptualized the book. From Prometheus, I would like to especially thank Linda Greenspan Regan, whose advice and excellent editing improved every aspect of the book.

Over the years, my research has been supported by a number of organizations. I am grateful to the Spencer Foundation, the William T. Grant Foundation, the National Institute of Mental Health, and the National Institute for Child Health and Human Development. Without the support of these organizations, the work would not have been possible.

Finally, I am grateful to my daughters and husband, who supported me throughout the writing process and are a source of love and inspiration every day. Allison and Rebecca allowed me to use their stories—some great times were had recounting earlier events and some good laughs remembering my parenting mistakes. Finally, for the last twenty-seven years my husband, Jay, has supported my work in every way. Without his love and confidence, the book would not have been possible.

KATHY'S ACKNOWLEDGMENTS

I could not have coauthored this book without the piquant and poignant stories of friends and family—and their friends—who shared their parenting stories and opinions with us: Laurie Brenner, Megan Fishmann, Blanca Franco, Beverly Bienstock, Sarah Garrison, Jacob Garrison, Lisa Haberman, Monique Raphel High, Amy Neff, Anita Pulier, Joyce Rangen, Barbara Falk Sabbeth, Emily Simon, Elizabeth Stanley, David Stanley, Ann Shenkin, Elyce Wakermen, Pam Young-Wolff, Raymond Zhang, and Mary Zhang.

A number of professionals were also extremely helpful: Anne Adams, Dorothy Chin, Ingrid Clarfield, Anne Henderson, Rosita Mang, Christine Padesky, Dee Shepherd-Look, Tracey Shores, Linda Stump, Tom Tobin, and Jim Thompson and Jim Perry of the Positive Coaching Alliance.

And to my comrades in our writing workshop—Bruce Bauman, Leonia Kallir Kurgan, Pat Dunn, Monica Carter, Max Stevens, and Russell Avery—thanks for *your* stories, your critical examination of ideas and prose, and above all, your laughter and your support.

I second Wendy's gratitude to our agent, Barbara Lowenstein, our expert shaper and sharpener, Janet Goldstein, and our indefatigably speedy and skillful editor, Linda Greenspan Regan, who understood at once the worth of our project. Thanks also to the team at Prometheus—Steven L. Mitchell, Chris Kramer, Nicole Lecht, and Jill Maxick for your skill and professionalism.

Wendy—who often got up at five a.m. to squeeze in a few hours of reading and writing before a full day of teaching, meetings, writing grant proposals, mothering her two teenagers, and more—was an exceptional coauthor. She'd not only written a trailblazing academic book about parental control but also had a wealth of stories (and friends with stories) as well as an invaluable knack for explaining psychological concepts in everyday language. Adhering to her own research findings, she afforded me an amazing amount of autonomy, so that I felt a very enjoyable sense of ownership and creativity while writing this book.

Finally, thanks to Zach and Jeff, who, despite my years of yelling at them for wrestling on the living room floor, had the good grace to grow up fine anyway. I appreciate greatly their replies to my e-mail queries (*Do kids nowadays still use Walkmen? What do kids today call someone who doesn't do well in school?*) and their childhood memories. As always, I'm grateful to Jim, who answered my question "Which sentence sounds better?" numberless times, even when busy with his own work, and whose sage and supportive counsel and love make my work possible.

CHAPTER 1

PARENT PANIC
It Takes You by Surprise

One day as I sat on the bleachers at our local pool waiting for my daughter Allie to swim time trials, I saw Susan, another mother from our team, running along the edge of the pool. A stopwatch in her right hand, her left arm pumping by her side, she bent over, screaming to her son Seth as he swam. "Faster, *faster!*" I heard her shouting. "Come on! Go!"

As Seth touched the wall, Susan snapped her stopwatch button and checked the time, frowning. Shoulders hunched forward and muttering to herself, she came to sit on the bleachers in front of me, as I waited in the steamy air for the girls' eight-and-under fifty-yard backstroke to begin.

"Congratulations," I said with a smile. "Seth had a great swim!"

"He can do better," Susan said, her face drawn and tight. "He should've been two seconds faster. I wish I'd made him practice more this summer, instead of going to camp." She sighed.

As Seth climbed out of the pool, his body looked tense and he glanced over at Susan with a worried look on his face. I felt sorry for him. He so clearly hadn't enjoyed the swim.

At the same time I understood Susan's behavior. Seth was a talented swimmer, and she wanted him to be the best he could be. When Allie started swimming, I'd been tempted to push her too. It's a decision we all face: *when should you encourage your kid to work hard and excel, and when should you just let her be a kid?*

It's so hard being a parent sometimes, I thought. You want to do what's best for your child, but sometimes it's difficult to figure out exactly what that is.

I wondered about saying a few words to help Susan relax, but I couldn't think of anything. Besides, she didn't seem open to suggestions.

Just then I spotted Allie in the water, holding the starting bar. My stomach fluttered and I felt edgy. *What if she forgets to touch the wall with both hands?* I thought. Dread suddenly invaded my stomach. I desperately wanted Allie to qualify. I'd never run along the side of the pool as Susan did—and yet, I wanted my kid to stand out too!

Allie clocked in at about a second slower than a year before, but she still qualified. *Maybe I don't push her enough,* I worried. *I don't even know the difference between a good time and a bad time. Maybe I should get a stopwatch and time her, the way Susan times Seth.*

Then Allie walked up to me, smiling, a towel around her waist. My self-doubt vanished. *She likes swimming,* I realized, *and she feels fine about herself.*

But that wasn't the first or last time that I panicked before my daughter's performance or second-guessed my parenting. This mix of anxiety and the nagging feeling that I'm not doing enough visits me often. Not long ago, however, I realized that I'm not alone. This brew of worry is so widespread in this age of advanced parental anxiety that I call it the Pressured Parent Phenomenon, or PPP.

While this phenomenon has always been with us, it has intensified in the last decade or so as competition has invaded our children's lives more than ever.

The PPP is a visceral anxiety, triggered when the ever-increasing competition—academic, athletic, social, or artistic—that our kids face today switches on our physiological hardwiring. It's an internal pressure so strong that we can't rest until we feel our child is safe—has gained admission to that certain magnet school or won a spot in the school orchestra. It brings on tears of empathic hurt when we see our child snubbed by a clique or crying on the basketball court, and it makes us do things that we thought we'd never do—such as pull strings to get our child into a special arts program. The Pressured Parent Phenomenon often kicks in after an incident that affects us more than our child. As one mother remembers about a coach refusing to give her son playing time, "I was definitely more emotional about it than Travis. He wasn't really unhappy.

"But I felt like killing the coach, *I* was so angry."

Since the Pressured Parent Phenomenon gives us an urge to push our kids, it alienates our children from us—a result exactly the opposite of what we intended. Because, ironically, it's the absence of pressure that allows our kids both to remain close to us and to succeed.

Now let's explore the Pressured Parent Phenomenon. What is it? Where does it come from? Why is it so strong? Why is every parent prone to it?

PRESSURED PARENTS ARE EVERYWHERE

Both in my research and in talking to other parents, I've found that anxiety from the competition our kids face has reached epidemic proportions. We all want our kids to excel for their own sake, to feel happy and good about themselves. Most of all, we love and care about our kids and want the best for them. And most often the best means "winning." So when they compete in any way, we're filled with nervous anticipation, fear, anxiety, and even panic. Our children's increasingly competitive lives drive us to emotional heights and depths more extreme than those evoked by our own lives. Even though it's only a question of getting into a certain kindergarten or making the traveling soccer team, we *feel* as though our child's life is at stake. And despite all we do, we worry that we're not doing enough to help our kids succeed.

Many parenting experts criticize parents for these feelings. Stop hovering over your children and living through them, they say. Stop basing your self-esteem on their achievements! Lay off the overscheduling and helicopter parenting. Don't relive your childhood through your kids, they warn.[1] Stop trying to "perfect" them.[2] One psychologist accuses parents of using their children like Prozac, to gain the satisfaction they're not getting from their own spouse or job.[3] *Newsweek* chimes in by scorning parents' "one-upmanship" and "fanaticism" over college admissions, saying it's a "self-serving desire to announce their own success."[4] A recent book even blames excessive devotion to their children for ruining parents' sex lives.[5] We're supposed to cease and desist, to get hold of ourselves, to control our emotions. In other words, we should bury those strong feelings, get rid of them somehow. Begone, scat, good-bye. As if we could do that!

We can't, because these feelings are normal and natural. We all want our kids to shine. These desires are quintessentially human. In fact, if you never feel that way—never feel like pressuring your child—*that's* when I'd worry. As embarrassing as it may be to admit feeling "pushy," that urge simply means you're a parent.

That's why the experts' criticism has done little to stop the pushing; nor has it calmed our anxiety. There are only two strategies that can help parents. The first is banding together and changing institutions—insisting, for example, that schools focus less on grades, or that sports leagues don't keep score or don't have younger children practice too often. The second is using the three-part framework of Autonomy, Structure, and Support (detailed in chapters 6 though 9) as tools to turn your anxiety into positive parenting.

STRESS

The Pressured Parent Phenomenon is closely related to stress—the tension we feel when our children refuse to go to bed or won't stop wrestling on the living room floor. It's similar to the stress we experience while driving our kids to ten different places in a twelve-hour period though horrendous traffic and squeezing in a parent-teacher conference on the side. Stress makes us desperately reach for the same solution of taking over and ignoring our child's autonomy, whether or not that's a good idea. But the two phenomena are also very different, because stress comes from conditions of the outside world while the Pressured Parent Phenomenon emanates from within.

True, we may focus on the kind of success that eluded us when we were young. A mom who was excluded from the popular clique in high school might wish fervently for her daughter to join the high-status group in her school. A dad who never played for the varsity may obsess over his son's making the football team. But these personal histories only add emphasis to this general desire we all share for our kids to succeed.

NARCISSISM AND ENMESHMENT

What about parents who *force* their children to take music lessons or play a sport so that they, the parents, can live through them or brag about them? Some people, after all, are psychologically unable to separate themselves from their kids. Capable of focusing only on themselves, they can't take their children's perspective or see them as individuals rather than as extensions of themselves. Suffering from narcissism, they use their children to fulfill their own needs. These parents have a psychological illness that is quite different from the Pressured Parent Phenomenon.

In the past, psychiatrists and psychologists believed that the roots of controlling parenting lay solely in psychological disorders such as narcissism or family enmeshment. In *The Drama of the Gifted Child*, Alice Miller tells of parents who—perhaps raised by abusive parents as she was—try to shore up their shaky self-esteem by pushing their children to fulfill their own unfulfilled hopes and desires.[6] They can't recognize, let alone meet, their children's separate needs, since they are so focused on their own neediness.

The championship swimmer who forces his daughter to compete because he misses the glory of his youth or the mother who commandeers her daughter's social life and mesmerizes her boyfriends because she feels unloved would both fall into this category. If her daughter does pursue her own interests, the narcissistic parent scolds her as selfish and inconsiderate. Gazing into their own Grand Canyons of emotional deficit, narcissistic parents can't muster empathy for their kids.

Another pathological cause of parents' controlling their children appears in families that therapists label "enmeshed."[7] The boundaries between members of these families are very porous or nonexistent, and no one has an individual identity. Parents truly "live through their children," feeling their kids' emotions for them, not allowing them to experience their own lives. They are both too close to and too far from their children, intruding in the kids' lives on the one hand but not, on the other, recognizing their distinct identity.

When I worked in family therapy as a clinical psychology trainee, I saw several enmeshed families. Here's the story of one very much like those I saw:

Five-year-old Amy refused to go to kindergarten. Every time her mother tried to walk her to school, the little girl threw up on the sidewalk.

"I don't know why we have any problems," began the mother. "We have such a close family."

The therapist turned toward the little girl.

"Does going to school frighten you?" she asked gently.

"No, I'm sure it doesn't frighten Amy," answered the mother. "We go everywhere—the playground, the mall, the mountains. She loved her playgroup!"

"I'd like Amy to tell me how she feels about going to school," said the therapist.

The mother moved closer to her daughter on the couch and put her arm around her.

"But I know exactly how she feels," said the mom. "We're a *very* close family."

Enmeshed families aren't to be confused with families who value the collective over the individual, as in several Asian cultures.

Enmeshment is very problematic and requires professional help. It doesn't explain any more than extreme narcissism does the far more widespread and everyday feelings of the Pressured Parent Phenomenon.

Most parents are not narcissistic, and few families are as enmeshed as Amy's. Though protective of their children, the majority of parents can separate themselves from their children and focus on them as individuals. Most parents can empathize with their children's feelings and desires. But they are still not immune to the PPP.

POUNDING HEARTS, SWEATY PALMS: *IT'S THE BIOLOGY*

For normal parents, when our kids compete, these feelings of anxiety and the desire for control can be very strong, even overwhelming. When our children take a math test or try out for a singing group, we may feel an anguished desire for them to succeed. We want them to do whatever it takes, come what may. Sometimes I feel—as I did at Allie's swim trials—as though an alien has invaded my body, filling it with anxiety, fear, and dread.

That's because the Pressured Parent Phenomenon has a robust physical component. It's one form of the human stress response. The brain, as though sensing danger, sends the stress hormones cortisol and adrenalin rushing into the bloodstream. That gives you a dry mouth and a wildly beating heart. Your muscles tense as the body shifts into its "fight-or-flight" mode. You might even feel as if you're having a panic attack. Even though your child simply has try-outs for the soccer travel team or is taking a qualifying test for the gifted program, you may feel as though his life hangs in the balance.

That's how I felt the second week of first grade when Zach got in the car and I asked him about his reading group. Was he a bluebird, a sparrow, or a cardinal? Was he as smart as I thought? My heart thumped under my T-shirt as I waited for him to answer. I felt as though his placement would determine his success as a student over the next sixteen years of his education. And, secretly, I wanted him to be the best reader in the class!

Of course, at the same time, the rational part of my brain knew that kids develop in fits and starts, but that didn't lighten my heartbeats. Knowing that his reading group placement wouldn't really predict whether he'd become a brain surgeon didn't keep me from wanting him to be a star in first grade. Such competitive feelings are so overwhelming that you can't let the facts get in the way.

POWERFUL FEELINGS

The fierceness of these feelings generated by the Pressured Parent Phenomenon often surprises us.

Gina Kelly, a Newton, Massachusetts, mother of three, remembers her intense reaction to a playground incident when her daughter Nicole was two years old. Nicole hadn't yet said one word. Her best friend, Anna, was two weeks younger. One day, as the two toddlers sat on the seesaw in the park, Anna squealed, "I go up!"

"I couldn't stand it!" Gina told me. "I wanted to push her off the teeter totter! I'm glad that I didn't—Anna is still Nicole's best friend—but I sure felt like it."

SOMETIMES WE CARE MORE THAN THEY DO

The power of the feelings generated by the Pressured Parent Phenomenon can make us care about certain incidents more than our kids do. Social snubs are a good example. When I was about five, I remember how furious my mother was when Bo, my daily playmate who lived next door, ignored me when another friend of hers came over to play. I was unfazed, perhaps because both girls were two years older than I was. But it infuriated my mother so much that she forbade me to play with Bo ever again.

Parents similarly hold onto their feelings long after the child has forgotten the triumph or the rejection. My friend Sheila's daughter, Katie, for example, is a successful lawyer, but Sheila still smarts from her daughter's rejection by her first-choice college, which apparently didn't weight her grades for the many AP courses she'd taken.

"Katie had a fabulous experience at college," says Sheila. "She loved UC Santa Cruz—it had everything she wanted.

"As Katie would say, she moved on a long time ago. But I haven't completely," says Sheila, laughing at the apparent absurdity. "I'm still mad she didn't get into Northwestern."

Of course, it's ridiculous for a college to turn down a student for taking challenging courses, but that fact only incenses Sheila more.

THEY SNEAK UP ON US: SURPRISING FEELINGS

We're usually unprepared for these strong feelings and the sweaty palms and heart palpitations that come with them. They sneak up on us unaware.

I don't expect to feel nervous whenever my kids' report cards arrive in the mail, yet sometimes I find my hands shaking. I try not to buy into the hysteria about college and I genuinely believe that my goals are for my children to work hard, enjoy learning, and be kind and ethical young people. Yet every spring, the high school newspaper list of where that year's seniors are going to college stages a surprise attack on me. I avidly scan the page, wanting to know which student won which brand-name admission, where the children of parents whom I know "got in." The thrill of the competition sucks me in, just as do the Oscars or *Dancing with the Stars*. All the while I realize that my interest is frivolous. I've seen enough kids go on to college and graduate to realize that a degree from a prestigious school doesn't make anyone successful, happy, or rich. After a few minutes of intense absorption, I laugh at my silliness—but I haven't stopped looking at that list yet.

DOING WHAT WE THOUGHT WE'D NEVER DO

A teacher once told me that she used to have many parent volunteers in her classroom. However, she noticed that some of the parents craned their necks to see the grades of other people's children. One day the teacher left the room for a minute. When she came back, she saw one of the volunteers peeking into her grade book. That was the end of *that* volunteer system. Now she allows parents to help her only if their children are in different classrooms.

Can you imagine yourself peeking into the roll book of your child's teacher? No, of course not. Yet when your child tells you how he did on a test, don't you sometimes find yourself asking how his friends did?

The fact is that sometimes these surges of competitive feeling make us act in ways that we never thought we would. My friend's daughter Juliet, who lives in Manhattan, was applying to preschools for her three-year-old daughter. Competition was fierce—there were four applicants for every spot in the schools that everyone said were "the best."

"I never thought of myself as trendy or status conscious, but suddenly I was determined to get Zoë into the best school I could find," says Juliet, a theater administrator. "For a few weeks, nothing else mattered. I was like a remote-controlled missile homing in on a school. Nothing would stand in my way. I even called someone I knew who was on the board of the 'best' school and asked her to pull strings.

"I hate it when people throw their weight around and exert influence, and I felt *so* embarrassed," she sighs. "Humiliated is not too strong a word.

"I *never* thought I'd beg for a special favor like that, from someone I barely knew.

"But I felt compelled to do it, and I did.

"It worked.

"Now that Zoë's eleven, I realize that she could have learned what she needed to at any number of fine preschools. But back then it seemed like she *had* to go to one of the well-known places all the other mothers wanted."

Civic-minded, socially conscious parents, who theoretically believe in an equal chance for everyone, suddenly find themselves doing whatever it takes to jump their child to the head of the line—to get their kid into a coveted magnet school kindergarten or a special science program. It's so hard to care about democracy, integration plans, or school board mandates when it seems as though your child's entire future is at stake.

MORE TABOO THAN SEX

We seldom talk to each other about these competitive anxieties. Discussing them is more taboo than sex. Have you ever heard anyone say, "I could hardly sleep worrying about whether Brandon will make symphony band," or "I can't stand it that his best friend is a shoo-in!"

That's because we feel ashamed of our competitive angst. In our culture, parents are supposed to nurture, to model for our children that kindergarten lesson about sharing and cooperating. Women, especially, are expected to put others first. We're not *supposed* to wish for our own child to win and leave other kids in the dust. In some cultures, boasting about your children feels especially shameful and unseemly because parents don't want to humiliate other parents. "I feel horrified when I see one of those bumper stickers saying, 'My child is student of the month,'" a Chinese American father once told me after a talk I gave in Boston. "It's embarrassing if your child is better than someone else's. It's like you're bragging, and making others feel bad." Asian cultures, he reminded me as we chatted, value harmony and uniformity rather than individualism. "That's why the Japanese have the saying 'The nail that sticks out gets pounded down.'"

These competitive feelings also embarrass us because they seem, well, ridiculous. Who will admit to panicking over a child's reading group? How humiliating is it to crave a certain birthday party invitation for your child? We're not supposed to be so insecure, so vulnerable to the judgments of others—particularly those of other kids! Likewise we know that small achievements such as learning to ride a tricycle early mean little in the grand scheme of things and don't indicate whether our child will have a good life— let alone whether he'll have a great future in athletics. So we don't want to let on how much we hang on to our child's every little step forward or back.

I know that I also hesitate to discuss these anxieties because I worry that another parent will claim that he (or she) never panics, and I'll feel ridiculous rather than understood. Even worse, my listener may zero in for the kill, implicitly criticizing me with, "I try not to live vicariously through my child." Or maybe the other parent will brag competitively: "My son is so brilliant that I don't worry about him. The only problem is that he's bored in school."

So when these gut-wrenching emotions overwhelm us, we tend to keep them bottled up inside.

Instead we talk indirectly about our own anxious and competitive feelings by chatting about how *other* parents are pushy, criticizing them for acting on the feelings that we find shameful in ourselves.

"My neighbor has her son scheduled twenty-four/seven," you say, to the clicking tongues and disapproving groans of those sitting nearby at a birthday party. "He goes from Suzuki lessons and Kindergym straight to preschool admission test prep. Oh, and she's got him auditioning for TV commercials, too.

"He's only four. That boy is going to have a nervous breakdown by the time he reaches first grade!"

None of us wants to admit that we feel pushy sometimes too. We defend ourselves if accused, as did a mother who takes her five-year-old to tutoring. Her preschool didn't teach reading, she explained to a *Wall Street Journal* reporter, and the local school system had only a half-day kindergarten.

"I'm not pushy," she said, "but reading is such a critical skill."

We all know someone who is playing Mozart CDs to her pregnant belly.

I'm not immune. When Zach was two, I'm embarrassed to admit, I tried to teach him to read by using the Glen Doman method. ("What for?" asked my mother, to her credit.)

TV reality shows like *Show Biz Moms and Dads* and *Sports Moms and Dads* rivet us because we sense a bit of ourselves in the parents' emotional intensity. They allow us to explore our own feelings without admitting that we have them. Fascinated, we watch other parents act on the same emotions we try to keep a lid on.

Yet we parents face a quandary, because examining only *other* parents' feelings leaves us dealing alone with the panicky gut emotions that emerge as we watch our children competing in an increasingly cutthroat world.

ANXIETY AND FEAR CAN MORPH INTO RAGE

When we don't air these feelings, the trapped anxiety can morph into a "hard" feeling, such as anger, cloaking the underlying "soft" emotion of worry. That's why we shout furiously at the child who isn't doing his Spanish homework. ("I don't care how late it is! I don't care how sleepy you are! You put off your homework, now sit down and finish it!")

That's also the reason parents erupt in rage at a coach, referee, or teacher who they think is shortchanging their child. I remember seeing the father of a high school soccer player who often followed the referee off the field, waving a finger at him and screaming so furiously that others worried he'd have a heart attack. Another dad's internal pressure brought out his racism. Face flushed crimson, he cupped his hands around his mouth and shouted, "Go back to Mexico!" at a referee who had ruled against his child's team. The parents of his child's teammates said nothing.

This same parental rage periodically turns violent. In 2000, a dad in Massachusetts killed the father of another player on his son's ice hockey team. Three years later, a retired French army helicopter pilot drugged twenty-seven of his children's tennis opponents, one of whom crashed his car and died on the way home from a tournament. And remember the Texas mother who tried to murder her daughter's cheerleading rival *and* her mother? Wanda Holloway's 1991 crime spawned a documentary and two made-for-TV movies.[8]

We like to dismiss these people as mentally unbalanced nuts who live through their children. Clearly, they're abnormal because they act on antisocial impulses rather than reining them in. I'm not suggesting that if you don't soothe your anxieties they'll morph into such violence. But these extreme, pathological examples of the Pressured Parent Phenomenon demonstrate how important it is to understand these feelings and learn to deal with them—as I'll show you later.

IT'S CONTAGIOUS: OTHER PARENTS FAN THE FLAMES

The Pressured Parent Phenomenon is contagious. Often I feel just fine about my kids until a casual conversation on the soccer sidelines turns into a comparison fest.

"We go to Kumon once a week," a mom wearing a Dartmouth sweatshirt told me one day as we watched our kids play. "I didn't think I could fit that in, what with Benjamin's oboe lessons and Cub Scouts, but we're going on Tuesdays, right after soccer."

"And what are you doing over Christmas vacation?" I asked with masochistic verve.

"We're sending him to soccer camp in Brazil.

"And this summer we're going to do our regular road trip. We'll visit every state capital by the end of junior year. That will give Benjamin great material for his college application essay!" she exclaimed.

College application essay? I think, my throat tightening.

But our kids are only twelve years old!

As the halftime whistle blew, the competitive conversation infused me momentarily with the same "Am I doing the best for my child?" anxiety as I had felt finding out about Zach's reading group. My mind spun off into absurd worries. *Maybe I should be taking Zach to tutoring to pull up that B minus in Spanish,* I thought. *Hmmm, I'd better get going on his summer plans, and oh, my gosh, what would he write his college application essay on?*

"I know just what you mean," says my friend Sheila. "When Katie was applying to college and I talked to other parents at school meetings, they were in such a frenzy that I often felt like, 'There must be something I should be doing.' But I couldn't figure out exactly what that something was."

At other times we know exactly what "that" is, as at a school meeting I went to when Jeff was in eighth grade. Every question from parents dealt with honors classes. I barely knew they existed. I started to panic. What did these parents know that I didn't? Clearly I was out of the savvy parenting loop. Should I set up a teacher conference and insist Jeff take honors classes? Make an appointment on the spot? The PPP had me in its grip.

I tried not to spiral down into the abyss of parental terror, imagining Jeff facing a stack of twenty college rejection letters because he hadn't taken AP calculus by junior year. Eventually I realized that regular ninth-grade geometry would fit Jeff just fine, but it was very difficult for me to resist the anxious wave that swept over the meeting room that night.

Sometimes parents catch the anxiety over practices that begin healthily enough but then morph into a social trend or even an epidemic. Though some parents are advised by schools to hold their children back in school to benefit from an extra year of development, you hear that many people are deciding themselves to hold their kids back from kindergarten for a year or "redshirting" them to give them an "extra advantage."[9] It's hard not to get caught up in the frenzy. You think, *What do these parents know that I don't? I don't want my child to miss out!*

TV commercials for "educational" toys and computer programs set off similar alarms, as do advertisements blaring, "Soccer for Tots: Intro to Soccer for Preschoolers" and "Keep Learning in the Summer! Innovative and Creative Tutoring!"

It makes you wonder whether you're keeping your child from developing a competitive edge. If you don't send her to Soccer for Preschoolers, will she start out behind the other kids when they all begin league soccer?

WHERE PARENTAL PANIC COMES FROM AND WHAT TO DO ABOUT IT

Parents have always felt such anxieties about their children, but today these emotions are skyrocketing to new heights of intensity.

There are ways to turn that anxiety into positive parenting, however. Here's how two parents I know did just that. Both Lucy Pollard and her husband, Rich, had been athletic growing up. But when their son Travis was eleven, Lucy noticed that when two "captains" chose up teams at club soccer practices, he was always chosen last. "My heart used to go, 'Oh, my God, how can Travis stand that?'" remembers Lucy, a former teacher. "I wanted to die." On weekends the club team traveled all over Los Angeles for games, but Travis was lucky to get ten minutes of playing time.

One night at a meeting, the coach told the parents that every boy would play at least half of every game.

"I couldn't take it, so I piped up, 'How about Travis?'" Lucy remembers. "He hardly even gets to play."

"Well, Travis has a stride problem," said the coach. "He can't coordinate his legs."

Lucy burst into tears. "I could not stop crying," she remembers. "It was horrible. You get so caught up in this stuff as a parent. It was so humiliating. I was hurting for Travis, but I felt like it was happening to me."

At home Lucy drew Rich into the kitchen while Travis watched TV in the living room. "I want Travis to quit," she whispered. "This coach is so mean to him. I can't stand it anymore."

"I don't think he wants to quit," said Rich. "He's not unhappy. We're the ones who are unhappy."

Lucy and Rich continued driving long distances every weekend for the club games. "We suffered," Lucy says, especially since she'd have rather spent that time hiking and camping as a family. But still Travis barely played in the soccer matches. It didn't seem to bother him though. "I was definitely more emotional about it than either Travis or Rich," says Lucy. "I felt like killing the coach, I was so angry.

"What really bothered me was that the coach didn't say 'Let's figure out how Travis can get a better stride.'"

The Pollards didn't talk to the coach. "Both Rich and I played varsity sports in high school and college," explains Lucy. "We loved being athletic and both knew that you have to work hard to get good at a sport and it's up to you alone to achieve that, not having your parents talk or complain to the coach.

"We would have helped him improve his stride," adds Lucy, "but we didn't really know what the coach meant. We didn't think he would enlighten us if we asked."

Besides, Travis didn't want them to.

Lucy and Rich never told Travis about their concerns that he didn't get much playing time, nor did they tell him he had to improve. "Basically we were encouraging—trying to find something he did that was good," says Lucy.

The following year after the coach said at a meeting that the kids should consider soccer more important than school, several of the families decided to pull their sons out of the club. One of the dads said he'd be willing to coach a new team for those boys.

As they drove home from the meeting, Rich asked Travis what he wanted to do. "I don't know," he answered.

"Do you want to stay with the club? Go with the other dad?" asked Lucy.

"I guess I want to stay with the club. But I don't get much playing time," said Travis.

"You could go with the new team," suggested Rich.

"I don't know," Travis said again. He seemed confused.

"You know, there's always the American Youth Soccer Organization [AYSO]," said Lucy. Travis had played AYSO before he'd made the club team.

When they got home Lucy said, "You know, Travis, whatever you decide is fine with us. We'll support you in club, AYSO, or even taking a year off from soccer. We'll help you find a good AYSO team if you want and I'm sure your dad will be happy to go out and practice with you too. Whatever you want, we'll back you."

A few days later on the way to school, Travis told Rich he thought he might want to try AYSO. Some of his friends at school played in that league, he said.

Rich felt disappointed because he knew the level of play was higher in club soccer, but he kept that thought to himself. When he told Lucy, she pointed out that the low-pressure atmosphere of AYSO might give Travis more playing time. Plus there would be only one practice a week and much less driving to the games.

They told Travis he'd made a very good decision.

"Leaving the club was the best thing he ever did, because that club situation was hurting him," says Lucy. "It was like he knew he needed to go back to AYSO."

The AYSO coach switched Travis from offense, which he'd always played in club soccer, to sweeper, a defense position. Lucy praises that coach, who had played varsity soccer in college. "He was wonderful, very nurturing and very specific about how Travis could get better."

Travis improved greatly. "He just blossomed," says Lucy. He won a spot on the AYSO tournament team, and made a lot of friends.

When he went to high school, Travis made the varsity team and soon became a star. The original club coach asked him to return to his team. Travis agreed, and this time around he got lots of playing time. He also played varsity volleyball and won the Best Athlete of the Year award during his senior year.

As I write, Travis is a twenty-six-year-old college graduate who works as a graphic artist. He played club soccer through college and now plays on a weekend team with a group of friends from his high school.

"After you and I talked yesterday," Lucy told me recently, "I asked Travis how he felt about the sports he played growing up, and he said that he absolutely loved them. He also said that—though he realized his dad had been sad when he quit baseball in high school—he never felt pushed. It was all his self-motivation and interest."

Despite the turbulent emotions aroused in them by the club soccer coach, the Pollards managed to focus on how their son felt and what he wanted. They respected his autonomy by not insisting he quit the club team and directed their energy toward supporting and encouraging him.

Lucy and Rich's daughter Kristen, two years younger than Travis, also played club and high school soccer and volleyball. "We did it because the kids wanted to do it. We kind of followed their lead," says Lucy.

Even though competition in our children's lives is mounting, the Pollards' story shows how parents can cope effectively with their resulting fear. In later chapters we'll see how—ironically—eliminating pressure helps kids excel.

CHAPTER 2

WHY NOW?

"Our Kids Are Competing All the Time"

Gina Kelly's older daughter, thirteen-year-old Danielle, plays basketball year-round. Last spring she tried out for state and national teams sponsored by the Amateur Athletic Union.

"It's tough competition," says Gina, who sat through the tryouts. "She missed a couple of lay-ups and another girl beat her down on the boards."

Danielle made the state team. But when she got in the car, she started crying.

"What's the matter, honey?" Gina asked.

"I wanted to make the national team!" Danielle sobbed.

"I felt like crying right along with her," remembers Gina. "I know how much she loves basketball. And whenever I see her with tears in her eyes, I want to wrap my arms around her. She wanted to make the national team *so much*. And I want her to be happy!"

Danielle's AAU tryout wasn't the only competitive mini-crisis the Kelly family weathered that week. The next day, eleven-year-old Brandon admitted that his two best friends had made the school orchestra, but he had missed the tryouts because he'd forgotten and had gone to Boy Scouts instead.

"That's OK, honey," said Gina, anguished at the disappointment she heard in Brandon's voice and wishing he'd told her about the tryouts ahead of time. Then she had an idea.

"Maybe you could explain what happened and ask for a separate audition. I bet Ms. Wu would let you! She's so nice." Glancing over at Brandon, Gina saw his face brighten.

Then, on Friday, her younger daughter, Nicole, came home furious at her friend Phoebe, who sat in front of her and always got straight As.

"Every time the teacher hands back a test," Nicole fumed, "Phoebe turns around and says to me"—Nicole's tone rose tauntingly, in singsong imitation —"'I got a ninety-eight. What did you get?'"

"I'm sick of her!" said Nicole, and Gina didn't know whether to laugh or cry.

Parents have always had to cope with their children's competitive standing, but weeks like the one Gina Kelly experienced are now increasingly common. Kids face tests for admission to gifted programs, AP classes, and magnet schools, auditions for concert bands and school plays, and tryouts for Olympic soccer development teams. The profusion of standardized and high-stakes tests; competitions for beauty, dance, chess, skateboarding, and surfing; and even interviews to win a place in community service projects throw kids into a competitive whirlwind. And casting its shadow over ever-larger areas of children's lives is the race for a brand-name college with its frenzied compilation of attractive résumés, the pursuit of high GPAs and SATs, and more!

As Gina Kelly says, "It seems like our kids are competing all the time now."

With competition escalating in every arena of our children's lives, we find ourselves forced to "manage"—plan and plot—our children's academic, athletic, and arts "careers." We also have to cope more frequently than ever with the entire family's emotional ups and downs.

CULTURE OF COMPETITION

Why the frenzy?

America venerates competition. It's endemic to our culture. Think *American Idol.* Competition, we believe, keeps our economy strong and healthy by generating low prices, endless innovation, and excellence. Where would Apple be without Microsoft? Sampras without Agassi? How would we have mapped the human genome if two teams hadn't raced to do so? And how many millions of us—fortunately for the networks who charge millions of dollars for a thirty-second spot—enjoy our annual über-competitive epics, the World Series, the Super Bowl, and the Final Four? Add to that the trumpeting of champions such as Tiger Woods or Lance Armstrong, as well as the steady ratcheting up of celebrity consciousness by proliferating multimedia. It becomes hard to distinguish parents' legitimate wishes for their children to succeed and be happy from media-fostered desires to thrust stardom on them.

And as America races to maintain its number-one world economy, is it any wonder that the culture of competition filters down into our children's lives? That's what researchers studying the Silicon Valley culture in California have found—that the heightened competitiveness in parents' careers spills over into their kids' lives.

"A number of women we've interviewed say a version of, 'I've been a project manager in my company,'" San Jose State anthropologist Chuck Darrah mentions, "'and now my kids are my projects and I manage their lives.'"[1] As parents work in companies that compete globally, they may feel they have to manage their children to do the same.

"People are absolutely frantic," says Darrah. Even in research done before the dot-com bust, parents seemed "very fearful" of losing what they had, he explains. "There's a palpable sense that getting your kids into the right schools is really important and that the race starts very early and you have to pay a lot of attention to this."

The tremendous expansion—however uneven—of wealth in the United States ups the competitive ante too, as parents lavish their disposable income on their children's extracurricular lessons. Between 1965 and 2004, the median income for families increased from $35,311 to $54,061 in 2004 dollars.[2] The number of high school graduates from families earning more than $100,000 was expected to jump about 12 percent between 2002 and 2007.[3] Also, families now have fewer children, giving parents even more money to spend on each child.[4] That means more and more people can afford to pursue what sociologist Annette Lareau calls "concerted cultivation"—the upper-middle-class child-rearing style of fostering kids' academic, athletic, and artistic talents and skills.[5] More families than ever before have the money to travel to music and sports competitions and to give their children the competitive boost of private coaches, tutors, specialized camps, and even full-time sports academies.

On the other hand, many families hit by the disappearance of decent-paying jobs have to struggle to prepare their children for getting a good education and perhaps climb up a rung in the economic ladder. With less disposable income, they have to hold tag and garage sales and other fund-raisers and work extra jobs or make other sacrifices to pay for computers and calculators, musical instruments or team fees, and the many other "extras" that help their kids compete. That pressure can add to their anxiety all the more.

While thirty years ago only a small number of top students aimed for prestigious colleges, today increasing numbers of families contemplate brand-name schools far from home, which in turn intensifies the battle for distinction in academics, athletics, the arts, and even community service. The colleges have encouraged this competition with branding and marketing practices so aggressive that a fourth grader I know is already aiming for Yale. This marketing hype helps promote the myth that only a few select institutions are the very best at the same time that the number of applicants is peaking because the baby boomlet—children of baby boomers—is reaching college age. Three point one million students graduated from high school in 2006, up more than 20 percent from 1995, and the Federal Department of Education projected that the number of high school graduates would rise to 3.2 million students in 2007.[6]

Behind all this frantic competition also lies a backdrop of dazzling changes in the economy. The severe shrinking of American heavy industry, the flourishing of high technology, and the offshoring of not only service but now even some professional jobs mean that we are sending our children out into a workforce that is much more volatile than the one we have known.[7] Serial employment is replacing lifetime employment, and the cost of health insurance, college tuitions, and housing are skyrocketing, while efforts to improve public schools seem to face an uphill battle. As employer-paid health insurance, pensions, and Social Security disappear, personal wealth is increasingly necessary to replace them. It's a more fiercely competitive and individualistic world than ever before. Whereas a college degree used to seem like plenty of educational insurance for young people, today it hardly seems enough.

"Lifelong competition has replaced lifetime security," writes UCLA psychiatrist Peter C. Whybrow, "and a new age of fiscal uncertainty has fallen on the average American family."[8]

This uncertainty falls particularly hard on the increasing number of families in the United States living at or below the poverty level. For many of them, the competition for family survival leaves no time to worry about any competition in their children's lives. Their lack of means eliminates some competition, too. Your child can't compete for a chair in the violin section when you can't buy her a violin, let alone pay for lessons. Chances are the school in an economically disadvantaged area doesn't have an orchestra anyway. Yet middle-class parents don't have a monopoly on aspirations for their children. Less privileged parents also have great hopes for their kids. Many want them to lead lives easier and more comfortable than their own. But their children may have to compete even more fiercely than wealthier children, because their opportunities are fewer. And so their parents' hearts also beat quickly as they open the envelope of a letter informing them of a magnet or charter school acceptance, or a parochial school scholarship, or whether they've won the lottery for a voucher. Mothers and fathers may well feel the pressure of their young teenagers practicing basketball or football, competing against tremendous odds for a spot on a college team, or studying hard, hoping for college scholarships and other financial aid. The specifics of the competition may differ, but the pressure is just as real.

Consciously or unconsciously, well off or economically struggling, many parents think that the best way to protect their children against future ups and downs is to make sure they're at the top of the heap. If there are fewer good jobs to go around, at least *our* kids will get them. If there are no more social benefits, we'd better groom them to make as much money as possible.

Terrorism and war also foster fear. Parents may not be aware of it, but an underlying fear of suicide bombings and airplanes diving into office towers can make polishing a child's competitive skills feel like equipping him for survival. We want to do all we can to keep our children safe, as though his success—skills, money, and prestige—may somehow protect him. Of course, no amount of money or prestige under those extreme and unlikely circumstances will be useful.

All these factors—real or imagined—add up to a culture steeped in competition.

IT BEGINS AT BIRTH

Feelings of competition begin almost at childbirth. We feel terribly proud when our children start crawling, walking, and talking. Even the first time a baby turns over is an event to report. Then, sooner or later, the Baby Milestone Game begins. Comments like "Devon said 'Da-da' at seven months" bounce off the walls at first birthday parties. "When did Matthew start sitting up?" another mom asks, and the race is on. No kid is always ahead, so sooner or later even the most confident parent worries, perhaps because another child is walking and his is barely crawling.

SCHOOLS: DRENCHED IN COMPETITION

Competition is a defining feature of American schooling. The belief that competition promotes motivation and excellence usually remains unspoken, but it explains why competition is so engrained in our schools that we take it for granted.

Perhaps we do so also because competition begins very slowly. Preschool activities aren't structured competitively. You can't easily compare one child to another when kids move fluidly from the sand table to the dress-up corner, from block-building to story time. Furthermore, preschoolers often work alone, one child putting together a jigsaw puzzle while another strings beads, or they play in small groups. Too young cognitively to compare themselves with each other, they are absorbed in their own efforts as they learn how to write their names or to ride a tricycle. And as long as a child works on a project for a fair amount of time, preschool teachers usually say that it's fine.[9]

However, that pleasant state of affairs doesn't last long. Competition starts ramping up in kindergarten, especially since the curriculum now includes the reading and arithmetic taught not so long ago in first grade. Some schools screen kindergarten children with a skills test, which helps identify any children who need extra help. Although the kids may not notice, some parents are already acutely tuned in to the competition and send children as young as three to private tutoring. Enrollment at the Junior Kumon program, for example, which teaches preschoolers and kindergartners basic reading and math skills, has surged by about 27 percent a year since its inception in 2003.[10]

Kindergarten children still aren't aware of competition, however. They know the difference between winning and losing and can compare themselves to another child even if they can't accurately judge their competitive position in a group. In fact, if you ask kindergarteners how they rank, most will say they're the smartest in the class![11] If you ask why, they'll say, "Because I can say the alphabet" or "Because I can count to 100." That's because they define success as learning a skill and achieving their own goals. In addition, they often include social behavior and conduct in their definition of who's smart.

Five-year-olds also don't compete to see who's smarter because they don't distinguish between effort and ability. They don't conceive of smartness as a fixed quality. They judge how smart someone is by the result, not differentiating between those who tried hard and did well and those who didn't try hard but still did well. That's what the late researcher John Nicholls of University of Illinois at Chicago realized when he showed some kindergartners a video of two young actors working on identical projects. One boy obviously tried very hard, while the other breezed through the work. The children didn't think the laid-back boy was smarter than the hard worker. Most of them couldn't believe that he hadn't expended more effort than they saw on the tape. He "must have been thinking while he was fiddling around," said one child.[12] Other children believed he'd begun working before the videotape began.

But by about age seven or eight, kids can actively compare themselves to the rest of the group. In first grade, children learn in larger groups than in kindergarten—sometimes as an entire class. So it's easy for a child to compare her progress with another child's. And by age ten or eleven, children not only are able to compare themselves to others, but they also have developed a firm concept of ability. So at this age they begin to use the performances of others to judge themselves and their own abilities.[13] And this is just when competitive academic practices start kicking in with a vengeance.

With the best of intentions, teachers start to award stickers and gold stars, and schools give out "My Child Is an Honor Student" and "Proud Parent of an Accelerated Reader" bumper stickers. Teachers adorn papers with red Xs and comments like "poor," "satisfactory," "very good," and "excellent." They may try to protect fragile feelings with thinly veiled negatives like "that's close," "good try," "keep working," or a smiling head shake, but that fools no one. In an effort to motivate students, teachers tack the best essays, art work, and 100 percent spelling tests on the bulletin board. Now children start entering high and low reading and math groups, resource classrooms, and gifted programs. Less obvious sorting mechanisms also start to appear. Which student will the teacher ask to help her? Help other children? Whom does she call on when there's an observer in the room? These subtler signs escape no child's notice.

In addition, teachers start to praise kids for finding the right answer, not simply for trying. Children raise hands to answer teachers' questions, and their answers are either right or wrong. It's the same scene we remember so well from our own childhoods: the teacher asks a question. Kids who don't know the answer feel like dummies and wish they could hide under the desk. Those who *do* know the answer hope the others don't. The teacher calls on one child after another until one student answers correctly and triumphantly.[14]

The older the children get, the more schools emphasize grades, and the more teachers base grades on tests and quality of work rather than on effort, concentration, and persistence. They may even hand the papers out in order, highest grade first, or read the best papers out loud.

Children respond to all this ranking by comparing grades with their friends and enemies. By age eleven or twelve, they're fully able to judge themselves against others and have developed the concept of ability. They're quite capable of recognizing the hierarchy that emerges from the drumbeat of competition: the "smart kids," "overachievers," and nerds on the one hand, and on the other, the "dopes" (or as my fourth-grade teacher used to call them, the "klunks").

Some students become grade grubbers, as described by a recent graduate of a private high school: "Most of the kids argued over every little point they got wrong on a test so they could jump up their grade from a B plus to an A minus. Every time we got a test back they would go over it and argue with the teacher to get their score higher."

As kids move on to middle and high school, competition intensifies. Some grades are calculated on a curve, rather than by an absolute standard. Honor rolls and dean's lists, class rank calculations, spelling bees, geography contests, awards assemblies, Daughters of the American Revolution prizes, and college book awards inject ranking into the consciousness of kids and parents alike. Honors and AP classes, as well as national and statewide high-stakes tests like the PSATs, SATs, ACTs, and the Regents in New York and Golden State tests in California also provide ways for students to compete and for parents to compare their children with others. The pressure cooker is turned on high.

THE BATTLE FOR ADMISSIONS SETS PARENTS' TEETH ON EDGE

But competition isn't only for grades and test scores. Increasingly, parents take part in another contest—the battle for admission. In large cities, that marathon begins with admission to preschool.

In 2002 the press told a story of the rich and famous that illustrated the rabid competition for preschool slots faced by parents in large cities. Desperate to get his twins into the well-regarded Manhattan 92nd Street Y preschool in 1999, stock analyst Jack B. Grubman upgraded his recommendation of AT&T stock from "neutral" to "buy." Allegedly, he wanted his boss, Sanford I. Weill, then chairman of Citigroup and a member of AT&T's board of directors, to talk to members of the 92nd Street Y's board of directors about his twins' applications. After the children were admitted to the preschool, Weill reportedly arranged for Citigroup to donate $5 million to the Y over five years. Both men denied any quid pro quo—or, as the *Wall Street Journal* dubbed it, "kid-pro-quo"—and the New York attorney general didn't press criminal charges against either Weill or Grubman.[15]

Celebrity and money stories are always titillating, but this one hit a nerve because it was emblematic: neither you nor I could leverage $5 million for a preschool slot, but when caught up in the anxiety of getting our kids into a good preschool—one that ironically might be more playful than academic, and therefore less pressured—we might, if we had the means, at least *consider* that solution. Media stories may make cracks about egotistical, status-driven parents who think certain preschools lead directly to Harvard. But even low-profile folks can face tremendous hurdles as we compete for scarce slots in quality child-care centers and preschools. The number of public and private slots in New York City, for example, is only one-half the number of the city's preschool age children.[16]

Admissions competition only escalates after preschool, as the educational stakes rise ever higher. Housing prices in communities with good schools are often very expensive. That means students in many public districts have to compete for admission to magnet schools, specialized public academies, selective high schools, and coveted music or art programs. If a voucher system or charter school shows up promising better education, families have to compete, often by lottery, for a small number of places. Parents regularly camp out overnight to be first in line on application days. In many districts, children take tests to qualify for the "gifted program" or the "honors program"—code words for a really good public education.

Competition for admission to private and some parochial schools is just as frenzied or even more so. Parents deluge private school admissions offices with plates of brownies and tubs of popcorn, and they create novel strategies. At the UCLA laboratory elementary school that my sons attended, one enterprising mother, hoping to gain an admissions edge, volunteered in the parent-school association *before* her child was admitted. Non-Catholic couples have been known to suddenly join a Catholic church and attend services, at least until their children graduate from a good parochial high school.

"I was phony," laughs Loretta Carson, a psychotherapist whose two daughters graduated from a well-regarded Catholic school in Los Angeles. "Baptized the babies there, and attended periodically, hoping to fool the system."

We parents simply want our kids to get a good education. But after studying the intense vying for admission, grades, test scores, credits, and degrees at prestigious schools, sociologist David Labaree concluded that the goal of education today is less about students "gaining useful knowledge" and more about gaining a competitive advantage by acquiring various badges of merit.[17]

SPORTS COMPETITION

If kids faced only an academic arms race, that would provide competition enough. What's driving parents crazy, however, is the parallel rise in competition in every other arena of our children's lives.

Thirty-five million boys and girls—the highest number in history—played organized team sports in the United States in 2006.[18] Programs have proliferated not only in baseball, basketball, swimming, soccer, field hockey, softball, and tennis, but also in volleyball, lacrosse, ice hockey, and even paintballing. So many American parents devote such large portions of their lives to kids' sports—as chauffeurs, coaches, fans, nutritionists, physical therapists, and fund-raisers—that sociologists have coined a new term, the *athletic family*, for families whose lives revolve around their children's sports.[19] It's an emerging social system of parents focusing their time, money, and emotional energies on the kids' athletic games.

Much of that emotional energy concentrates on the growing competitiveness of kids' athletics. To be sure, formal competition has been a feature of children's sports for many years. Little League baseball, for example, began in 1939 for eleven- and twelve-year-olds. But in the last few decades, organized competition for kids has expanded exponentially. Little League rosters, standings, and championships now start at age seven. American Youth Soccer Organization teams start at age four and a half. Kids start gymnastics at age one and attend classes without a parent by age three. In some communities lacrosse teams start in first grade, and swimmers can enter competitive meets at ages six and seven.

In some other sports, teams of young children practice two to four hours a week. The age for travel or club teams and elite programs is dropping lower and lower. There are traveling under-eight soccer teams and club lacrosse teams for fourth graders. Championships, tournaments, play-offs, and all-star teams maximize competition. Contests are multiplying even for action sports such as skateboarding, surfing, motocross, and snowboarding. MVP trophies, varsity letters, and school spirit rallies, which lionize a select few athletes, heighten rivalries.

THE SPORTS PYRAMID

In addition, sports are organized like a pyramid: the higher you go, the fewer the spots.

"On the bottom of that pyramid are all the wonderfully talented kids who play youth sports," observes Rick Wolff, a former professional baseball player and coach, who hosts a sports radio talk show about parenting child athletes.[20] "But as you begin to climb that pyramid you find that only a certain percentage of those athletically gifted kids ever go on to become high school players."[21] Only one out of four top youth league players become high school sports stars.[22] In other words, as sports psychologist Terry Orlick says, sports programs operate as "failure factories" that, as time goes on, weed out more and more players.[23]

PARENTS MORE COMPETITIVE THAN CHILDREN

All this competition affects parents as much or even more than the children. Just like the classroom volunteers who couldn't help peeking into the roll book, we get hooked into the competitive mind-set of organized sports. We don't want our kids to feel bad when they're cut from the team or lose a game. We want them to have positive self-esteem and can't stand it when they suffer humiliation.

"I know Heather wants to do well—that's why I want her to win," says Eliane Cortez, a mother of two in Los Angeles. "I want my child to be happy."

We all feel that way, yet often the children care less about winning and losing than we do. When my friend Janet's daughter, Kristin, was ten, she played on a traveling basketball team. Since many other girls had better skills, Kristin was given little playing time. One Saturday, Janet drove more than forty miles to a game. It was a great match-up—Kristin's team won in the last minute—but she and another girl didn't play at all. As they were leaving, they saw several of the girls talking to the coach. "It's not fair if everyone doesn't get to play," Janet heard one of them say. "We'd rather lose than leave someone out." The other girls nodded in agreement.

Janet couldn't believe her ears. It was quite a speech for a ten-year-old! "I felt like crying," she told me. "And at the same time I felt so happy."

Later when my son Zach coached youth basketball and worked as a Little League baseball umpire, he also noticed how the competitive structure of sports affected parents more than their kids.

"The parents always paid attention to how good each kid was and put kids in groups—the good ones [players], the average ones, and the bad ones," Zach e-mailed me recently. But their children felt less competitive. "Kids on all the teams I played on were—surprisingly—not mean to bad kids and not super kiss-ass to the good kids," he wrote. "They were very mature, always treating each other as equals, no matter what the other kid's playing ability. I saw this also as an umpire. It's really amazing how supportive young kids playing sports are—boys and girls. It's actually pretty sweet."

PROFESSIONALIZATION OF YOUTH SPORTS

The professionalization of youth sports also intensifies the competition. Some families focus their lives around sports for their fun and social life and pour money into camps and coaches because they want their kids to "be the best they can be." Many others do so because they hope sports will boost their child's college admission chances. A few hope for scholarships to cover soaring college tuition costs.

All these hopes and dreams have produced a "downward creeping specialization rush," says Jim Thompson, executive director of the Positive Coaching Alliance (PCA), based at Stanford University.[24] Kids as young as ten now concentrate on one sport, with college or the pros in mind. Affluent families pay private trainers and professional coaches up to $150 an hour to build kids' sports skills and overall fitness.[25] Specialty sports camps are proliferating, and some kids may attend as many as three such camps in a summer.

"We used to criticize the East German sports model, which emphasized the elite athlete," says Thompson. "To a certain extent, I think the United States has adopted that model."[26]

Most parents can't afford private coaches and specialty camps—many scramble simply to scrape up team fees. But a handful of highly trained children ratchet up competition for all.

And as American sports have become billion-dollar industries, some parents even groom their kids for careers in sports. They're enticed by expanded professional leagues, the astronomical rise in salaries since free agency began in the 1980s, and athletes' mega-million-dollar endorsement deals.

"I was at a kids' basketball game the other day and heard a dad say, 'My son has narrowed his choice to Duke, Kentucky, UCLA, and Texas.' The kid was twelve years old," says the PCA's Jim Perry, who has coached high school and college sports teams since 1975.

"The dad next to him said, 'We're not worried about college—we're going straight to the NBA.'

"Lebron James has done more to screw up parenting than anyone else in America," commented Perry, referring to the first basketball player to go directly from high school to the NBA. James also signed a shoe endorsement contract with Nike for more than $90 million before he'd even played a game.

We could shake our fingers at parents for this "professionalization" of youth sports. But it's not crazy to hope that your child's lacrosse or basketball skills will ease his way into college. Nor is it a crime to dream big about your child's future, especially when the media trumpet professional glory so loudly. However, the media rarely if ever mention that there are only 1,200 basketball scholarships every year in the United States and only 59 players drafted by the NBA—and a half dozen of those are from other countries.[27] Even with expanded US leagues and the possibility of playing basketball in Italy, baseball in Japan, or soccer in the Netherlands, the odds of pulling down a decent professional salary remain minuscule. Yet by promoting the dreams of parents and their sports-minded children, television and other sports media are, inadvertently or not, ramping up competition in youth sports to unprecedented heights.

DEMOGRAPHICS CONTRIBUTE

Demographic changes have also contributed to the burgeoning sports competition. Working parents need after-school activities for their kids, especially with our fears of dangers for latchkey children. Replacing casual after-school play with competitive programs may also appeal to parents who feel less guilty about working if their kids are honing their skills in adult-organized games, learning how to win, and doing what it takes in today's world to build self-esteem.

The hypercompetition in children's sports makes it hard for parents who simply want their kids to exercise and have fun while playing several different sports. "It's like, if your kid isn't good by age eight, forget it," says Leslie Dennis, a friend of mine since college who now lives in Philadelphia.

Shrinking budgets add to that problem, because they have forced many public high schools to largely eliminate freshman-sophomore teams, "B" teams, and intramural sports programs. And many community recreational leagues stop at age fourteen; they assume that kids that age will play on their high school teams.

HOW ONE FAMILY COPED WITH THE COMPETITION THAT PUT THEIR DAUGHTER IN A TOUGH SPOT

Bill and Marie Docter's daughter Devon has loved swimming ever since her dad taught her to dog-paddle as a six-year-old in a calm, lapping bay on the New Jersey shore. When she was ten, Devon joined the local YMCA swim team, and now at fifteen she swims the backstroke and the fifty-yard freestyle in a summer league.

"I'm glad Devon swims," says her dad. "It's a really healthy sport. She's got good friends on the team, and we love watching the swim meets."

But the family hit a snag as the season ended. "At the end of the summer everyone started asking, 'Where are you going to swim in the fall?'" said Bill, an assistant superintendent in a suburban Baltimore school district. "I thought childhood was about being exposed to different sports in different seasons. But if you're going to remain competitive, you now have to stick with one sport throughout the year."

Bill and Marie worried—what if Devon couldn't make the team next summer? Devon at first decided to swim at a local indoor club for two months in the winter, but then decided to run track instead. "She enjoys being in different sports, and we encourage her to mix it up," says Bill. In June she returned to the YMCA team, which Bill describes as "competitive, but not overly so." She had a good season, and the Docters breathed a collective sigh of relief.

With the support of her parents, Devon managed to keep swimming and to play other sports—despite many teammates who specialized only in swimming. But not every kid is that lucky.

"On our [Chino Hills High School] softball team, if you haven't played travel ball for a good length of time, you're not going to make the team," said Mike West, athletic director of Chino Hills High School in Chino Hills, California.[28]

COMPETITION IN THE ARTS

Competitive frenzy has even spread to the arts, with children as young as four entering piano competitions. Music organizations and singing teachers hold local and national competitions. Local music groups hold scholarship contests. Kids compete for places in school choirs and singing ensembles that have names like the Madrigals or Lyrics, and for chairs in the orchestra and places in regional and state ensembles.

"The music world of kids revolves around competitions," says Rosita Mang, who teaches piano in Alexandria, Virginia. "There is an explosion of competitions at the local, national, and international levels. The teachers are measured by how many contests their students win. The stakes are high, the tension builds, and only a very few can win."[29]

"Right now," she adds, "the competitions have also become a fashion statement, so the parents spend fortunes on the proper dress for each level and each day of the contest."

Musical competition within schools can also be brutal. For example, a girl I knew who sang first soprano in the choir worried that she could have one bad day—and drop to third soprano!

COMPETITION IN THEATER PROGRAMS

Competition for roles in school theater productions is especially fierce. Most plays and musicals offer only a handful of meaty parts. Since girls usually outnumber boys in theater programs—except at all-male schools—they find snagging a plum role particularly difficult. Unlike sports, where there's a game every week and substitutions allowed, schools usually stage only one or two productions a year.

At my local high school, the drama director has a reputation for extreme democracy. He likes to choose plays with many parts and practices multiple casting. For example, he staged *Little Shop of Horrors* with four different girls playing the lead of Audrey on four different nights.

But in many theater programs, competition for scarce good roles rages, with casting subject to the whims, artistic or otherwise, of one all-powerful teacher who chooses each year's production. A student who works hard has no guarantee of a play that fits her skills and talents.

"You could pay your dues for four years, and if they pick a dancing play and you're a singer not a dancer, you can be a senior and have seniority, and they'll pick a dancer who was never in a play before," says Cynthia Notley, a physical therapist and mother of three in Fremont, California.

"It's heartbreaking."

IS COMPETITION GOOD OR BAD FOR KIDS?

Gina Kelly's older daughter Danielle loves riding horseback, but competing makes her anxious.

"Last summer she'd get up at 4:30 a.m. for competitions," says Gina, "but she got so nervous before one show that she got scratched from jumping—her coach pulled her. She jumped beautifully in practice or lessons, yet during shows I could see her sweating it out.

"She couldn't enjoy it because she worried she'd make a terrible mistake and then feel so inadequate. No matter how much I told her mistakes didn't matter, or that they were part of the process, I could still see her shaking before every contest."

Finally one day as they drove home after a show, Gina asked Danielle, "Did you have fun?"

"No," she answered.

"Why are you doing it then?" Gina asked.

"Because my coach expects it," said Danielle.

Both were quiet for a while.

Then Gina said, "If you don't want to do competitions, I'll support you."

"I *don't* really want to do competitions," said Danielle, brightening. "I guess I never realized that I didn't have to."

The following summer Danielle took lessons and competed once, in her barn's event, when her coach wanted 100 percent participation.

"What a relief!" says Gina. "I was *so* happy. I could see her stress level go down. It's a terrible thing to watch your child not succeed at something they love. And she'd been so nasty beforehand because of the stress.

"My husband and I told her, 'It's OK to love what you're doing and not compete in it. Why can't you just enjoy it and work to get better?'

"It really took stress and pressure off her and me."

Like Gina and Danielle, many parents—and kids—aren't always happy about living in a culture of intensifying competition. There's a strong countercurrent among parents who would like to see their children less stressed and would like to slow down their lives.

That's not a bad idea, suggests the research on competition.

RESEARCH TRUMPS FOLK WISDOM:
COMPETITION DAMPENS MOTIVATION

Even though many of us would guess that competition increases kids' motivation, research has shown the opposite—that competition today often dampens kids' eagerness to learn and play.

Psychologist Ed Deci and his colleagues zeroed in on this phenomenon in a 1981 experiment at his University of Rochester laboratory.

Tall and slim, invariably dressed in comfortable corduroys, Ed usually looks serious, as befits a world-renowned expert on motivation psychology.

As soon as I arrived at Rochester to start my graduate work, Ed became an important mentor, warmly welcoming me into his group of motivation researchers. Those of us who study human motivation, bound by our commitment to enhancing it, care for each other like family. We feed on each other's work, discussing and teaching everyone's ideas endlessly. It was in one such graduate seminar discussion that Ed suggested competition undermines intrinsic motivation. "But competition is fun," some of the students objected. "Especially when you win!" So in 1981 Ed launched an experiment, hoping to find out whether competition chills motivation or heats it up. He recruited a group of college students to work on SOMA puzzles, which are similar to Rubik's cubes. You have to fit seven different-shaped pieces together into one cube, and they can be lots of fun.

Ed sat the students down at tables, each with a partner. He told half the students simply *to solve the puzzles as quickly as they could,* and the other half *to try to beat their tablemate.* The students didn't know that their partners were ringers, instructed by Ed to keep the competition close but to let the student win.

After twenty minutes, Ed told the students the experiment was over. Of course, they had all won. And so, whether or not they'd *tried* to best their tablemate, they had all received the implicit positive feedback of winning.

Then Ed said that he had to leave the room for a few minutes. The students could do more puzzles, he added casually, or read magazines. Ed then watched through a one-way mirror to see what would happen. The students who had been instructed to compete—to *try to beat their* tablemate—spent less time playing with the puzzles than those who had been told simply to do their best. (The women who had competed and "won" spent even *less* time on the puzzle than the male "winners.") The pressure of competition—of trying to beat their tablemates, Ed concluded, had dampened their intrinsic motivation.[30]

A story told by Rosita Mang illustrates how excess competition does just that to kids. "I know of an eight-year-old girl who has won most of the local contests," says the piano teacher. "She has a keyboard in her parents' car. She practices to and from school. She comes home in the afternoon and there is no TV, no computer games, no playing outside with friends. She has to do her homework, plus six hours of piano practice.

"Yes, she wins all the time—but if you talk to her, there is sadness, an emptiness of soul, a lack of awareness that is frightening."

Competitive excess can also harm musicians' playing ability because they haven't had enough time for everyday experiences. "Once I had a student playing a piece that required a tingling kind of sound," she says. "I told her to imagine that a very soft rain would just tingle on her face. She told me that she had never felt rain. Outside we went, I turned on the hose and let her feel it . . . her eyes were bright with excitement. She understood what I meant!"

We often think that teachers who inject little races into the classroom are clever because they know how to "make learning fun," but the research trumps this folk wisdom. In one of many relevant studies, University of Iowa researcher Margaret M. Clifford set up a competitive game in hopes of motivating fifth graders to learn a list of vocabulary words.

"Contrary to prediction," said Clifford, the game improved neither the students' performance nor their retention of correct spellings. The game did spark a bit of interest, she found, but mostly among the winners.[31]

WHEN COMPETITION HARMS KIDS

What goes wrong when competition crushes kids' souls, as it did the eight-year-old pianist's in Rosita Mang's story? Is it simply a matter of too much competition to the exclusion of other activities? Maybe winning or losing makes the difference. Or does competition discourage people, no matter what?

Three years after Ed Deci's experiment, psychologists Carole and Russell Ames surveyed the then burgeoning research on competition and realized that no one was studying how competition affected children. Nor were any researchers examining how it affected people of all ages emotionally. "We wondered," says Carole Ames, "if perhaps competition generated negative feelings that in turn discouraged kids." And if that were so, she and her husband asked, exactly which negative feelings did competition generate?

The Ameses assembled a group of about a hundred children in grades five and six.[32] As Deci had done, they divided them into twos. Then, the researcher told half of the pairs: "The one who solves the most puzzles will be the winner." They told the other half, "Solve as many puzzles as you can."

The Ames also fixed the competition, but differently than Deci had. They gave some children very easy puzzles and others impossible ones, so that one child in each pair solved most of the puzzles and the other solved none.

Then they interviewed the "losers"—the kids who had been told to compete but who had solved none of the puzzles. These kids tended to blame the loss on their own incompetence, and some even checked "yes" next to statements such as "I am stupid." Interestingly, the kids who blamed themselves *most* were those who considered themselves the smartest. The kids who were not competing did not get down on themselves whether or not they were able to solve the puzzles.

It's hard not to blame your incompetence when you lose. And no one likes to feel incompetent. But competition, the Ameses pointed out, almost always creates at least one loser. So that accounts for another problem with competition—losers can feel bad about themselves. It's easy to see how that could depress their motivation to play again.

Competition and Dropping Out of Sports

Perhaps this production of losers is one reason why youngsters steadily drop out of organized sports starting at age ten, with about 50 percent dropping out by age thirteen, and 75 percent by age eighteen.[33] Indeed a raft of studies has found that when it comes to sports, kids put winning quite low on their list of reasons they like to play. They want to learn and sharpen skills, build physical fitness, make friends, and have fun. They also say they like the excitement and the sense of personal accomplishment.[34]

"We surveyed thirty thousand kids eight to twenty-two years old about why they participate in athletics," says the PCA's Jim Perry. "The number one reason from kids was 'Fun.' Winning came in ninth on the girls list, and seventh on the guys list."[35]

What a shame that emphasis on winning so often saps the fun out of sports in the long run!

THE ROLE OF PRESSURE IN COMPETITION

But, as Deci's students reminded him, millions of people like and even passionately love to play games that produce winners and losers. So about a dozen years after the Ameses' experiment, he decided to look for a "good" side to competition. Does it ever benefit people, he wondered, or at least not hinder their motivation? Perhaps a quality or condition such as *pressure to win* determines whether competition motivates or discourages people. In his 1981 experiment he had pressured *all* the competing students to win. Perhaps that pressure squelched their intrinsic motivation, not the competition itself.

To answer these questions, Deci and his colleague Johnmarshall Reeve had one hundred students work on "Happy Cube" puzzles.[36] Created by the Belgian inventor Dirk Laureyssens, Happy Cubes are made of sage-green foam divided into six parts. Players take them out of their frame, fit them together into a perfect cube and then put them back into the frame.

Again, Deci paired each student with a ringer. The experiment began with everyone working on two practice puzzles. Deci had told the accomplices not to finish the first puzzle in three allotted minutes but to finish the second one within one minute. That made the students think that they and their ringer partners had about the same ability, and so they would feel good when they won. Next Deci told the students that everyone now had to work independently and that all partners and their opponents would work in separate rooms.

He then told some of the students to "just do your individual best"—that is, to strive but not to compete—and the others to "outperform your partner by solving your puzzles faster than he or she does"—in other words, to compete. Then he gave half of this "competing group" these directions: "The only thing that matters is which of you wins the competition. *So focus all your attention on being the winner.*" In other words, he pressured half of the competing students to win.

Next the students did four rounds of puzzles. After each round, Deci came in and told each student that he or she had won.

As in the 1981 experiment, Deci then made an excuse to leave the room, telling the students they could do whatever they felt like doing until he returned. Then he watched them through the one-way mirror. Which students would still be interested in the puzzle and enjoy it? he wondered. The results were complicated but interesting: on the one hand, students who'd been *pressured* to win played with the Happy Cubes much less than those who'd competed but had *not* been pressured. The pressured competition had undermined their intrinsic motivation.

On the other hand, Deci had also included several other groups of competing and noncompeting students in the study who were put under different conditions. When he compared *all* the competing students with *all* the noncompeting ones, on average Ed found no difference in how long these two groups played with puzzles when left alone. In other words, on average he found no difference in intrinsic motivation between the two groups. That showed that competition in and of itself hadn't undermined enjoyment and interest. But *pressure* to win had made players focus on winning and losing, undermining their intrinsic motivation.

This study and many others that followed show that it's not competing by itself that determines motivation and enjoyment as much as the ideas and feelings people have about the competition. If the emphasis is on winning—if they feel pressured to come out on top—they are more likely to lose their interest and not enjoy learning or playing. If in a contest you focus on something other than winning—say, how well you had trained or studied, or how much you're enjoying the moment—that focus can prevent competitive games from crushing motivation.

When applied to sports, spelling bees, or even beauty contests, this finding means that parents or coaches who pour on pressure to win are likely to stifle a child's enjoyment. So if you want to encourage your kid to love the game, instead of pressuring him with "Did you win?" you might want to ask, "How was the game?" or "Did you have fun?" Instead of "What did you get on the test?" you could try, "Learn anything interesting in school today?"

That's why the best and most beloved music teachers, for example, prepare both children and parents psychologically before competitions to make sure they don't focus on winning.

"It would be ideal," says Linda Stump, director of competitions for the Music Teachers National Association, "if everybody went into competition with the idea, 'I want this good experience. I want these comments from the judges. I want to grow from them. It doesn't really make any difference if I win or lose...'

"When I was putting my own students in, I told them 'If you're into winning, I'm not putting you in.'"[37]

The "winning is everything" notion contrasts sharply with many parents' and grandparents' childhood memories. Nostalgia can cast a deceptively golden glow over our own childhoods, but nonetheless Jim Perry believes that before adults began organizing most youth sports, kids had more fun. Their games downplayed the pressure to win, he explains.[38]

"When we were growing up, the two best or the two biggest players chose up," remembers Perry. "If the score got lopsided, we stopped the game and switched teams."

X-sports like inline skating, surfing, skateboarding, and BMX biking—as well as video games—have risen in popularity, he adds, because children typically play them without adult pressure to win.

"If you go to a skateboard park, two groups of adults *aren't* there: parents and coaches. A kid tries a move and falls. What happens? The kids say, 'Dude you gotta do that again.' A coach would say, 'No, that's not how you do it!' and a parent would say, 'Honey, are you hurt?'"

LIFE LESSONS

Several organizations have sprung up devoted to convincing coaches and parents to emphasize values other than winning. Among these, the Positive Coaching Alliance recommends that coaches adopt two goals—winning and life lessons—but that parents should focus only on the life lessons. These lessons include teamwork, the importance of respecting the letter and spirit of the rules, how to make and learn from mistakes, and self-discipline.

Positive Coaching Alliance workshops show parents how to do just that. One evening at a Los Angeles community recreation center, Perry posed a hypothetical question to a group of basketball league parents.

"Your child had a chance to make a winning basket in the game, but he goes to the free throw line and misses the shot," Perry tosses out to them. "The game's over. Your son says, 'The kids at school are gonna hate me. They'll never pick me to play again.'

"What do you say to him?"

The parents confer, turning their folding chairs to form little clusters of three and four. After a few minutes they rotate back to face the white-haired Perry, who stands in front, hands on the hips of his shiny blue warm-ups.

"Yes, they *will* pick you," says the spokesman for one group, "because they miss too."

Perry nods.

"I'm proud," the second parent reads from a sheet of paper. "It was an exciting game to watch. You did your best. The only way to get good is to have the opportunity to try. You'll go back out there and play tomorrow and there'll be another game next week."

"That's good," Perry says. "Help the kid put it in perspective."

"I think Michael Jordan has missed shots too. Even pros—all they can do is try their best," says another parent.

"Look how far we came," says another parent. "You made positive plays during the game. Your shot wasn't the difference in the game. If we hadn't kicked the ball that time or missed two lay-ups...if we'd made all the free throws we missed...if two guys hadn't fouled out...we'd have never been in that spot to begin with."

"I like that," says Perry. "Kids have to understand it's not just about that one play.

"And if we put incredible emphasis on winning versus losing, we'll drive kids away from the very thing we want them to participate in."

MORE REASONS WHY COMPETITION IS COUNTERPRODUCTIVE

Author Alfie Kohn has written eloquently about how competition alienates people from each other. In contests, he points out, "other people are not partners but opponents, not potential friends but rivals."[39]

Competing takes the focus off other goals such as learning and enjoying. It can produce anxiety that inhibits learning—and, ironically, winning—because it produces anxiety, as it did with Gina's daughter during horse shows. I have a similar memory of being a ninth grader, shaking as I took an exam to win the loving cup awarded to "best English student" on junior high school graduation night. I was so anxious to win that I went back to check my answers and changed so many that I did poorly on that test.

Likewise, athletes who concentrate only on winning often don't play their best game, because the narrow mental focus disrupts their mind-body coordination, interrupting their smooth functioning. Imagine a tennis player focusing only on winning the point: she might half-swing because she's worried she'll hit the ball out. Her fluid strokes become choppy.

In fact, as we'll see later, researchers have found that intrinsic motivation increases performance and learning more than competition does. As Kohn puts it, "We do best at the tasks we enjoy."

COMPETITIVE PRESSURE PROMOTES A CULTURE OF CHEATING

Emphasizing winning over other goals and attaching high stakes to it encourages people like an infamous high school football team coach who was caught by a video camera moving back the ten-yard marker so that his team would make a first down. His team went on to score a touchdown, winning the league championship—but at what cost to the teenage players' ethical education?

There must be a lot of pressure to win in America, because it's common to see a child fall on the ground faking a soccer injury, or dropping a water bottle on the basketball court to gain a time out. In fact, when the Josephson Institute of Ethics, a Los Angeles nonprofit institute, surveyed more than five thousand high school athletes in 2005 and 2006, nearly half of high school baseball players agreed it was fine for a baseball coach to order his pitcher to throw at an opposing hitter. (Only 10 percent of *girl* softball players agreed.)[40]

Competitive pressure sullies our academic culture too. When the Josephson Institute questioned thirty-five thousand students in 2006, it found that 60 percent had cheated during a test at school within the past twelve months. Thirty-five percent said they'd cheated more than once.[41]

"Kids today are more accepting of cheating, lying, and fudging than their parents ever were," says Los Angeles psychotherapist Dee Shepherd-Look. "They have really rationalized that it's OK for them. 'There's so much competition—you have to do it to get into grad school,' they'll say, or, 'I really need this GPA because I have a loan or scholarship and I really have to stay in school.'

"'Don't you know that everybody's cheating and you have to cheat to get the grade?'"[42]

Teenagers padding their accomplishments—lying on—their college applications, sometimes to the point of absurdity, shows how the competitive college hysteria promotes cheating. It also divorces students from their more genuine selves.

"I see kids who are so packaged it's depressing to have a conversation with them," says Bruce Poch, Pomona College vice president and dean of admissions. "They have this Botox look—like their face is frozen—as they try to tell you how much they love what they're doing. There's no emotion behind it."[43]

The fudging isn't limited to high school. A survey of more than five thousand students at thirty-two business graduate schools in the United States and Canada found that fifty-six percent admitted to cheating at least once in the past academic year. Students said they cheated to keep up with other students, whom they assumed were also cheating.[44]

The corner-cutting, cynical tricks, and outright fraud promoted by the heightened academic competition disturbs many parents. "They're worried their kids are going to grow up and be Mr. Enron," says Shepherd-Look, who also teaches at California State University, Northridge.

GOOD COMPETITION CAN BE THRILLING

Competition can be fun and exciting when children aren't pressured to win and when the stakes aren't so high that they cause anxiety. Parents can play a huge role in taking pressure off youngsters and helping them to value fun and skill-building more than winning.

My daughter Allison has adopted this mind-set. When she was twelve, she lost interest in soccer but had a slightly older friend who loved field hockey.

"Sure," we said when she asked if she could go to the hockey camp her friend was attending at a local college.

When we arrived at the first day of camp, the scent of chlorophyll from the freshly mowed, dewy lawns and the hard thwacks of sticks against white balls filled me with excitement. But soon the sight of fourteen- and fifteen-year-olds rotating their sticks expertly sent panic rising in my throat. This camp was too advanced for Allie. She was going to feel lost and discouraged among these highly skilled girls.

"Maybe we should find another program for girls like you who are just beginning to learn hockey," I whispered to her.

"Oh, no, Mom, I don't think so," she said, eagerly watching the older girls warming up. "I'm sure I'll learn a lot here."

Every day of that camp, Allie brought home stories about what she'd learned. Her excitement kept mounting. Four years later, she still loves hockey for the pure joy of playing the sport well. She especially enjoys learning skills, and if she succeeds with a new tactic or move, she feels great.

Once after losing a game she said, "We lost, but it was the best game ever. Did you see that reverse chip? And our passing game was magic. Everyone on our team played so well together. It was beautiful field hockey. That was so cool."

Music competitions likewise provide a great chance to build skills and create beauty. They give students "a reason to polish their repertoire—to finish something and get it to the highest level possible," explains Ingrid Clarfield, who teaches piano in Princeton, New Jersey.[45]

IS THERE AN ALTERNATIVE TO COMPETITION?

What can we do about the excessive competitive pressure in our kids' lives? One solution is to promote cooperation whenever and wherever possible. A slew of studies have shown that cooperation produces higher achievement, lower anxiety, better self-esteem, closer relationships, and more motivation than competition.

Volleyball, basketball, field hockey, and other team sports give kids an opportunity to enjoy the benefits of cooperation. Since the group sinks or swims together, players can encourage excellence in each other. The same principle applies to academics. Rather than encouraging students to vie against each other, research has found that fostering cooperation strengthens learning.

For example, University of Minnesota psychologist David Johnson examined hundreds of studies that compared cooperation and competition in school. He found that in 316 out of 351 cases cooperative activities among students produced significantly higher academic achievement. He also discovered 98 examples of pupils liking their lessons more while working cooperatively but only 12 such examples when they were working competitively.[46]

Other researchers have pointed out that when kids cooperate as a team, and if teams are organized fairly, everyone has an equal chance to win.[47] Teams also promote feelings of friendship rather than hostility and reduce performance anxiety.

When I speak at schools and suggest that kids learn well when they work in a team on an academic project, parents often bristle. "Ughhh," they say. "There'll always be one or two who do all the work and the rest kick back and do nothing" (most people remember themselves as carrying the load).[48] But if the teacher structures cooperation properly, that's not what happens. Teachers have to divide roles, material, resources, and information among group members in a way that requires everyone to contribute and to hold students individually accountable. For example, a teacher might tell a team of students that one of them will present their solution for a math problem to the whole class—but she won't tell them *who* will present it until the last minute.

Contrary to popular belief, grouping the "bright" kids and the "slower" kids separately doesn't yield the best learning for either group. As the fictionalized Anna told the king of Siam,

> *It's a very ancient saying,*
> *But a true and honest thought,*
> *That if you become a teacher,*
> *By your pupils you'll be taught.*

That applies to cooperative learning. Research has shown that helping another student to learn makes kids organize their thinking better and stimulates them to explain their ideas more fully. As they recognize and fill in the gaps in each other's understanding, all students benefit. This form of learning can also teach the social skills of communication and managing conflicts. That's one reason study groups work, and why it's not a bad idea for kids to study together (so long as they stick to studying).

When a group of students investigates a topic—"Why is there no snow in Maine this December?" for example, or "How do cell phones work?"—they can decide together on their division of labor for conducting their investigation. They'll present a final report to the class—perhaps using PowerPoint—and may even propose the questions for testing how well their classmates learned from their presentation. This model, called Group Investigation, yields high academic achievement.[49]

Psychologist Elliott Aronson of the University of California, Santa Cruz, invented a similar "jigsaw method" of learning in 1971.[50] Here's how it works: the teacher assigns a group of five or six students to learn, say, about World War II. Each student is responsible for researching one piece of the picture—Hitler's rise to power, concentration camps, Britain's role in the war, or the development of the atomic bomb. Students who are investigating the same topic for different groups meet and test out their presentations on each other. Finally, each pupil reports what she's learned to her original group. Then the teacher tests the entire class on what they've learned about World War II.

This method has been shown not only to boost student achievement but also to soothe racial tensions. "When the structure of the classroom is set up so that students must cooperate with one another in order to do well, they begin to see positive things in each other that they wouldn't have seen while competing against each other," says Aronson. "This creates a climate where prejudicial attitudes can begin to fade."[51]

But cooperative learning takes simpler forms too. A teacher can assign a group to answer a question ("Why are scientists excited about finding water on Mars?"). Or she can form a group of students with differing abilities or knowledge and ask them to help each other until everyone understands how to solve a particular geometry problem.[52]

NATIONAL COMPETITIONS

Some national student academic contests provide good examples of cooperative learning and fulfill many of the criteria for fun, fair, and motivating competition. The Future Problem Solving Program (FPSP), for example, is designed to balance cooperation and competition. One goal of the contest is teaching students to pool their knowledge with others and to play up each other's strengths. It involves about two hundred and fifty thousand students annually from the United States, Canada, Australia, New Zealand, Korea, Malaysia, and Russia. In its Team Problem Solving contest, groups of four students, guided by a teacher/coach, use a six-step model to propose action plans to complex social problems. The topics of competition in 2007–2008 were Body Enhancement, Simulation Technology, Neurotechnology, Debt in Developing Countries, and Child Labor.[53]

In the *FIRST* Robotics Competition, high school students work cooperatively in teams. Each group receives a standard "kit of parts" and rules. Working with professional mentors, they have six weeks to solve the engineering design problem of building a robot from these parts. Then they enter their robots in competitions designed by engineers. Judges rate the teams according to excellence in design, demonstrated team spirit, gracious professionalism and maturity, and ability to overcome obstacles.[54]

The success of these programs belies the stereotype of inventors and scientists as men working alone in a laboratory late at night. You might think that it's crucial for your son or daughter to learn to compete as an individual, but the ability to work in a diverse group may well be more important. Today especially, with the crossovers and synergies between disciplines—often as the result of new technology—"the exciting developments come out of interdisciplinary working groups," says the Nobel Prize winner Paul Greengard.[55]

A study by psychologist Robert L. Helmreich of the University of Texas backs up that de-emphasis on competitiveness. Helmreich rated 103 male PhD scientists on their orientation toward work, their preference for challenging tasks, and their competitiveness. Then he rated their achievement by how often colleagues cited their work. The scientists who had the most citations rated high in work orientation and preference for challenge but low on the competitiveness scale.[56]

Our children are bathed in competition, and some of it is exciting and fun. Very often however—especially if adults stress winning as the number one goal—it dampens kids' inner passions and increases their anxiety. It also takes their focus off the goals of learning and building their skills. When competition has high stakes, it can encourage shortcuts like cheating. Rivalry injects hostility into relationships, while cooperation creates friendships. Schools, parents, and coaches should examine with skepticism the widespread belief that competition is motivating and look around for ways to foster cooperation.

But as much as you might like them to, our kids can't avoid competition, especially in academics. And when these competitive threats collide with your parental hardwiring, that's what creates the Pressured Parent Phenomenon.

CHAPTER 3

IT'S AN ANIMAL THING
When Our Hardwiring Goes Haywire

Last year, my friend Leslie e-mailed me:

> This morning at Maya's middle school graduation I sat hoping she would win one of the awards, that someone besides me would notice how special she is. She got an award for being on the honor roll three straight years, but so did fifty other kids. Why am I not satisfied with that in my heart? I wanted her to get the Best Math Student award!!

I wrote back:

> I know just what you mean.
>
> I remember sitting on the edge of my seat hoping Jeff would win an award at middle school graduation. Nada. Tommy MacDonald won almost every award. He also played a violin solo with the orchestra, and was president of the class. Everyone laughed as he kept jumping down from the stage to the orchestra and back up again. I wanted *my* kid to get all those honors, not him!
>
> Later when Jeff graduated from high school he got the "Most Improved Student" award. I felt wonderful for three days. Now that he's finished college, I never think about it.
>
> These awards are meaningless in later life, so why do schools keep giving them out? And why do we care so much about them?

"Yeah," Leslie answered. "I can't believe how much this upset me. I never would have thought I felt so competitive!"

Every parent at one time or other experiences fierce emotions like Leslie's and mine. They make us feel uncomfortable, even ashamed. "I try to be kind, to wish other kids and their parents well," you think. "So why do these selfish and competitive feelings come over me?"

Our culture fosters this shame by regularly criticizing us. We're trying to one-up other parents! the media tell us. We're overscheduling our kids in an effort to perfect them!

It's the popular sport of parent-blaming that experts resort to when they lack a better explanation. No wonder we feel guilty and confess our feelings only to a close friend or partner who won't criticize us, or anonymously in cyberspace on a chat board.

But with competition expanding exponentially in our children's lives, our minds and bodies have to cope with these intense feelings almost daily.

"We put Josh in preschool at twenty-one months," says David Breitweiser, a Los Angeles father of three sons, "because everyone insisted we had to, if we wanted him to get into this particular school.

"It was crazy—he was too young—but we felt we *had* to do it. Like something awful would happen if we didn't.

"I felt a pull inside me," he says, rapping a fist on his breastbone. "Right here. I'd give anything to understand what that was."

Fortunately, the new science of evolutionary biology explains where these powerful and irrational feelings come from: they emanate from our evolutionary hardwiring. Our hunter-gatherer ancestors who carried children on their backs had to protect them from a world full of dangers, such as ravenous lions and monkeys vying for meat. Those who encouraged their children to compete for scarce resources including food and shelter helped their kids survive and reproduce, passing their genes down to succeeding generations.

Over millions of years, this trait piled up in the population and spread throughout our gene pool. We're the modern recipients, hardwired to want our children to win whatever battles they may face. Whenever our kids meet a competitive danger, our minds and bodies go on high alert. We receive signals of anxiety and alarm, inciting us to push our children forward to compete. When they do well, we're thrilled, but when they don't, we worry what it means for the future. *What if he misses out, falls behind?* Occasionally the intensity of our alarm is justified, but often it outstrips the magnitude of the danger.

That's not all. Nature has also reinforced this protective hardwiring with a second intertwining filament—an affectional system that fills us with love for our children and prompts us to care for them. This love makes us want the best for our kids; we want them to lead happy lives. It provides a daily pull inside of us so deep and strong that we invest a great deal of time and energy in our children, making sacrifices for them along the way.

This sturdy cord of protective and loving hardwiring is the force that drove David to sign up his toddler for that preschool, while another part of his brain participated only under protest, shouting, "This is nuts!"

Such strong, irrational feelings are normal and absolutely understandable. They're just activated in today's competitive environment too often for our own good and for the good of our children. While having such powerful emotions doesn't create problems, heedlessly acting on them does.

Let's explore the source of these feelings. Knowing where your turbulent emotions come from will help you feel comfortable thinking about them. That in turn will prepare you to master them for your own benefit and your child's. Maybe you'll even chuckle at this relic from our animal past.

FIGHT OR FLIGHT, THE PARENTAL VERSION

The pull that took over David's chest when he thought about getting Josh into preschool illustrates the strong bodily component of the Pressured Parent Phenomenon. It's not a rational train of thought that overwhelms us at such moments. To the contrary, we often feel that our guts are pushing us on a path that our minds don't want to take. You don't *think* that your three-year-old really needs a soccer skills prep clinic—in fact, it seems ridiculous—but when you hear that her friends are signing up, you panic.

"They'll play better than Sarah!" you think. "Next year when they start league soccer she won't know how to kick! Maybe she'll *never* catch up to them!"

The pounding heart in your chest, as your thoughts spiral catastrophically downward, comes straight from your hardwiring. It's a variation of the human stress response, triggered by the competitive "menace" facing your child.

Whenever we sense our children at risk, our minds and bodies respond automatically. That gene inherited from our ancestors alerts neurotransmitters to activate our reptilian fear center, the amygdala, bypassing the brain's rational intelligence region and flooding us with anxiety and fear. Our muscles tense up just as our ancestors' did when they eyed a hungry hyena tromping toward their babies.

That's how Gina Kelly feels when Nicole plays soccer goalie and faces a penalty kick alone.

"I'm sitting on my lawn chair," says Gina. "My head feels like—like it's got a clenched fist in it. When they kick the ball and Nicole dives for it, I shift to the left or the right, like *I'm* going for the ball."

That parental muscle movement results from what biologist Robert Sapolsky calls "physiological uproar." The body's own emergency team springs into action: your muscles need energy, STAT! Brain, blood, hormones, and organs mobilize to deliver it in the form of glucose to your arms and legs. The brain's hypothalamus sets off a cascade of chemicals, releasing hormones which in turn prompt the pituitary gland, just underneath the brain, to release the hormone corticotrophin, or ACTH, into the bloodstream. The ACTH instructs your adrenal gland to release the stress hormones cortisol and cate-cholamines (also called adrenaline and noradrenaline), which tell the liver to generate new glucose and shoot it into the bloodstream.

To speed up the glucose delivery, some major arteries constrict, which raises your blood pressure and speeds up your heart. Breathing quickens, helping the lungs pump the increased oxygen needed to accelerate circulation. Finally, blood delivers the energy to your muscles, which, if you don't use them to fight or flee, clench.

Other hormones simultaneously shut down unnecessary processes including digestion, so your saliva dries up, parching your mouth and throat. You may go pale as the blood diverted to your muscles drains from your face. Your palms and armpits get clammy as sweat surfaces to cool down your body, which has just been heated by the sudden rush of action.

FINDING THE ROOTS OF OUR PARENTING
AND OF THE PRESSURED PARENT PHENOMENON

But why do relatively small competitive situations like a penalty kick in soccer set off this powerful fight-or-flight response? Why can trivial events put us through such extreme physical and emotional anguish? To understand this Pressured Parent Phenomenon, we'll use evolutionary psychology, which explores the development of human systems and traits over millions of years. Also called sociobiology, it relies on the theory of natural selection first elaborated by Darwin in his 1859 *Origin of Species*. As you undoubtedly know, this theory proposes that organisms with genes that are best adapted to the environment are more likely than others to survive and reproduce and will pass those genes on to future generations.

Since parenting, like sexuality, is key to survival and reproduction, it's not surprising that evolution has shaped it. Nature wouldn't leave this crucial behavior pattern to chance! To figure out how this shaping developed, evolutionary psychologists have studied the parenting strategies of different species.

Leading the way in this research is Edward O. Wilson, often called the father of sociobiology. His interest in animal habits blossomed at the age of seven when his divorcing parents sent him to board for the summer with a family in Paradise Beach, Florida. There Wilson fell in love with the natural world of jellyfish and needlefish, of blue crabs, sea trout, and stingrays. He spent many hours angling for pinfish, a species that has ten needlelike spines on the dorsal fin that stick straight up when it is threatened. One day, feeling a pull on his minnow hook, Wilson yanked so hard that a pinfish flew into his face, and one of its spines pierced the pupil of his right eye.[1]

Not only did Wilson lose half his sight, but as a teenager, he lost his hearing in the high registers, probably because of a hereditary defect. These combined sensory losses prevented him from watching birds and frogs, so Wilson turned to insects. As he studied the social behavior of ants, especially their communication through chemicals, he began to wonder about the genetic basis of the social behavior of animals in general. In 1975 he published *Sociobiology: The New Synthesis*, a hefty tome that includes an examination of the parenting behavior of dozens of animals.

Some species, Wilson saw, live in short-lived, unpredictable habitats such as the mud surface of a new river bar or the bottom of a nutrient-rich rain pool. They maximize their brood's survival by quickly reproducing many small offspring, giving them very little time, care, or food. That way they use up the resources of this ephemeral habitat swiftly, before it disappears or another species horns in on it. Not big fans of quality time, they stake their genetic bets instead on reproducing in quantity.

Similarly, hemipterous bugs, like bedbugs, simply deposit their eggs on a plant or a mattress and take off.[2]

Wilson and his colleague Robert MacArthur called this parenting pattern "r-selected," the "r" standing for "rapid."[3] Other r-selected animals include voles, or field mice. Living in meadows and along rivers, they are prey to voracious killers including the red fox and the striped skunk, so their survival strategy also involves mass reproduction with minimal nurturing. A female field mouse has as many as twelve litters of two to nine babies. She cares for her young in the nest until they're two weeks old and then moves away, never to return.

Many other animals, including humans, follow a diametrically opposite parenting pattern, called K-selected ("K" stands for "carrying capacity" or "saturation level"). They live in a stable, predictable environment such as a cave wall or an old climax forest, where animals have lived for a long time and populated it at or near its saturation level. These species follow a survival strategy of grooming a few large offspring to be highly competitive. Their babies are born spaced apart rather than in a litter. Their "survivorship is improved," wrote Wilson, "by special attention during their early development."[4]

The great parent tit bird is a poster child for this special-attention feature of the K-selected strategy, bringing its nested babies a tasty new morsel of food every thirty minutes. Other animals that nurture their young intensively include emus, the eider duck, and the golden pheasant, which sits on its eggs and goes without food until the baby birds hatch.[5] Some K-selected insects even carry around their newly hatched young in abdominal pouches.

Like other K-selected species, we live in an old, relatively stable and predictable habitat that is at or near saturation point. We raise a small number of children but invest large amounts of time and energy in them so they'll be competitive in the race for survival. This pattern has evolved as the most successful parenting strategy for humans and many other animals. Wilson called it "high investment parenting," using a term coined by Robert Trivers, an idiosyncratic sociobiologist whose work on the evolutionary basis of human relationships made Harvard psychologist Steven Pinker dub him "one of the great thinkers in the history of Western thought."[6]

Dropping out of Harvard as a freshman, Trivers found a job writing children's books on animal behavior. As he watched films about baboons, he noticed that they disciplined their young similarly to humans but without language. The root of this shared behavior, he concluded, had to be evolutionary. As he explored these ideas in the early 1970s, Trivers used the phrase *parental investment* for the special way that humans treat their children. He defined it as whatever resources parents invest in their children that increase their chance of surviving and reproducing. It's the time and energy it takes to have and raise kids.[7]

Human physiology has evolved in a way that demands high-investment parenting. As our species became ever smarter, babies' heads grew ever larger. But the narrow human pelvis, necessary for walking upright, affords women a narrow birth canal. If the rest of the infant body were as large and well developed as the head, it couldn't navigate this passage. So human babies are born relatively prematurely and helpless, and they stay that way for a long time. They demand an extended learning period (one that seems to be getting longer and longer) and high investments of time, energy, and—increasingly—money.

Why do mothers feel so conflicted about returning to work when their children are young? Why do parents look so obsessively for a good school for their children? Why do we take so much pleasure in teaching our children how to set the table, or fish, or find a square root? Why do we feel so good when buying them warm clothes for winter or making them hot soup?

All of these "taking care" behaviors have a genetic root. Evolution has selected for those genes that propel us to protect and nurture our relatively helpless children during their long preparation for independent adulthood.

But, you might say, how do we know our genes propel us to invest only in our own children so intensively? Maybe parents care equally about the upbringing of *all* children. How do we know that they take their own children's behavior to heart more than other children's? A study by Canadian researchers Tess Dawber and Leon Kuczynski addresses that question.[8] Do mothers feel differently when their children's playmates and their own kids misbehave? they asked. Do they treat the playmates' disobedience the same way they treat their own children's naughtiness?

Dawber and Kuczynski asked mothers of six-to-eight-year-olds what they would do if they saw their own child, their child's friend, or a child they'd just met disobeying. How upset would they feel if these kids ran across the street without looking or stole candy from a store?

"What discipline would you apply?" they asked the mothers. "What would you hope it would accomplish?"

The researchers found that the mothers would scold their own child more strongly and care far more about teaching him a long-term lesson. They would feel much more distressed when their own child misbehaved.

We may like and enjoy, even love our friends' children, but since our own kids share 50 percent of our genes, evolution makes the parent-child relationship special. Caring for nieces, nephews, and grandchildren is likewise favored by evolution because they, too, share our genes, although not as many as our children do.

That's not to say that adoptive parents don't love and nurture their children just as intensely as biological parents do. Studies show, for example, that female rats at first may ignore and even push away other mothers' babies placed in their cages. Eventually, however, they start to look after these children, keeping them warm and piling them up with their other babies. "They do everything except give them milk," says Rutgers University neuroscientist Tracey Shors.[9] That suggests an evolutionary psychological basis for parents' strong feelings of love for their adopted children.

BOTH PARENTS ARE HARDWIRED TO PROTECT THE TIGER BAIT

Charles Darwin kept a diary in which he mused about his family life and the light it cast on his emerging theory of natural selection. A few months after his wedding day, and not long after he and his wife, Emma, had conceived their first child, the naturalist posed a question in this journal. Why, he asked, does a husband's "kindness to wife and children…give him pleasure, without any regard to his own interest?"[10]

While Darwin did not fully answer this question in his lifetime, evolutionary biologists have recently done so. Men, they've concluded, are hardwired to love and nurture their children—similar to women, but (and this will not surprise you) not in an identical way.

Primate fathers supply evidence for this conclusion. Biologists have found that when male primates know which children are theirs, they usually take care of them.[11] A few primate dads even provide extreme amounts of childcare. For example, until the combined weight of his two offspring rivals his, the male marmoset carries them around all day, handing them over to their mother only at mealtime. Male siamangs—small, acrobatic advanced apes from Southeast Asia—lug their infants around while the family forages for food together. And some Japanese macaque fathers babysit for their one-year-olds while their mates take care of their newborns.[12]

While these particularly stellar primate fathers outstrip the average human dad, evolution has nonetheless shaped men to take care of their children far more than the average primate.[13] The vulnerability of human babies largely accounts for this hardwiring of paternal nurturance. As author Robert Wright puts it, for many months our babies are "mounds of helpless flesh: tiger bait."[14]

This helplessness means that a second parent around the cave went a long way toward protecting babies from predators. And—just as male birds hunt worms while females warm the eggs in the nest—someone needed to go hunt for food while human mothers nursed their babies. Tellingly, while most primates (gibbons are an exception) don't pair up for life, every human culture studied by anthropologists encompasses some form of marriage.

Evolution has selected out fathering genes for a third reason in humans: as the brain grew, educational input from a second parent gave the baby an edge. "Information is power" operated even in primitive times, as the children most likely to survive and reproduce were those who had *two* parents showing them how to shake fruit down from trees and where to hide from rampaging saber-tooths. Trivers termed this help that dads supply in feeding, defending, and teaching their children "male parental investment."[15]

THE FILAMENT OF LOVE

What makes mothers and fathers invest so much time and energy in our children? No one pays or forces us. It comes naturally. That's because to set in motion our high-investment parenting, nature has equipped us with a system of "affiliation," or love.

Parents' love for their children ranks high in the hierarchy of human emotions. Our fierce feelings of affection prompt us to give our children the intense care they need over their long period of vulnerability. Love makes us *want* to invest our time and energy in our children. It not only makes the world go around, but it also ensures the survival of our genes.

Since babies need such intense care, we feel especially tender toward them. That affection spills over into the animal world, explaining why we also adore kittens, puppies, and other baby animals and enjoy petting or "grooming" them. How beautiful, how adorable are our babies! Don't you just want to cuddle them? These feelings ensure that we respond to our infant's every cry, sacrificing our work, play, showers, and sleep. Love fills us with such a surge of responsibility that on the day his first child was born, my brother-in-law ran out and bought life insurance. Nor is it uncommon today for highly educated women to quit lucrative careers—at least temporarily—and throw themselves wholeheartedly into mothering, so potent is the loving hardwiring that switches on with childbirth.

Evolution has also given us instincts to help our children grow and learn.

Our baby talk, with its exaggerated intonation, helps babies learn words faster than a monotone would.[16] We automatically play games like peek-a-boo that teach the basic scientific fact that objects exist even when we don't see them. The modern obsession over our kids' schooling has the same instinctive source. Formal education is another stage in the long period of learning that children need to move away from helplessness and into adulthood and eventually to parenthood.

An Internal Reward System

Many studies have shown that laboratory rats, well known for pressing a bar to receive food, will also tap that bar to bring their babies closer. Now that new technology can document human neural activity, researchers are investigating similar mechanisms in parents, using photographs and magnetic resonance imaging rather than bars and food pellets for their studies. Two British neuroscientists, Andreas Bartels and Semir Zeki, of University College London, have examined how love affects the human brain. Recently they scanned the brains of mothers as they looked at photos of their nine-month-old to six-year-old children. As the moms gazed at their kids, brain areas showing activity included the basal ganglia, which release dopamine, the neurotransmitter that gives us a feeling of pleasure. That's the same reward system that makes us feel good when we eat chocolate, win money, or even abuse cocaine.[17] These reward areas didn't light up when the mothers looked at pictures of several other people, including other children they knew.

While the mothers looked at pictures of their children, the brain scans also showed deactivation in regions "associated with negative emotions and social judgment," which might account for why we sometimes think our children are perfect.

"Human attachment," conclude Bartels and Zeki, "...bonds individuals through the involvement of the reward circuitry, explaining the power of love to motivate and exhilarate."[18] In other words, our loving feelings bring with them a physiological reward system that makes us feel good when we're close to our children. That helps explain bonding with our kids and why (as much as we'd rather not be around our whiny two-year-olds) their presence so often brings us a feeling of calm well-being. Separation, on the other hand, can evoke intense feelings of loss, as anyone who has had to leave a premature baby in an incubator knows. Similarly, taking a child to a babysitter or to childcare for the first time can cause a psychological ache along with the physical pain of very full breasts. No wonder parents across the country have protested school district bans on cell phones, which make us feel near to our children.[19]

We also feel pleasure in taking care of our children as they grow. Love makes us *want* to feed and clothe our kids, and the reward system often makes us happy to do so. We feel satisfied when they like the food we give them and eat well. It feels good to buy them school notebooks, computer equipment, ballet slippers, and baseball bats. The proverbial high-powered executive may feel a sudden surge of joy wrapping a birthday present for her child. That's why politicians who drop out of races so frequently claim "more time with their families" as their reason. Whether or not they genuinely want to return to the hearth, they know that the voters will understand, because they're expressing such a widely shared emotion.

Seeing our kids succeed and thrive thus brings us immense pleasure. We want the best for them. That's why we provide all the opportunities we can for them to learn and grow. Giving them music lessons and museum science classes, signing them up for scouting or religious school gives us pleasure, because it's the modern equivalent of teaching a child which berries to pick or how to hone an arrowhead. Most of us don't want our children to win best math student awards so that we can brag obnoxiously about them. We want them to win because our hardwiring knows that the more competent our children are, the more likely they will pass on our genes. As Ellen Garfield, a Pittsburgh mother of a six-year-old, put it, "It's very hard to resist that temptation to have the perfect child."

We enjoy caring for our children even when they are semi-independent. A few years ago I attended a talk by psychologist Michael Thompson for parents of high school students. The approaching separation from their teenagers, said Thompson, feeds parents' anxiety about college admissions. He recounted his own compulsion to care for his daughter during her freshman year at a Florida college. The area had already undergone two hurricanes, losing its electricity temporarily, when he heard reports of a third storm approaching. He called his daughter, wondering how he could protect her when she was a thousand miles away.

"Do you have a flashlight?" he asked.

"Dad, don't worry," she said. "They have an emergency generator for each residence hall."

The next morning Thompson shipped her a flashlight. The audience laughed, recognizing this primal urge to care for our kids their whole lives long.

Since we care for our children so deeply, we want them to feel good about themselves, achieve their goals, and have thriving and wonderful lives. When we say, "I want Jeremy to do well in school because I want him to feel self-confident and happy," that's our affiliation system talking. It's most often not the narcissistic, boastful egotism that some parenting experts love to criticize. It's our love combined with our protective hard-wiring that makes our kids' feelings become our feelings. That's why our hearts break when they're sad, as Gina Kelly's did when her daughter didn't make the national basketball team.

"I love my child, so when she competes at something she enjoys, I'm there supporting her," says Gina. "Out of love for her I'm saying, 'Make that team! Score that goal!' Because I want what she wants.

"I want her not to fail for her own happiness. It's empathy for her."

That's why hearing that a child will get an incompetent sixth-grade teacher or won't make the traveling hockey team can dis-

PRIDE STEMS FROM OUR FEELINGS OF LOVE

In the preface I mentioned wanting to tell everyone I knew when Rebecca started walking at eight months. This "I want to tell the world!" pride comes straight from our affectional system. Nature draws us into intense investment in our children by rewarding us with surges of delight when our baby takes his first steps, says his first word, and connects his bat and the T-ball for the first time. How bright our children seem to us. How ingenious, how clever, how amazing! Of *course* we want to tell the world!

I realized the primordial roots of this pride the first day that my kitten came and pawed on my shoe to tell me she wanted breakfast. A wave of smugness washed over me. "My cat is so bright!" I thought happily for a few seconds. Then I laughed, realizing the absurdity.

When we share these feelings of pride with others, it's called bragging. Most of us recognize this universal sign of love and therefore empathize with others' desires to boast: 94 percent of those polled in 2006 by *Parenting* magazine said that other mothers brag about their kids, but only 16 percent said they were "sick of hearing it." At the same time, probably because they don't like admitting their competitiveness, a smaller number of parents—70 percent—admitted that *they* talk about their children's feats, but only if asked.[20]

Published in the *New York Times* January 10, 2006

To the Editor:

I agree completely with "Honk If You Adore My Child Too" (Thursday Styles, Jan. 5). But I want to add that grandparents are much more guilty of bragging about their grandchildren than even their parents.

I am a grandmother, and I, too, brag at times, but not as much as any of the other grandmother friends of mine. Everyone I know has the most intelligent grandchild in the world—the highest SAT scores ever, the best Ivy League colleges seeking them out.

All are in honor classes from kindergarten on. Everyone's child is a valedictorian. Of course, all these children are the most gorgeous and friendly as well as talented.

I am so sick of listening to these braggarts that I am giving up my social life. After all, it is only my grandchildren and not theirs who are brilliant, talented and beautiful.

Elaine Smith Leonard

Hartsdale, NY

tress us so much. All these loving feelings converge toward the same goal: producing children who will be strong and capable, who will have the qualities to survive and reproduce.

So whenever the overheated culture of competition enters our kids' lives, we want them to win, but we also want them to do well because we love them. Our protective and loving hardwiring intertwine. They meld in our minds and hearts. These are the complex feelings that unite to produce the Pressured Parent Phenomenon. They explain why, whenever our kids compete, we watch anxiously, hanging on their every move, exulting when they do well, and worrying when they don't.

Now let's examine why even the tiniest bit of competition facing our children can bring on our panic.

PROTECTING OUR KIDS: IT'S IN OUR GENES

An Anxiety Doctor's Worry Leads to Discovering the Smoke Detector Principle

While many beetles hardly care for their young at all, the *Bledius spectabilis*, a species of rove beetle, lavishes an exceptionally high degree of care on her young. That's because it inhabits an extremely difficult environment for an insect—the intertidal mud of Russia and other northern European coasts, which are highly salty and short on oxygen. So to protect her offspring, the *Bledius spectabilis* digs a burrow and deposits her larvae there to protect them from ravenous insect intruders. She scours the land for food, frequently delivering to her young delicious meals of fresh algae. Nature has given this beetle the ability to tailor its parenting to the fierce competition in its harsh surroundings.

Since our ancestors also evolved in a highly competitive and harsh environment we are, like this beetle, a K-selected species intensely focused on the welfare of our children. That means we are highly sensitive to the merest hint of threat to them. How often we fear the worst, and how easily we panic! How often our alarm system goes off!

Sometimes even the mundane challenges of childhood frighten us. Whenever Zach or Jeff walked to the mound to pitch in Little League, for example, I felt a flash of dread. My heart beat wildly, and if either of them walked a few batters to first base, I silently moaned with anxiety.

Why did I feel such major angst over a ten-year-old throwing a small white ball? It wasn't a matter of life or death. Why did I feel as if it was?

The answer lies in what University of Michigan psychiatrist Randolph Nesse calls "the smoke detector principle." Nesse compares our response system to a smoke detector that goes off every time you burn a bagel.[21] Our hardwiring is similarly supersensitive because the cost of *not* responding to a threat was so high in our dangerous ancestral environment.

A teddy bear of a man with a graying beard and a ready chuckle, Nesse practices in the university's anxiety clinic. One summer afternoon while seeing patients there, he began to question whether he might be harming patients by ridding them of their anxiety. Hmmm, you might think, that's odd—a doctor worrying because he cures his patients. Had he caught some of their angst?

But Nesse also researches the evolutionary origins and functions of the emotions. So his musing wandered to the idea that natural selection has shaped and tuned the body's reactions for the best possible self-defense. In other words, our negative physiological traits have a purpose: fever protects us from infection, coughing prevents a surgical patient from getting pneumonia, and vomiting rids the body of poisons. (Pregnant mammals feel nausea and vomit, especially early in pregnancy, when the fetus is most vulnerable to toxins and resulting miscarriage.)[22] Anxiety, too, as we've just pointed out, is extremely useful, since it triggers the physiological responses needed to fight or flee from danger. Nesse worried that by ridding his patients of anxiety, he was removing a signal wired into people for their own survival.

A few days later, as Nesse wrestled again with this disturbing thought, he looked out his office window, where he saw birds at his backyard feeder repeatedly startle and flee for no apparent reason. That reminded him of the excessive defense mechanisms he'd observed in people. For example, you might feel a stab of fear in the summer at the spot of sidewalk where you'd slipped on ice the previous January. Similarly, many of our defenses against disease seem equally unnecessary. Taking aspirin to suppress the pain of a smashed finger or to lower fever from the flu doesn't prevent the body from healing. So perhaps, Nesse thought, curbing anxiety with therapy or drugs doesn't harm people.

But why does the body produce these unnecessary defenses?

This "overresponsiveness" is an illusion, thought Nesse. Natural selection has calibrated the expression of this response to the point of optimal benefit to us. A defense—such as fleeing—will pay off whenever the harm from that defense is less than the harm from the feared catastrophe times the probability of its occurring.[23]

In other words a defense pays off as long as it doesn't damage you more than the injury it's protecting you from. The smoke detector's false alarms are annoying but a minor nuisance compared to possible injury or death from a fire. You might panic many times at your child's running out into the street, even though there is no car coming toward her at that moment.

This fear is a relic from our primitive past, when there wasn't time to think—your child would be dead by the time you thought about protecting him from a pouncing tiger. So evolution selected out a sensitive trigger that provokes our anxiety at the tiniest little dimpling of grass in the savannah—or at Jeremy's tiniest little math quiz. Ninety-nine times out of one hundred, our kid's life isn't at stake—we just feel as if it were.

"Many defenses," Nesse explains, "are inexpensive compared to the potential harm they protect against."[24]

Our ability to tolerate false alarms comes in handy, especially since we frequently don't have complete information on a danger. The rustle our ancestor heard in the bush was ambiguous, just like the rejection of our child from a special arts program: we're not certain that it will make it harder for our child to earn a decent living, but with our economy in such flux, who knows?

"The vast majority of the time," says Nesse, "especially in our very safe modern environment, we benefit from only a tiny proportion of the anxiety and stress we experience."[25]

In other words, worry about our children is natural, a trait passed down to us from our ancestors. Parents' fierce desire for our children to beat out the competition and shine originates in our evolutionary hardwiring, which over the centuries has ensured the survival of our species by making us react viscerally whenever our children might face a threat. Our protective antennae are always up, reacting to any shift of signals in the atmosphere around our children. We fret over every hint about our child's progress in school, as Ellen Garfield did when her son Jack came home with a book that his teacher, Mrs. Lee, had given him to read. She couldn't help wondering what that meant.

"Why did the teacher give you that book?" Ellen asked Jack in as breezy a tone as she could muster.

"I dunno," he answered, munching on a graham cracker.

"Is it because she thinks you didn't read well enough?" Ellen blurted out, regretting her words immediately. Jack stopped chewing and gave her a confused look. But Ellen was dying to know whether the book was more advanced or less advanced than those chosen for the rest of the class!

Not only does the smoke detector effect sensitize us to any shift in the wind, but it also makes us react to small hazards as though they're life threatening. Laurie Shellenberger, who lives in San Francisco, obsessed about whether her son Oliver's name would be drawn in the lottery for the school's Spanish immersion program. Her friend Karen tried to soothe her.

"Look at it this way, Laurie," said Karen, who didn't have children. "Will the world come to an end if Oliver doesn't get in? I don't think so. Don't you think you're blowing this out of proportion?"

Yes, that's exactly what Laurie was doing, especially when she worried about Oliver losing out on a future job opportunity because he wasn't bilingual. In her worst moments, she fretted over the couple she had read about with kids in a Spanish immersion program who had also hired a Mandarin-speaking nanny. Their children would be *tri*lingual! Laurie was overreacting—but that's just what our hardwiring is designed to do.

Laurie realized that families in other countries face war and famine, and she felt tremendously privileged to have such relatively small worries. But none of this rational thought affected her relentless anxiety. The competitive environment had switched on the mental and physical sirens of her protective hardwiring. Only the admission letter to the immersion magnet, which Oliver finally received, calmed them.

Laurie's protective anxiety was also fueled by the uncertainty of the danger she felt facing her son. There was no way to predict the effect of his not learning Spanish. Sensitively tuned into just such a situation, her alarm system went off—just in case the danger proved grave.

"We live in Star Wars civilizations," explains Edward O. Wilson, "ruled by Stone Age emotions."[26]

The whisper of a social problem can also set off these protective alarm bells. When my daughter didn't receive an invitation to the birthday party of the most popular girl in her preschool class, I felt as though someone had punched me in the stomach. It didn't help that I knew the popular girl's family couldn't afford a large party. Hyper-vigilant, my mind asked anxious and even irrational questions. Was my daughter too shy? I wondered.

Trading information and gossiping with other parents at school meetings or while waiting for afternoon dismissal gives us valuable information and a warm feeling of community. But at the same time it allows you to scan the horizon warily, like the mother tiger scanning the veldt for predators. What test scores did other kids get? How can you maneuver your child to get the best teacher next year? Some parents are supportive when you speak to them, but others bristle with competitive anxiety. We come home from the encounter frazzled. Like a car alarm brushed by the merest gust of wind, our hardwiring goes haywire.

THE PRESSURED PARENT PHENOMENON: WHEN HARDWIRING MEETS COMPETITION

When Ellen Garfield and her husband, Steve, went to the first parent-teacher conference at Jack's new school, they didn't harbor any specific hopes or fears. So far, their first grader seemed to like his new teacher, Mrs. Lee, and had found some kids to play with at recess. Yet, sitting on the tiny chairs in a small area just off the classroom, the Garfields knew that first grade was more competitive than the low-key kindergarten that Jack had attended, and a vague anxiety enveloped them. Mrs. Lee laid out some of Jack's math work sheets and a paragraph he had written. As the teacher began talking about her curriculum goals for the year, Ellen felt tense, as though a question hung in the air, preventing her from paying full attention. Suddenly she realized why she felt so anxious.

"It was all I could do not to blurt out, 'So what do you think, is he a genius or not?'" she laughs.

"I think Jack is pretty special," Steve admits. "I was wondering if the teacher was going to say something about his great sense of humor.

"Not to mention," Steve smiled, "that he can already dribble left-handed."

Fortunately, Jack's teacher began to praise Jack's reading skills, his interest in the fish tank and turtles in the classroom, and his empathy for a girl whose grandmother had died. Ellen and Steve looked at each other and smiled. It seemed as if the teacher really appreciated their son. But when Mrs. Lee pulled out a paper with Jack's initial diagnostic test scores, Ellen's heartbeat sped up like a metronome set on allegro. It didn't slow down until the teacher showed them that Jack had scored in the ninety-fourth percentile in math and eighty-ninth in verbal. When Mrs. Lee said she thought he would be a good candidate for the gifted program that began in fourth grade, Ellen began breathing again.

THE PRESSURED PARENT PHENOMENON TAKES CENTER STAGE

Parent-teacher conferences provide a perfect stage for the Pressured Parent Phenomenon. The spotlight is on our child as we wonder protectively how she ranks competitively with the other students—academically, socially, athletically, and artistically. Any complaint from the teacher about our child's behavior or comments that he might "need extra help" drops a boulder into the pit of our stomachs. Anxiety zooms into the stratosphere, and if the teacher doesn't immediately add some praise for our child, we begin to catastrophize. ("Maybe she's a slow learner!") Some parents may seize on a conference as a chance to rework their own childhood, preventing hurts and filling in holes. ("I want her to be popular!") Our loving hardwiring lights up too, provoking anxiety as we wait for the teacher to confirm the wonderfulness of our child. "I was so conscious of my need to hear only positive comments about Jack," remembers Ellen. "And really, I wanted more than that. I wanted exclamation points for every aspect of his work and his behavior!"

The hardwiring that makes us love and nurture our children is both useful and beautiful, bringing us profound joy. The competition proliferating in our children's lives is a fact of modern life. By themselves neither the hardwiring nor the competition would produce the Pressured Parent Phenomenon. But when the two collide, sparks fly. Anxiety grips our insides, and we go ballistic over matters minor and major, obsessing irrationally and fearing catastrophe.

In chapters 4 and 5, we'll start to examine the results of the Pressured Parent Phenomenon. We'll look at the desire it gives us to override our children's autonomy, blocking their inner passion to grow and learn. We'll explain why your child's intrinsic motivation is so important. In ensuing chapters, we'll show you how to nurture it while staying very involved in your child's life.

CHAPTER 4

THE BIG TAKEOVER
How Our Feelings Pull Us to Push

When my son Zach was nine, we rode our bikes to school together every day. One morning he couldn't find his bicycle helmet. It was almost 7:45 a.m., and I worried he was going to be late for school.

"Wear this one, just for today," I said, rummaging in the back of the closet and pulling out a funny-shaped Darth Vader helmet that looked like a refugee from the *Star Wars* wardrobe room.

"OK," said Zach, grabbing the helmet without looking at it.

It was a beautiful November day and we rode steadily in the chilled air, musty with the scent of decaying leaves. Biking past groups of children walking with adults, we approached the school. As I stood watching Zach tuck his bike into the school's rack, I noticed Ben, a boy who had been teasing him since school started, on the steps in front of the door, staring at us.

"Zach, everybody's laughing at you," said Ben.

Zach's head jerked up from fastening his bike lock, his face stricken. I wanted to grab the helmet off his head and hide it behind my back.

My heart started to thump. I was furious. How could this pipsqueak be so cruel to my son? I walked over and stood in front of Ben with my hands on my hips. It was all I could do to keep from pushing him, hard.

"That was a very mean thing to say," I managed to get out. He shrugged and walked away.

"Mom!" Zach shrieked at me, his forehead flushed red and a hurt look in his eyes. He turned away and trudged into school.

"Oh, my gosh, what have I done?" I thought, tears flooding into my eyes. I wanted to run after Zach and apologize. I realized I had just made the situation worse.

I cycled back home sadly, no longer enjoying the fine weather. At work the incident kept popping up in my mind. I felt depressed. Far from solving Zach's problem, I had only made him angry at me.

When an incident like this one threatens our child, fight-or-flight anxiety courses through our veins. It's the same stress response that would gear your body to kill a lion that is leaping to devour your child. That's how we react when another kid teases our child: our protective and loving hardwiring fills us with anguish. The urge to take control often becomes almost irresistible. Blood rushes to our muscles. Reflexively, we want to use that fuel to take action, as I did by scolding Ben. "Doing something—anything" discharges your muscular energy, relieving your physical anxiety as though you're removing the cause of the problem and saving your child.

As competition escalates in our children's world, these impulses to take action multiply. The extremely unpleasant anxiety of the Pressured Parent Phenomenon mounts, and we want to jump in and solve the problem *now*—whether it's academic, athletic, artistic, or social. Increasingly we feel the urge to pressure our children, telling them exactly what to do and when to do it, even jury-rigging the situation behind the scenes. ("Mrs. DiRocco, *please* give Stella the lead in the play! She's worked so hard toward it!") When the love, fear, and compulsion to protect our children kick in—along with the stress and pressure in our own lives—we feel this desire to take control. Who hasn't felt at least once like grabbing your child's homework and correcting it for her? When my daughter was eight, one night I almost did just that. I couldn't bear the thought of her handing in a math work sheet unfinished. My fingers itched to pick up a pencil and fill in the answers for her.

But such taking over is counterproductive. It squelches kids' autonomy, which damages them. Pushing, pressuring, or controlling ends up stifling kids' internal desire to do and to achieve. It also undermines their performance and their creativity and hurts our relationship with them.

Remember the babies and mothers I watched on videotape mentioned in the preface—the ones who spoiled my vision in 1982? This experiment showed for the first time that taking control affects even one-year-olds. The videotapes were fuzzy, but as I mentioned, they showed one phenomenon very clearly. When the babies whose mothers had directed their every move were left alone with the toys, they played with them lackadaisically and soon stopped—they didn't seem to have the desire to learn how to work the toys.[1]

Over twenty-five years of studies since then have shown that this squelching of intrinsic motivation is only one of the problems created by pushing kids rather than nurturing their autonomy.

PARENTS DON'T WANT TO TAKE OVER

Parents' hardwiring is at war with their desires, because if you ask whether they *want* to pressure their children, they rarely say yes. Most parents say that they want their children to determine their own destinies. When I was a grad student at the University of Rochester, psychologist Rich Ryan and I asked a group of parents in rural Dansville, New York, their hopes for their children. Almost every single one said basically, "I want my children to be happy doing what interests them—whatever that may be." The author Alfie Kohn similarly asked parents at one private school in Texas and another in Minnesota about their long-term goals for their children. They wanted them to be "happy, balanced, independent, fulfilled, productive, self-reliant, responsible, functioning, kind, thoughtful, loving, inquisitive, and confident," reports Kohn.[2] "Championship," "top college," and "Nobel prize" didn't appear on the list.

But there's a mountain of pressure on parents today to push their children. Even the most conscientious parents who truly want their children to choose their own paths fall prey to the cutthroat environment. Stressed out by modern life and by the anxiety from their child's hypercompetitive world, at times even the most selfless parents feel like pressuring their children.

I know. I've been there myself.

THE PRESSURE TO TAKE OVER: STRESS

To understand this harmful feature of the Pressured Parent Phenomenon— the urge we feel to control our kids—let's first examine a related theme familiar to us all: the effect of stress on our parenting. Like the Pressured Parent Phenomenon, stress in our lives often compels us to take over. The story I told you in the preface about screaming at Allison when she wouldn't get dressed for preschool wasn't the only time that stress overpowered my better judgment. It happened a lot. For example, when my kids were little and I was in a rush, I was much more likely to say, "C'mere, let me tie your shoes," than "Sweetheart, your shoes are undone again. Why don't you retie them?"

Not letting my child take responsibility for tying her own shoes didn't stem from a personality quirk. It simply illustrates a principle that applies to us all. Stress in our lives often leads us to run roughshod over our child's autonomy.

The morning rush to get everyone off to school and work is especially fierce when parents work, volunteer, or have other commitments outside the home. You have lunches to pack, a dog to feed, laundry to throw in the dryer,

"It's too hot to strive for autonomy."

and a note to write to the teacher, not to mention helping with breakfast and getting dressed yourself. To top it off, your mind is on that difficult 10 a.m. meeting at work and your mother's broken hip.

When you have a million things to do in fifteen minutes, following the best advice of parenting experts seems ludicrous. Who has time to stop and think, "How can I ask Willie nicely to hurry up, while respecting his autonomy?" It's all you can do to command, "Willie! Hurry up and finish your cereal!" while you're pouring soap into the washing machine.

And then, kids will be kids. Instead of eating breakfast, Willie and Sophie are throwing Froot Loops at each other, and tears are spilling down Sophie's cheeks.

"Stop it, Willie!" you shout.

"She took my Spider Man bowl!" says Willie.

"*Please* finish eating, go and turn off the TV and put your homework in your backpack," you sigh or scream, depending on whether you've had coffee yet.

Willie throws a Froot Loop at Sophie, who shrieks, tears flowing.

When kids drive you crazy, can anyone blame you for turning into a marine drill sergeant?

But today you manage to say evenly, "Willie, Sophie, hurry up. We have to leave in five minutes."

"No, we have seven minutes!" replies Willie. "Anyway, it's OK to be late today.... It's a Schedule B day. My teacher has a meeting."

You glance at the school calendar and panic. Willie's right. But you didn't arrange to drop the kids off at a friend's who will take them to school with her own kids, and you have to prepare for that meeting at work, pronto. The phone is ringing. It's probably your mother.

Somehow you get everybody off, but at night the pressure mounts again. In the scant hours before bedtime, you have to organize dinner, supervise homework, read notes sent home from school, and arrange childcare for Martin Luther King Day, which leaves you no time to take a hot bath or watch *Grey's Anatomy*.

It's easy to see how this everyday stress leads to control. Stress narrows our focus. Rather than seeing the big parenting picture, we concentrate on the immediate goal—getting our child out the door or getting that homework *done*. "Get in here right now and finish your math!" doesn't seem unreasonable coming from a harried parent who is trying to pry a child away from the second straight hour on his Game Boy.

I remember issuing commands to my children whenever I was at the end of my rope. "I don't care *what* level you're almost at. Turn that off and get in here right now!" and "If you're not in here by the count of three I'm going to..." are lines I remember clearly.

Even parents who work from home feel stressed.

"I'm a full-time mom, keeping the house and scraping together a living," says Kelly Campbell, who has an eighteen-month-old and works as a publicist from her home. "It's like I'm doing three jobs at once!

"My patience wears pretty thin."

One of our studies showed that you can, in fact, predict how much control a parent will exert over a child by the amount of stress that the parent has undergone.[3] We interviewed ninety-one parents of children thirteen to eighteen years old. Spending hours in their homes, we asked about a wide range of situations. How did they react to their teenagers' report cards? What did they do when their children stayed out after curfew? What was the latest disagreement they'd had with their teen?

Then we asked the parents if they'd suffered from any deaths, illnesses, economic setbacks, or other stressful events in the past three months. We found that the more stressful events the mothers had, the more they tended to control their children. For example, they yelled at them, rather than discussing bad grades. They changed curfews without listening to their children's input and set extreme punishments, such as "You're grounded for the next two months!" without discussing this consequence ahead of time.

Although we found no correlations for fathers between such life stresses and parenting, we did find that those who had endured more stressful events tended to spend *less* time with their children. Maybe, we speculated, dads can take off for a while when they're stressed. Mothers usually don't have that luxury. So they stay involved with the children but resort to controlling methods.

THREATS IN A CHILD'S FUTURE

As I'm sure you know, stress also seeps into us from the "outside world"—the economic and political problems we face. But you may be surprised to learn that even such seemingly distant threats affect our parenting.

In my lab we investigated what kind of world parents thought their children would inhabit and how those ideas affected their relationship with their child.[4] If parents expected a harsh world with scarce, insecure jobs, would they control their children more than parents who worried less?

Just before the 9/11 terrorist attacks, we asked a group of forty mothers how much they agreed with statements such as:

- "It makes me nervous to think about all the dangers kids are exposed to these days."
- "It's getting harder and harder all the time to make a decent living."
- "It's scary to imagine what the world will be like for our children in the future."

We also asked these parents to help their third graders learn how to give directions from a map and to label and write quatrains—four-line poems with different rhyming patterns (e.g., in an *abab* pattern, the last word of every other line rhyming). Sure enough, those who had envisioned a threatening world in the future tended to take over and tell their kids what to do more than the less-worried parents. Some put the work sheets in front of themselves rather than the child, and others read the directions out loud instead of letting their child read them. But the calmer parents were more likely to allow kids to lead, stepping in only when they needed help.

And those results were before 9/11. We don't know how many of the more relaxed parents remained that way. We live in a difficult world. The challenges it presents can send our protective impulses into overdrive, provoking us to pressure our children. That's an understandable response, but not a helpful one. I hope that by understanding this dynamic you will be able to avoid it.

A TWO-WAY STREET: CHILDREN PULL YOU TO PUSH

"Yes, but my kid *makes* me control him," you may be thinking to yourself. "If I don't tell him exactly what to do, and make him do it, he doesn't do what he needs to."

And you'd be right, because as any parent of more than one child well knows, different children elicit different parenting skills. Temperament counts. After you ask once, your son helps you bring in the groceries, but your daughter helps only after you ask her three times, and maybe not even then.

One child stops banging her spoon on her plate as soon as you ask, but another won't stop until you take the spoon away. How can this different behavior *not* affect your parenting style?

Indeed it does, and these temperamental differences, like stress in our lives, explain an urge to push and pressure our children that's related to the Pressured Parent Phenomenon. John E. Bates, a psychologist at Indiana University, has provided some valuable evidence. He found that mothers don't respond differently to difficult children at six and thirteen months, but by the time these kids are two, their mothers use more controlling methods than do mothers of easier kids. When their children cried a lot, demanded attention persistently, changed moods frequently, and broke rules mothers scolded, spanked, and took away toys more often than parents with less difficult children.[5]

Other researchers have likewise found that active children provoke more power struggles with their parents than quieter children do. In other words, parenting is a two-way street. We affect our children's behavior, but they also affect ours.

This dynamic of kids "pulling you to push them" operates between teenagers and their parents too. In the study of families with teenagers I mentioned earlier, we asked the parents to rate statements, such as "my child is even-tempered and not moody," on a scale ranging from "very true" to "not true at all."[6] That told us how difficult the parents found their teens, and we had learned from our interviews how they motivated and disciplined their kids. The more difficult the mothers rated their children, we found, the more controlling their methods.

Of course, when parents try to control their children, it often escalates into a cycle of mutual instigation. Your child says "No!" to irritate you, and you bark back, "Oh, yes you will!" That response in turn generates the even more resistant "Oh, no I won't!"—and so on. (In chapters 6 through 9, we'll advise you how to stop these useless and exhausting power struggles by using the Three-Part Framework.)

THE PRESSURED PARENT PHENOMENON

It's easy to understand how everyday stress and worries about the future can lead to pushing our children and trampling on their autonomy. The Pressured Parent Phenomenon, however, affects parents more subtly. Unlike work stress and political or economic threats, which come from outside, the PPP comes from within. When our child faces competition, it nags at us internally. Rooted in our primal fears, it compels us to protect our children. When your son risks not getting into that special magnet or charter school program, or not making the basketball team; when the popular clique suddenly drops your daughter; when only a handful of students will "make it" into a community service program—all these threats to our children trip that internal hardwire, flooding our minds and bodies with anxiety. But since researchers have found that we don't *want* to push and pressure our children, where is the evidence that the Pressured Parent Phenomenon makes us do so?

THE PRESSURE TO TAKE OVER

Competition and Judgments

Experiments in our lab have demonstrated that competitive situations pressure parents to violate their own goals. Whenever we create competitive threats in the laboratory, many parents take control of their children.

Some of the behavior we've generated will surprise you. In one study, for example, we gave sixty public school fourth graders an "About Me" questionnaire to fill out.[7] It asked questions like "How many brothers and sisters do you have?" and "What is your favorite thing to do on the weekend?"

We told *half* of these children's mothers that another group of kids would meet their son or daughter. These new acquaintances would use the "About Me" answers when rating how much they liked their child.

We told the *other half* of these moms, however, that the new children would simply read the questionnaires before meeting their children (we didn't mention any rating to these mothers). Knowing that parents care deeply about whether other children like their kids, and that any hint of rejection pulls at their heartstrings, we guessed that the "pressured" mothers—those who were told that other children would rate their child—might try to take control. Sure enough, many of these moms directed and pressured their kids.

"No, video games aren't your favorite activity," one told her child. "Put down baseball."

"Don't write your favorite toy is a doll!" said another, anxiety making her voice quiver.

The mothers we hadn't told about any rating, however, simply watched their kids fill in their answers, helping them when asked.

Some of our questions posed social dilemmas, such as: "If you're playing with one friend and another one asks you to play, what would you do?" Another question asked how children would respond to this situation: "Two of your friends are in a fight, and both want you not to talk to the other. What would you do?" These questions clearly had more and less "appropriate" answers, so wouldn't you think that they'd provoke the *most* anxiety from the "pressured" group of mothers? Indeed they did. The mothers in that group intervened more on these social dilemma items than on any other questions. They fired directions at the child, or even took over and gave broad hints about how they wanted the child to answer the questions.

"No, no, no," said one mother impatiently to her little girl. "You wouldn't leave your friend. You would invite the new girl to play, *wouldn't you?*" She raised her eyebrows and stared at her child as she emphasized those last two words.

This experiment showed us quite clearly how the Pressured Parent Phenomenon overpowers parents' better judgment and squelches children's autonomy.

PRESSURED PARENT PHENOMENON INTENSIFIES EGO INVOLVEMENT

When my kids' report cards arrive, I focus on their grades more than I ever imagined I would. Likewise, when Allison swam on the community swim team, I found myself as time went on paying a suspicious amount of attention to her times—and to those of other kids. And the night that Zach's fourth-grade teacher read the opening of his scary ghost story to a roomful of parents, without identifying the author, I wanted to stand up and blurt to everyone, "That's Zach's!"

As strongly as I believe in supporting children's autonomy, as my kids have grown, I've found it surprisingly difficult to keep my ego out of their activities. You don't have to be narcissistic or enmeshed to fall prey to this phenomenon that psychologists call "ego-involvement." Ego-involvement is a tendency to wrap our self-esteem or "ego" around our successes or failures. Psychologists usually talk about ego involvement as hinging our feelings about *ourselves* on our own achievements. For example, if I'm ego-involved in this book's success, I'll feel like a worthless person if no one buys it. But we can also involve our egos in the successes and failures of others who are closely connected to us. And no one is more intensely connected to us than our children.

So we all occasionally wrap our egos around our children's achievements. We feel as though their success or failure reflects on us.

Haven't we all dreamed of our children winning at Wimbledon, capturing a Pulitzer, or starring on Broadway? Wouldn't we all feel proud if our child were accepted by an Ivy League school? Maybe, we think, being a "good parent" includes pressuring our children to accomplish such feats. Haven't we all wondered something like: "Maybe I should push Elena to practice her ice skating in the morning before school—maybe that's what the Olympic ice skaters Sarah and Emily Hughes's parents did."

(For the record, they didn't. Here's how the Hughes's dad views his girls' competing: "The tough thing for a parent isn't the sport itself," John Hughes says, "but how does your kid replace it with something else they have as much passion for when this is done? Because it will be done. The real measure of their success is whether there are other things they love, know, can continue with.")[8]

Ego-involvement occurs when our protective and loving hardwiring collides with the competition in our children's lives, prompting us to wrap our own self-esteem around our children's achievement. That gives us our own stake in how well our child performs. If you feel bad about yourself when your child doesn't move up a chair in the orchestra, that's ego-involvement. When we worry about how others will judge our parenting—what the teacher will think of *me* if my child's homework isn't neat—that's ego-involvement, too.

Since it sensitizes us to other peoples' opinions, ego-involvement puts an extra layer of psychological pressure on us. By making us vulnerable to the judgments of others, it subjects our self-esteem to frequent ups and downs. The accompanying waves of emotion not only feel unpleasant, but they also weaken our parenting ability because they distract us from concentrating on our children's needs. For example, if you're worried about how your child scores on a standardized test because of how that will make you feel about yourself—and what others will think of you—that can sidetrack you from helping her feel calm and competent the day of the test. If she does poorly and you fall apart—thinking you're no good—that diverts you from figuring out what she needs to help her do better next time.

If, worried about criticism you might receive from other adults, you make your first grader change her mismatched clothes—a nuance that escapes six-year-olds—that wastes time and energy better spent talking to her in the car about the field trip she's about to embark on.

Why do we parents become so ego-involved in our children's achievements? The answer lies in our understanding of the need for self-esteem, which has long been a hallmark of American psychology. Philosopher and psychologist William James coined the word *self-esteem* in 1890 in his pioneering *Principles of Psychology.*[9] More than half a century later, pathbreaking American thinkers including Gordon W. Allport in the 1950s, Abraham Maslow, and Carl Rogers a decade later emphasized self-esteem as a significant feature of human personality.

"The pursuit of self-esteem is so pervasive," psychologists Jennifer Crocker and Lora E. Park of the University of Michigan write, "that many psychologists have assumed it is a universal and fundamental human need."[10]

Self-esteem gives us a very pleasant feeling, so it's no wonder we pursue it daily. We like to feel worthy and valuable, especially in those arenas that matter to us—work, or sports, or beauty, or moral virtue. Since natural selection has disposed us to invest large amounts of time and energy in our children, parenting matters to us deeply. So of course we want to feel good about it. Like Mr. Goodwrench, we take pride in what we do.

EGO-INVOLVEMENT MAKES US PUSH

Increased competition in our children's environment intensifies the ego-involvement in our parenting. We showed that link in the same map and poem study mentioned above, in the section on the threats in a child's future. As you'll recall, we asked the mothers in this experiment to help their third graders learn how to label rhyming patterns of several poems and then to write a quatrain, and how to give directions using a map.

We tried to arouse ego-involvement in half of the mothers by telling them we'd judge their child's work and then suggesting that the parents were responsible for that work meeting certain criteria.[11]

"Your role," we told them, "is to *ensure that your child learns to write a poem.* We'll be testing him/her afterward to make sure that he/she *performs well enough.*"

We didn't mention any criteria to the other half of the parents, nor did we imply that they had any responsibility for their children's performance: "Your role is to help your child learn how to write a poem," we told them. "We will be asking him/her some questions afterward, but *there is no particular level* at which he/she needs to perform."

The ego-involving instructions had a big effect on the first group of mothers. Many of them took over. "Do that one now," they'd demand. Some even showed their children the answers.

One of the moms in this ego-pressured group at first seemed determined to let her little girl write the poem herself. When her daughter hesitated, she gave her hints. That didn't help. So the mother reached out to snatch her daughter's pencil, stopping herself at the last second. But the little girl remained stumped, and we saw the mother's hand leap toward the pencil several more times. Finally, unable to contain herself, the mother grabbed the pencil and finished the girl's poem. As the session ended, both she and her daughter looked frustrated and unhappy.

This study showed how, when egged on by competitive judgment, parents tend to lapse into ego-involvement, which in turn makes them control their children. It's as though the mothers who felt pressure from the upcoming judgment relieved it by transferring the pressure to the child.

Of course, not every parent subjected to judgments of their child falls prey to ego-involvement. Most moms and dads will *not* grab a pencil out of their child's hand. Some parents are more vulnerable than others to ego-involvement and control, and some situations provoke it more than others, as we found in the next phase of the map and poem study.

Before the experiment began, we had asked the mothers and children to fill out questionnaires to show us the parents' underlying style. Did they tend to control their children at home or to allow them autonomy?

During the poem assignment, the pressure we applied provoked ego-involvement and control in almost all the parents. But the map task went differently. It elicited outright "taking over" from the parents who had controlling styles at home. But those who usually allowed their kids autonomy continued to do so during the experiment, regardless of the pressure we'd put on them. In fact, some of the parents who believed *most* in kids' autonomy reacted to the pressure by allowing their children to take the lead even more. That showed us that, as difficult as it may be, parents can fight off the impulse to control.

Why did parents pressure their children more while writing poems and less while giving directions on the map? We weren't sure. The map task was cut-and-dried, but the poem assignment was more unusual and creative. That may have put additional pressure on the mothers, causing more of them to clamp down on their kids.

What's Your Pressure Point?

To a greater or lesser extent, we're all ego-involved in our children's lives. It's only natural. But we hitch our self-esteem up to different arenas of our children's lives. Some parents get wrapped up in how their child gets along with other children, while others link their self-esteem to their children's grades. We hook our egos onto our children's lives differently for many reasons. Perhaps your child has had trouble making friends, and you've tried to help him improve his relationships, so when he has a "good day" at school, that boosts your self-esteem, while a "rough day" plunges you into a mini-depression. Or maybe you think that parents play an important role in their kids' athletic success, and so you take it personally when your son spikes a volleyball over the net or when the coach takes him out of the game.

Your own experiences can feed into your ego-involvement too. Maybe you're determined that your child succeed in football because you always wanted to and didn't, or you want her to get a singing role in the school musical because you loved having that experience yourself.

When judgment looms in one of those activities in which you've invested your own sense of self-esteem, the Pressured Parent Phenomenon really unleashes its fury. That's what we found in the "About Me" study described a few pages back, when we asked the fourth graders to answer questions about themselves before meeting a group of new children. Before they filled out these questionnaires, we asked their mothers how ego-involved they felt in their children's popularity: how much did they agree with statements such as "When my child does well socially, I feel good about myself" and "Although I care about what happens to my child, his/her social successes do not reflect on my worth as a person"?

The mothers who said they sometimes hinged their self-esteem onto their children's social success didn't necessarily apply pressure when their kids filled out the questionnaire. But when we added the factor of judgment—when we told these ego-involved mothers that the new children would judge their kids according to their questionnaires—the PPP kicked into high gear. These moms pushed their kids the *most* to answer in a certain way.

It is not abnormal to wrap our self-esteem around our children's achievement. We all do it to one extent or another. But *where* and *when* we do it varies, and knowing which activities in your child's life push your self-esteem button can alert you to an urge to pressure her before it happens. Understanding that dynamic may help you head it off.

MODERN URBAN LIFE INTENSIFIES EGO-INVOLVEMENT

We're highly invested in our children, but just exactly what "return" we expect on our investment changes from one era to another. Traditional American farm families, for example, were larger than urban families because parents needed them to help around the farm, often from an early age. But today universal schooling and advanced farm technology mean that children work on the farm far less, and farm families are no longer as large.

Parents also used to expect their children to take care of them in their old age, another return on their investment. As late as the 1940s, only about 25 percent of people older than sixty-five lived alone. Today, while the tradition of caring for elderly parents endures in many cultures, fewer children overall take care of their parents, financially and practically, than in past generations. Social Security, Medicare, and pension, IRA, and 401K plans as well as our revved-up geographical mobility have all contributed to weakening this extended family tradition.

So, in return for their high emotional and financial investment in their children, parents today unconsciously expect to feel proud. If children returned love in past eras by working alongside their parents and caring for them in their old age, today they might do so by succeeding in the world. The new independence in old age makes us anticipate all the more pride and pleasure in our children's achievements or, as it's called in the Jewish culture, *naches*.[12] I've seen that phenomenon at my father's retirement community, where talk about children's and grandchildren's achievements, especially the colleges they attend, bubbles up regularly at lunch and dinner. It's one way for my father and his friends to feel close to children who often live thousands of miles away.

However, such sharpened focus on children's accomplishments makes our hardwiring especially vulnerable to going haywire.

Faced with the anxiety generated by the Pressured Parent Phenomenon, parents have a choice. Will we give in to our impulses and pressure our children, even though we may not want to? Will we fall into the trap set for us by nature and society? Or is there another way to help children excel without pressuring them? In the chapters that follow, I'll show you that there is indeed another way. You'll learn how to turn your anxiety into positive parenting, guiding your children without controlling them, so that you can remain close and savor the joy as they grow into competent and happy adults.

CHAPTER 5

BEYOND THE CARROT AND THE STICK

Fanning the Flames of Your Child's Inner Passion

W hy do babies kick the mobiles hung over their cribs? Why do they play with their toes and pop objects into their mouths? Almost sixty years ago, psychologist Robert White decided that since this infant behavior is universal, it must have benefited the survival and reproduction of our ancestors. But what advantage did that playful behavior bestow? In his now-classic 1959 paper, White gave this answer: since humans are born so helpless and dependent, he said, our survival depends heavily on acquiring skills. So, natural selection has given us the genes that prompt exploration and curiosity, leading us to acquire competence. That's why babies explore and play the way they do, and that's why achieving competence is pleasurable in and of itself.[1]

White's theory helped explain the experimental results of a psychologist named Harry Harlow, whose research had tremendous implications for parents.

An outspoken and complicated man, Harlow defied the psychological mainstream with a series of experiments that demonstrated why people often explore and learn without any thought of gain or reward.[2] This research paved the way for modern psychologists to understand a child's intrinsic motivation. Later in this chapter we'll see how Harlow's research with rhesus monkeys in the early 1950s laid the basis for the Three-Part Framework that will help you turn the anxiety of the Pressured Parent Phenomenon into positive parenting. First let's look at Harlow's discoveries.

WHAT HARRY HARLOW'S MONKEYS
TAUGHT US ABOUT OUR CHILDREN

Before Harlow's midcentury experiments, most psychologists believed that a small number of basic biological needs, or "drives," motivated all human behavior. Freud had singled out two such drives, sex and aggression, and in the 1940s American psychologist Clark Hull expanded the number to four: hunger, thirst, sex, and avoidance of pain.[3] Only a reward satisfying one of these needs, psychologists thought, could motivate behavior. If you wanted a rat to run a maze you had to put food at the end of it, and if you wanted to motivate a child to read a book you had to offer him a cookie.

By the 1950s, however, a few psychologists began to question this theory of drive and rewards, dubbed behaviorism. Why, for example, do children play? Why do people enjoy reading books (even if there's no sex in them)? At the same time, scattered anecdotes were surfacing about hungry rats that would rather investigate a new space than eat. One researcher had even found that rats would cross an electrified grid to get to a checkerboard maze.[4]

Then along came Harry Harlow.

The University of Wisconsin psychologist scoffed at the behaviorist idea that only rewards and punishments can motivate primates to learn. In a group of experiments heretical for their time,[5] he set out to show another force at work. Fashioning a contraption with a hinged hasp held down on a wooden block by a pin and a hook, Harlow placed it in the cages of four monkeys, which he called Group A. He wanted to see if they'd remove the pin, allowing them to unhook the hasp and raise it. He also put the same contraption in the cages of a control group of four other monkeys— Group B—but with the hook and pin loose and the hasp already raised.[6]

Harlow checked the puzzles in each monkey's cage at regular intervals for twelve days. Each time a Group A monkey "solved" the puzzle, releasing the hasp, he noted

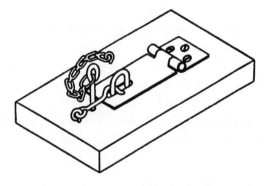

Harlow's Contraption

it down and reset the puzzle. If any Group B monkeys had "solved" their puzzles by assembling them, he would have reset theirs too, but none of them succeeded. Apparently the unassembled puzzle didn't provoke their curiosity in the same way that the hooked and pinned-down version intrigued the monkeys in Group A, provoking them to play around with it until they could raise the hasp.

Then he set the puzzle in all the monkey's cages, this time assembling it for both groups, and checked it for two more days. In forty trials, the Group A monkeys solved the puzzle thirty-one times and the Group B monkeys four times.

RHESUS PIECES

During the latter ten days of the experiment, Harlow also conducted a second protocol with all the monkeys. He let each one out of its own cage and into another that had food wells covered with an object. The monkeys could move the object and take a raisin from the food well.

On the fourteenth day, after the first phase of the experiment was over, Harlow let each Group A monkey into another cage, where the puzzle contraption now covered the food well. They all pushed the puzzle aside and gobbled up the raisin.

After five minutes, the monkeys went back to their initial cages. There Harlow had assembled the puzzle contraption, this time with a raisin crushed beneath its hasp.

Did this dangling of a food reward motivate the monkeys to solve the puzzle *more swiftly*? No—quite the opposite. The monkeys went to pieces. One of them couldn't free the hasp at all. The other three eventually did so and got their raisins, but only after making thirty-nine errors in three tests, far more than in the first phase. Furthermore, their errors were telling: the monkeys *always* attacked the hasp first, which they'd never done in the previous tests.

So Harlow concluded that, rather than motivating them, the raisin reward had distracted them and disrupted their puzzle solving.

That led to Harlow's pathbreaking conclusion: the monkeys had learned to solve the puzzles for no reward other than the pure pleasure of doing so. He coined the term *intrinsic motivation* to describe this internal energy propelling the monkeys to play with this puzzle until they solved it.[7]

Within the next decade, psychologists began examining intrinsic motivation in people. Human motivation theory, which proposes that humans are born with a desire to develop and to master the world, emerged from dozens of studies conducted over the next twenty years.

According to human motivation theory, the force that kept the monkeys working on their puzzles is the same inner passion that motivates babies to play with their toes. It's an internal urge to play and learn for our own satisfaction and enjoyment. We're all born with this curiosity to explore, this desire to build our skills and master the world around us. That's why we persist until we learn how to store phone numbers in our cell phones, finish Sudoku puzzles, or bake a flaky pie crust. That's what propels our children to read a Harry Potter book, scramble up the monkey bars, and climb to the next level in Tetris. A quarter century after Robert White identified the need for competence in the 1950s, psychologists identified two other deeply felt needs that fuel the engine of human intrinsic motivation. In addition to feeling *competent*, said Ed Deci in 1975, humans need to feel *autonomous*—that what they do comes from them, that they initiate their own actions.[8] And we need to feel *connected* to those around us.[9] In other words, to stoke their intrinsic motivation, children must feel autonomous, competent, and connected.

WHAT IS TO BE DONE?

This theory of human motivation provides the key to handling the Pressured Parent Phenomenon. As I described earlier, when the escalating competition in our children's world collides with our evolutionary hardwiring, we feel an impulse to take over. The extremely unpleasant anxiety of the Pressured Parent Phenomenon mounts, and we want to jump in and solve the problem *now*—whether it's academic, athletic, artistic, or social.

This wanting to take control is natural. Yet at the same time, it never feels quite right. Emergencies aside, I've usually felt terrible after pressuring or coercing my children. Nor do the parents in my lab ever look happy after they've told a child what to answer or showed him the solution to a puzzle. Furthermore, taking control infuriates kids. After I scolded Ben for taunting Zach in the Darth Vader bike helmet incident (at the start of chapter 4), I felt miserable, and Zach certainly was furious with me.

If you want to check that impulse to take over, then raising your child to be intrinsically motivated and responsible will help. Kids with those qualities study and practice hard. They're headed toward fulfilling their potential. Seeing that your child is "taking care of business" in this way will make it easier to check your urge to take over. Realizing that what your child needs to excel is his own inner passion—not your pressure—will go a long way toward easing the anxiety brought to you by the Pressured Parent Phenomenon.

Let's look now at all the ways intrinsic motivation benefits your child.

INTRINSIC MOTIVATION: AN ANTIDOTE TO THE PPP

Who cares *why* kids study, you might say, just so long as they study? What difference does it make what motivates kids to practice their music or play baseball?

It makes a huge difference.

The reasons are simple. First, the more intrinsically motivated kids feel, the more they achieve. Inner passion fosters both excellence and creativity.

Second, if you crack the whip, fighting and resentment are sure to follow. But encouraging your child's intrinsic motivation shows that you understand her and have her best interests at heart—and that will keep you close.

Third, intrinsic motivation promotes a child's happiness and general well-being.

The final reason to foster your child's inner passion is purely practical: you can't stand over her every time she needs to study. (That fact will become particularly clear when she goes off to college.) I'm sure you don't want to hover, either. How much better for your child to learn and achieve because she's fueled by pleasurable inner feelings!

A wealth of research points to these benefits of intrinsic motivation. Let's look at that evidence.

INNER PASSION IS THE KEY TO CHILDREN'S HIGH ACHIEVEMENT: *PEOPLE LEARN MORE WHEN THEY ENJOY IT*

Most children start school full of intrinsic motivation. If the conditions are right, they continue to enjoy learning all the way through high school. "When Maya was in elementary school," says my friend Leslie, "I used to glance at her when I volunteered in the classroom.

"She would be watching the teacher talking, a big smile on her face. She was *so* eager to learn. That's what her teachers said about her too.

"Now she's in seventh grade, and the other day I stopped by her school to drop off some forms. Of course, when I passed by her science class I peeked in. The teacher was performing an experiment in front of the class—and I saw that same smile on her face."

Obviously, if your child is happy, that makes you feel good, but does enjoying learning as Maya does make a difference in the quality of her learning?

Harry Harlow's rhesus monkeys helped answer that question. As we saw earlier, they solved their puzzles better when they worked on them for their own satisfaction, without the external motivation of a raisin beneath the hasp. That principle holds true for humans too. When kids do schoolwork, play sports, sing, or play the flute chiefly for their own enjoyment—propelled by their inner passion—that's when they achieve the most. Research has shown conclusively that—as you might guess—when a subject interests students, they pay more attention. That means they learn more, remember it longer, and understand it more deeply than topics that don't appeal to them.

Rich Ryan tested this principle experimentally in the early 1980s. A tall, friendly man with a shock of white hair parted in the middle, Rich himself is very intrinsically motivated. He loves his work so much that I remember as a grad student returning to my office late at night to pick up some papers and finding him working at his desk. Surrounded by tall stacks of books, one leg crossed over the other, he bent over his notebook, writing. He was so absorbed in his work that he didn't hear me until I shouted—"Hi, Rich! Hi!!"

Rich knew in the late 1980s that other researchers had pinned down the importance of intrinsic motivation to art, music, and other creative endeavors, but he wanted to find out how intrinsic motivation affected the kind of work millions of schoolchildren do every day—for example, learning from a textbook. So he gave a large group of college students some passages to read, one about a new blood analysis technique and another about the influence of Rudyard Kipling's experiences on his writing. Not wanting to distract them, Rich didn't mention that he would test them later. But after they finished reading, he did ask the students how interested they were in the passages and how much they enjoyed them.

A few minutes later, he asked the students to write down whatever they remembered from the passage they had read. Sure enough, the more they had enjoyed their reading and found it interesting, the more they remembered.

At that point the students thought the study was over. A week later, however, Rich asked them to come back in, presumably for another study. But instead he asked them to write down again all they could remember from the reading. The results barely changed—one more time, the students who had enjoyed their passage had retained more information.[10]

How about younger students—does intrinsic motivation help them learn too? To investigate this question, psychologist Adele Eskeles Gottfried of California State University, Northridge, gave questionnaires to 141 children, ages nine to thirteen. She asked them to agree or disagree with statements such as "I enjoy learning new things in reading, math, social studies, science"; "When I know I have learned something new, I feel good inside"; and "I think it is interesting to do work in [she named four subjects]." Then she gave the students standardized achievement exams. She found that the more the kids enjoyed academics, the higher they scored on these reading, social studies, and science tests.[11]

Learning for Its Own Sake or to Get a Good Grade?

Besides enjoyment, a second sign of academic intrinsic motivation is learning for its own sake rather than to look smart or to get a good grade. You can study, on the one hand, for intrinsic reasons—for the pure pleasure of it or because you want to learn—or you can study focusing only on results—because you want to impress or beat out others, win an award, or qualify for admission. Students who consider school a place for learning for its own sake, dozens of studies have found, get better grades, are more satisfied with school, and are less likely to drop out than those who study for grades or to "look smart" to others.[12] Psychologist Carol Dweck of Stanford University has found that students aiming above all for grades and to look intelligent tend to shy away from challenging work and quit easily when they face a bump in the road. But when children's top goal is learning, they're more likely to face a challenge with gusto. Dweck has linked these two kinds of goals to theories of intelligence: children who aim to "look good" often believe you're born with a certain amount of intelligence that never changes, but those who want first and foremost to learn usually think that you can "get smart" by working hard.[13]

That makes a big difference, because kids who think that their intelligence is fixed are easily discouraged. When they run into difficulties or make a mistake, they worry that maybe they're not smart enough. They tend to quit so as not to cast further doubt on their intelligence. On the other hand, kids who think that studying makes them smarter take a different attitude toward a tough problem. They don't see its difficulty as an indictment of their inborn ability. It's simply a signal to rev up and work harder (which can make them smarter). So believing that intelligence can grow fosters persistence.*

That's not to say students can't learn if they're aiming for good grades, because of course they can and do. Nor do I recommend that children forget about grades or test scores. I'm simply urging you not to make them the be-all and end-all. Because when learning tops their list of goals, research has found, children are less anxious and more comfortable asking for help—and therefore, ironically, get better grades.

Studies going as far back as the 1960s show that you can improve children's achievement by injecting intrinsic motivation into their learning. A classic study by Washington University psychologist Richard deCharms demonstrated just that.

In a year-long experiment, deCharms trained teachers to promote intrinsic motivation in sixth graders. He showed them how to promote their pupils' self-confidence, help them set realistic personal goals, and take responsibility for reaching them. He also gave the teachers workbooks and other materials that encouraged learning for its own sake. Finally, throughout the school year, deCharms and his colleagues coached the teachers to foster enjoyment of learning in their six hundred students. Stressing the impact of communication styles, they taught the teachers to downplay pressure on the children by not emphasizing grades and time limits. The instructors also learned to encourage students to theorize and generate hypotheses, to try new ways of doing things, and to work ahead if they liked. Finally, the teachers were advised to let the children express themselves, within the necessary limits.[14]

---

*Of course people who think that intelligence is fixed might think that studying can help them improve themselves to a certain extent. But the idea that their intelligence doesn't grow eventually limits their effort. These ideas shed light on why many Asian American students do very well in school. James W. Stigler and Harold Stevenson note in their book *The Learning Gap* (New York: Summit Books, 1992) that Americans greeted the invention of intelligence tests in the early twentieth century enthusiastically and have often used them to organize schooling. But "the notion of innate, fixed abilities rarely entered debates over educational policy in either Japan or China," wrote Stigler and Stevenson. Both Chinese and Japanese cultures, the psychologists found in their own research, emphasize the role of effort in academic achievement. Americans, however, tend to emphasize inborn talent. As Stigler and Stevenson point out in their book, when an American can't do math he's likely to say, "I don't have a head for numbers," but a Japanese or Chinese person will say, "I haven't worked hard enough at math."

Sixteen other teachers in the same district taught a control group of six hundred sixth graders using their usual methods.

That spring, tests showed that the students of the teachers trained by deCharms had not only increased their interest in learning but had also raised their Iowa Test of Basic Skills scores an average of a half year more than the students in the control group. They enjoyed school, missing it or coming late far less often.

Six years later, a follow-up study found that the "intrinsically motivated" group also graduated high school at a higher rate.[15]

But how can a *feeling* of enjoyment improve academic learning, which is largely rational? Don't emotions interfere with rationality? A story told by neuroscientist Antonio Damasio of the University of Southern California illustrates the emerging theory that feelings enhance rational thought. One of Damasio's patients, whom he refers to with the pseudonym Elliot, lost part of the frontal lobe of his brain, where surgeons had removed a tumor. Elliot's life spiraled downward as he fixated equally on all the details of daily living. Tests showed that Elliot had also lost his ability to feel emotions. But without feelings to guide him, explains Damasio, he could no longer make "rational" decisions.[16] That's because the insula, a small region deep within the brain, gathers sensory information from all over the body and generates a corresponding emotion. It then relays that information to possible decision-making parts of the brain such as the anterior cingulate and prefrontal cortices.[17] So, for example, the insula may translate a bad smell into disgust, leading to the decision to push away a rotten apple. So it's not surprising that feelings are essential for academic learning.

INTRINSIC MOTIVATION IS CRUCIAL TO SUCCESS IN SPORTS

In the fall of 2006, University of North Carolina freshman soccer player Yael Averbuch scored a goal with her opening kickoff.

That feat led sportswriter Harvey Araton, who lived nearby when Yael was growing up, to recall watching her "dancing with the ball at the bus stop, sending it across the street to a parent or her sister." But some parents in their suburban New Jersey neighborhood, he also remembers, gossiped that Yael's parents were pushing her to fulfill *their* dreams.

After that extraordinary 2006 goal four seconds into the UNC game,

Araton asked Yael's mother, Gloria, whether she and her husband had ever pressured their daughter to excel in soccer.

"What we did was create a culture at home for the love of sport for the recreational benefits," replied Gloria Averbuch, a long-distance runner.

"I knew what I was looking at athletically," she added. "But that last part that convinces you to let them try, I don't think we can know where it comes from or if we can even define it."

"How do you know if your child has it?" asked Araton.

"When she loves what she's doing like nothing else," answered Yael's mom.[18]

Former Olympic swimmer Summer Sanders would agree. Now a television personality, Sanders won two gold medals, a bronze, and a silver for swimming at the 1992 Olympic games in Barcelona. She has strong opinions about intrinsic motivation in young athletes.

"When a mother comes up to me at a mall and says, pointing to her kid, 'She's going to the 2004 Olympics,' I want to sit that mother down and set her straight," writes Sanders.

"I want her to understand that the only thing that'll take her daughter to the furthest edge of her potential is the sheer pleasure she takes in exercising her God-given ability."[19]

These are only two of a slew of stories illustrating that what motivates most successful athletes is intrinsic motivation—their love for the game. It's this same passion, research has shown, that keeps kids from dropping out of sports—not, as you might think, their win-loss record. That's what University of Ottawa psychologist Luc Pelletier found when he compared young swimmers who competed because they enjoyed it with children who swam for the trophies. The kids who swam for fun, Pelletier found, were much more likely than the others not to quit swimming.[20]

INTRINSICALLY MOTIVATED KIDS ARE HAPPIER

Scores of studies have found that intrinsically motivated kids are happier and feel better about themselves than children who are driven mainly by external pressures.

In one recent study, for example, we asked seventh- and eighth-grade students why they participated in after-school programs. Did their parents or other adults push them to sign up? Would they feel bad about themselves if

they didn't? Did they think the activity was important? And how much did fun
or enjoyment motivate them?

Some of the children said they participated for intrinsic reasons—such as
fun and skill building. They were more satisfied with their lives, we found, than
the children who took part for external reasons—because their parents made
them, for example, or because they felt pressured by their friends to join in.[21]

What about older teenagers? Psychologist Mihaly Csikszentmihalyi of the
Claremont Graduate University invented an ingenious way to check on how
intrinsic motivation affects them. Working with his colleague J. P. Hunter, he
gave 1,215 junior and senior high school students wristwatches set to go off
randomly within two-hour periods eight times during the day, for a week.
Whenever the watch beeped, the students wrote down the answers to two
questions about their most recent activity:

- "Was this activity interesting?"
- "Did you enjoy what you were doing?"

Then they rated on a seven-point scale whether they'd felt excited or bored.

The teenagers who reported lots of interest, enjoyment, and excitement—a great deal of intrinsic motivation—had higher self-esteem than those
who reported frequent boredom. The more intrinsically motivated students
also felt more effective in the world and more optimistic about the future.[22]

Other research has found that the more adults experience inner passion,
the more satisfied they feel with their lives. Lack of interest is a hallmark of
depression, but when people are propelled by the curiosity, enjoyment, and
excitement of intrinsic motivation, they simply feel good and even full of joy.[23]

INNER PASSION FUELS CREATIVITY

In this era when economists warn that our country needs innovative intellectual talent to thrive, intrinsic motivation takes on all the more importance,
because it promotes creativity.

Teresa Amabile, a Harvard Business School psychologist who has dedi-
cated her career to researching creativity, wanted to explore the relationship
between intrinsic motivation and creativity. So, over the course of eight years,
she investigated both these characteristics in twenty-four hundred college stu-

dents and working adults. First she asked them to rate on a scale of one to five how accurately statements like those below, which indicate intrinsic motivation, described them:

- "Curiosity is the driving force behind much of what I do."
- "I want to figure out how good I can really be at my work."

She also asked them to rate statements indicating extrinsic motivation, such as:

- "I'm less concerned with what work I do than what I get for it."
- "I prefer work I know I can do well over work that stretches my abilities."

The participants—who included hospital workers and secretaries, scientists and CEOs—then took two tests that measured their creativity. For the "creative personality" measure, she asked them to choose which adjectives described them. Are you:

- Capable?
- Clever?
- Confident?
- Humorous?
- Inventive?
- Original?
- Unconventional?

Or do you consider yourself:

- Cautious?
- Conservative?
- Conventional?
- Narrow in interests?[24]

The second creativity test measured their problem-solving style on a scale ranging from "adaptor" on one end to "innovator" at the other. It defined "adaptor" as someone who approaches problem-solving conservatively, tending to follow established pathways. An innovator, on the other hand, likes to find unique pathways, trying out different ways to solve problems. Questions on this test included this one: How easy or difficult is it for you to present yourself long-term and consistently as someone who:

- Conforms?
- Enjoys detailed work?
- Is stimulating?
- Is predictable?[25]

When Amabile compared the two sets of answers, she found that the higher people scored in intrinsic motivation, the higher they scored on the tests of creativity.

The twenty-four hundred people Amabile tested included four smaller groups of advanced student artists, advanced student poets, professional artists, and top-level scientists. The student artists and poets scored higher on intrinsic motivation than the other students, and the professional artists and scientists higher than the other adults in the study. And the more intrinsically motivated these artists, poets, and scientists, the more time they devoted to their pursuits and the more commitment they professed.

Amabile then looked at the writing samples of the student poets and found that their intrinsic motivation scores predicted the creativity of their writing. Furthermore, when she asked an independent panel of judges and the students' art teachers to rate the young artists' portfolios for creativity, the connection was striking: the higher the student artists' intrinsic motivation scores, the higher both kinds of judges rated their creativity.[26]

What Links Intrinsic Motivation with Creativity?

After finding that many successful creative people have high levels of intrinsic motivation, psychologists have tried to put their finger on exactly what creativity looks like. For example—finding a kernel of truth in the stereotype of scientists and philosophers who are oblivious to mundane activities such as eating—researchers have noted that creative people are totally absorbed in their work.[27] Intensely committed, they're energized by challenges and excited by complex problems. Furthermore, like the mathematicians who proved Fermat's last theorem in the early 1990s,[28] they're often fascinated by a tough, even risky set of problems over many years that "provide a powerful sense of pleasure for the opportunity to use their talents."[29]

Loving an activity is not too strong a synonym for feeling intrinsically motivated to pursue it, says Amabile. She likes to cite what Arthur Schawlow, a Nobel laureate in physics, said about the characteristics of scientific success: "The labor of love aspect is important," he said. "The successful scientists... are just impelled by curiosity."[30]

Although several streams of motivation flow into the river of creativity, that sort of personal involvement or love is essential for high-level creativity, say Amabile and her colleague Mary Ann Collins.[31] They also quote novelist John Irving, who spends as many as twelve hours a day writing. Why does he work so hard, Irving was asked, even after achieving fame, fans, and fortune? "The unspoken factor is love," he answered. "The reason I can work so hard at my writing is that it's not work for me."[32]

Indeed, a growing body of research supports the idea that the best way for people to maximize their creative potential is to do something they love. Several psychologists have found that people with creative jobs including artists and research scientists have more intrinsic motivation for their work than the general population.[33] One well-known study that spanned forty years followed into adulthood students who had attended elementary school in Minnesota from 1958 to 1964. The late University of Georgia researcher E. Paul Torrance (creator of the Future Problem Solving Program mentioned in chapter 2) gave these 215 students creativity tests each year and a questionnaire in 1980 that delved into whether they were maintaining their creativity and using it in their careers and child-rearing. Torrance contacted them again in 1998. The bottom line: those who were doing what they loved were more creative.[34]

Flow

People who are doing what they enjoy often experience a phenomenon called "flow." Flow occurs when intrinsic motivation reaches its peak. It's a highly creative state attained after you've put in hard work to build your skills. Flow frequently occurs as you're solving a complex problem or mastering a new task, when you're so deeply focused that you lose track of time. You can reach a flow state while running, playing a video game or the piano, working on geometry, or reading an engrossing book. Fed by challenges that are neither too easy nor too hard, flow provides a good petri dish for generating multiple solutions to a problem, some of which are usually creative.[35] Extremely pleasurable, flow brings a feeling of immersion, so joyful and deep it's exhilarating—a nonpharmaceutical "high." Flow gives you a feeling of great accomplishment.

Performing Arts

Creativity in the performing arts also thrives on intrinsic motivation. When you're performing mainly for the pleasure of it, you're more likely to let your feelings flood into your performance. Unlimited by fear of failure, you're more flexible, willing to respond to new impulses, and try out novel ideas.

Extrinsic motivation, on the other hand, tends to smother creativity because it narrows your focus. Concentrating on winning a role or pleasing a judge can make you focus uniquely on technique. That's why, observes singing teacher Anne Adams, a musician who places second in a competition often has a better career than the person who wins.

"People who win," she explains, "tend to do everything right but aren't necessarily the more adventurous or unusual." (I don't know if that explains

---

FLOW PROVIDES A CLUE TO DEVELOPING CHILDREN'S TALENTS: CSIKSZENTMIHALYI'S TALENTED TEENS

We've all known of child prodigies who crash and burn and more ordinary children who simply don't fulfill their early promise. What makes students persist in cultivating their talents?

Mihaly Csikszentmihalyi investigated that question by following more than two hundred teenagers identified at age thirteen as talented in math, science, music, art, or sports. Which teens, he wanted to know, would stick to developing their talent throughout high school and college?

He had the teenagers wear electronic pagers for a week. When their pagers received signals sent at random during the day—about fifty times in that week—they filled out a two-page questionnaire, revealing the challenges they faced at that moment and the skills they were using. Whenever the challenge and skills both rose above the weekly average, Csikszentmihalyi classified the students as experiencing flow.

His results? The teenagers who reported flow while pursuing the athletics, arts, or academics in which they showed talent took much harder courses in those subjects (or played higher-level sports) in high school. They also had much more commitment to cultivating their gifts in college. The best predictor of developing their talent, Csikszentmihalyi concluded, wasn't the students' SATs or IQs. Nor was it determined by their personality traits or their parents' income. The best predictor was how often they experienced flow.[36]

why Jennifer Hudson won an Oscar for the movie *Dreamgirls* yet placed seventh in *American Idol*, but it's certainly possible.)

Adams, who taught voice for several years at St. Olaf College in Minnesota and now teaches privately in Boston, counsels students to put the judges out of their minds and think of a contest as a concert and that they're entertaining an audience.

INTRINSIC MOTIVATION HELPS SOLVE THE PRESSURED PARENTS PHENOMENON

The more your child is propelled by intrinsic motivation, the easier you'll find it to deal with the Pressured Parent Phenomenon. When competition hits your hardwiring, you'll have a much better chance of calming your anxiety if your child is working hard and pursuing her passions. If she does her homework, practices of her own accord, exercises her creative potential, and sometimes achieves excellence, that will help you resist the urge to pressure her.

You'll feel less temptation to jump in and take over, because an intrinsically motivated child confidently takes on and solves problems, asking for your help only when necessary.

In addition, if you believe in her pursuing her interests, you'll feel less tempted to push her in a certain direction—toward a certain sport, a certain group of friends, a certain professional goal. If you realize that no amount of pushing will *create* a passion in your child, that will free you up to follow her lead and encourage *her* interests.

When the competition is intense and noisy, and kids all around you look like they are ready for the Olympics, it's hard to keep this faith. But doing so will give you the patience to wait and watch as your child discovers his own passions.

Following your child's intrinsic motivation won't end the anxiety and the urge to push him, but it will go a long way toward helping you cope with these feelings. You can say to yourself, "Sarah is doing what she *wants* to do and that's good for her. That's how she'll do her best and be happiest. It's not good for her or for me to push, pressure, or control. Even though that's what I feel like doing!

"What she needs most from me is guidance and support."

INTERNALIZATION: "GUN TO THE HEAD," "GUILTY," AND "I AGREE"

I now hear the thud of your coming down to earth after reading about all the enjoyment and creativity of children propelled by their intrinsic motivation. "That's really nice," I hear you saying, "but if I let my kid do only what she enjoys, she'll eat chocolate cake and play with the dog all day long.

"Inner passion is well and good," you might add, "but what about the SATs?

"Look, my child is intrinsically motivated to play video games, but what about the other things that I know he has to do to survive in this competitive world? Shouldn't I push him to do those things for his own good? I'm letting go of my responsibility as a parent if I don't."

Yes. You're right. Kids have to learn subjects and do chores that aren't fun. That includes many of the tasks that give rise to the Pressured Parent Phenomenon. It *is* your responsibility to make sure your child studies science and stays physically fit, even if he doesn't want to.

For those activities we turn to internalization: the process of children adopting their parents' values and goals and behaving accordingly.

Think about some of the work you do even though it isn't pleasurable.

VERA RUBIN: INTRINSIC MOTIVATION SURFACING AT AN EARLY AGE

As a child of seven, Vera Rubin saw the stars in the sky for the first time after her family moved from Philadelphia to the outskirts of Washington, DC.

"That experience was overwhelming," writes Mihaly Csikszentmihalyi about Vera. "From that moment on she could not imagine not spending her life studying the stars." Recognizing her inner passion, Rubin's father helped her build a telescope when she was fourteen. Today a research astronomer at the Carnegie Institution of Washington, Rubin is credited with establishing the importance of "dark matter" in the universe. A winner of the National Medal of Science, she's still motivated by her passion. "It's fun, great fun, to come upon something new," she told Csikszentmihalyi.

Not every child discovers an overwhelming passion at age seven, but all children have interests—a topic, or subject that fascinates them, to which they return again and again. Vera Rubin also had parents who took her early interest seriously and helped her explore it.[37]

Perhaps you work in a physician's office and hate filling out health insurance forms, but you do it anyway. Maybe you do it because if you don't, your boss will fire you. Or perhaps you fill out the forms because if you don't, your coworker will have to and you'll feel guilty. Or maybe you do it because you know these papers are important for the office to stay afloat and for the doctor to keep treating patients.

These motivations are forms of internalization, similar to a child's reasons for doing homework or cleaning her room. Your daughter might straighten her room because if she doesn't, she knows you'll get angry and maybe even withhold her allowance. This is *"gun to the head,"* or *coerced motivation*, similar to your doing paperwork to get your raise.

Your daughter might also clean her room because she knows you want to show it to guests, and she'll feel bad if you can't do that. This is *introjected* or *"guilty" motivation.*

On the other hand, perhaps one day she'll clean her room because she realizes that putting everything in its place will make it easier to find her favorite marking pen. This is an example of *"identified,"* or *"I agree" motivation.*

These first two kinds of motivation feel bad. "Gun to the head" motivation requires external prodding and lasts only as long as you apply that nudging. Kids with the second kind, guilty motivation, often get down on themselves.

The third kind, "identified" motivation, in which your child adopts your values for a long time and even permanently, is the strongest form of internalization. Your child has decided that doing her homework and cleaning her room are important *for her own reasons*. She wants to take on these chores to meet her own goals. They fit her values or standards. Doing her math homework may not be fun, but your daughter knows that it will take her where she wants to go. As with intrinsic motivation, your child feels a sense of self-initiation or autonomy.

This last form of "I agree" motivation is closest to intrinsic motivation—and therefore the best for your child's achievement and happiness as well as your relationship with him. Whenever intrinsic motivation isn't operating, you want your child to move toward this kind of "I agree" motivation. On a larger scale, it will help your child adopt values that benefit society overall.

The good news about internalization is that you foster it in your child every day without even thinking about it. When you treat a salesperson as a fellow human being rather than a servant, your child takes in the values demonstrated by your action. When you give to charity or refuse to cheat on your income tax, or when you take care of your aging parents, tell a family story, or solve an ethical problem ("Is it okay to tell a white lie?") in front of your children, they start to make your values their own.

"Your grandpa's older brother worked so that your grandpa could go to college" shows that your family values education. "I don't think we should go shopping today. It's Martin Luther King Day. Let's go to the celebration down at the park" demonstrates your beliefs, too.

Even when children hit the preteen years and act as though you know nothing, they still internalize your values. One day my daughter and I talked about a girl her friends had suddenly decided to stop talking to. I encouraged her to think about how she might feel if she were Zoë. "Zoë is mean and you don't know what you're talking about," she told me and stomped out of the room.

That afternoon I overheard her talking on the phone. "I don't think it's right to leave Zoë out," I heard her say. "I think we should invite her to the movie."

"I Agree" Internalization Works Better for Kids

Research has found that children who internalize "identified" or "I agree" motivation are more resilient and emotionally healthy than kids who internalize "gun to the head" or "guilty" motivation.

In one study, for example, Rich Ryan investigated how these three kinds of motivation affect children by asking several hundred third to sixth graders four questions:

- Why did they do their homework?
- Why did they do their class work?
- Why did they try to answer the teacher's questions in class?
- Why did they try to do well in school?

Some children's answers illustrated "gun to the head" motivation: "My teacher would yell at me if I didn't," or "I'll get in trouble if I don't." Others revealed introjected or guilty reasons: "I would feel bad about myself if I didn't." And still others showed identified, or "I agree" motivation: "I do my classwork because I want to understand the subject."

Interestingly, the children gave "I agree" reasons most often. That's good, because when Ryan looked at the other two kinds of motivation, he found problems.

When children with "gun to the head" motivation got a bad grade, they blamed others or sloughed it off. Throwing a bad test in the trash or forgetting about it was their style. Students with guilty motivation did try to find ways to do better, but the bad grade also sent their anxiety skyrocketing and made them feel stupid.

The kids who gave the "I agree" reasons for doing schoolwork were most resilient. When they got a bad grade, they used the test to figure out *how* to catch up, perhaps by asking the teacher or a parent for help.[38] They did not, like kids with guilty motivation, ruminate excessively over the bad grade.

When the Going Gets Tedious

"I agree" motivation is very important for helping kids get through the tedious moments and duties that are a part of even activities they enjoy tremendously. Sports, for example, demand physical conditioning. Football players have to lift weights and do sit-ups; field and ice hockey players have to strengthen their knees to prevent tears of their anterior cruciate ligaments. Schoolwork often demands memorizing a spelling word, definition, or formula; music demands practicing scales and breath control. Children can love these pursuits overall, but they still need to internalize the reasons for the boring parts, so they won't balk at them.

Acquiring "I agree" motivation is good preparation for later life, because, as Teresa Amabile points out, even highly creative adult work has its dull moments. Scientists may charge through an experiment or problem excitedly, fueled by intrinsic motivation even in a flow state. But to propel them through the dogged work of elucidating fine details and writing up papers for publication, they may need an additive of "I agree" motivation so they can meet deadlines.

FACILITATING INTRINSIC MOTIVATION AND "I AGREE" INTERNALIZATION

How can you ease internalization along when it hasn't happened naturally? How can you get your child to value his social studies homework or not skip basketball practice so as not to let down the team? To foster *both* children's intrinsic motivation and their "I agree" internalization, you can nurture three feelings inside them. These three feelings are autonomy, competence, and connection.

WHY CHILDREN GO CRAZY OVER VIDEO GAMES

Believe it or not, your child hunched over a keyboard or controller tells us something important about his passion for learning. Some of the most popular video games are intrinsically motivating because they fulfill one or more of the three needs—for competence, autonomy, and connection—that fuel intrinsic motivation. "People . . . play these games because they're intrinsically satisfying," says psychologist Rich Ryan, who, along with Scott Rigby and Andrew Przybylski, recently studied the effects of playing video games in both laboratory experiments and through a questionnaire answered by more than seven hundred players.

Often the game controls are intuitive, so players gain pleasurable feelings of competence when they master them at the very beginning of the game. Interestingly, initial studies show that boys master controls intuitively faster than girls.

Many video games also make players feel competent because they confront problems and practice solving them, gaining more skill along the way. They often meet successively difficult challenges, says linguistics professor James Paul Gee of the University of Wisconsin, Madison. "Good games stay within but at the outer edge of the player's competence," he explains. "They feel doable, but challenging."[39]

People almost always *choose* to play video games, too—and experience a sense of freedom or autonomy doing so. Some video games heighten that feeling by letting players decide the sequence of actions, strategies, and goals.

Ryan contrasts this kind of enjoyment to fun, which he believes is much shallower and doesn't "hook" people into playing as much as video games do.

Ryan and University of Rochester grad student Andrew Przybylski found that one type of video game—the massively multiplayer online, or MMO games, which are the fastest-growing segment of the computer gaming industry—provides a feeling of connection. Players, who are mostly age sixteen and above, chat with each other, make friends, and feel part of a group effort.[40]

"The psychological 'pull' of games is largely due to their capacity to engender feelings of autonomy, competence, and relatedness," says Ryan.[41] Of course, he warns, "Not all video games are created equal."

What's the best way to promote these three feelings in your child? That's where the Three-Part Framework—autonomy, involvement, and structure—comes in. To encourage intrinsic motivation and internalization, you can pay attention to:

- Granting your child **autonomy.** *Autonomy* lets him feel like he initiates his own actions and solves his own problems, rather than feeling pressured or compelled by someone else.
- Giving your child support through your **involvement.** A parent who affords his child his time and other resources fosters feelings of *connection.*
- Giving your child **structure.** Structure means the guidelines and information, rules and consequences that a child needs to act in the world. By showing her the effect of her actions and providing the tools she needs, structure gives her a feeling of *competence.*

We'll look next at autonomy and learn how to nourish that important feeling in your child.

CHAPTER 6

R_x FOR INTRINSIC MOTIVATION
Encouraging Your Child's Autonomy

I n the preface, I told you about my friend Beth Miller, whose ten-year-old daughter Jennifer wanted to quit ballet and start playing team sports.

"All my friends are playing basketball, softball, and soccer," Jennifer told Beth. "I'm tired of feeling left out!"

Beth and her husband, Mike, were beside themselves. Jennifer had started ballet at age four. She danced so beautifully. They loved watching her. She'd already appeared in the local production of *The Nutcracker* and would surely have a solo next year.

Thinking about Jennifer quitting ballet filled Beth with anxiety. How could her daughter throw away her talent, as well as the future opportunities it could bring? She didn't see how much she was giving up!

Also, Jennifer didn't play team sports very well. She didn't thrive on competition—her feelings were often and easily hurt.

After all the time and money they'd put into ballet, schlepping four times a week to a nearby town, the Millers felt blindsided. Maybe they should insist Jennifer keep dancing, they wondered. It gave her such a strong self-image. She was too young to understand the value of her dance accomplishments on her college application. Perhaps they should teach her the value of persistence.

"You know, it would be a shame to waste all the time and hard work you've put into ballet," Beth said to her daughter.

"If you stick with dance, you'll be glad you did," added Mike, before Jennifer could answer.

They don't understand, read the pout on Jennifer's face.

"All the other girls have been playing soccer for five or six years," Mike went on. "You wouldn't stand out the way you do in ballet."

"But I want to be with my friends!" Jennifer almost shrieked.

"What if you cut back on dance from three times a week to once?" tried Beth.

"No," said Jennifer.

They had never seen their daughter so stubborn.

That night after she was asleep, the Millers talked about how angry Jennifer would be if they forced her to keep dancing. Mike remembered his own fury when his parents had made him practice piano an hour a day, long after he stopped enjoying it.

The next morning they told Jennifer that the ultimate decision was hers.

"You know, I understand what it feels like to want to be with your friends," Beth told her. "I remember when my parents wouldn't take me to the other side of town for the meetings of the Girl Scout troop all my friends were in. I felt like I was missing so much. I was *so* mad!"

After telling me this story, Beth added, "I can't believe the way this upset Mike and me both. I never would have thought Jennifer's dancing meant so much to *us*!"

But she and Mike realized that their motives weren't purely altruistic. While they thought Jennifer should keep dancing for her own sake, they also wanted her to persist so *they* could feel proud. That was understandable, but it wasn't a good reason.

That year Jennifer played both soccer and softball. When she cried after one soccer game, Mike put his arm around her.

"I know it feels bad to lose," he said. "But you guys played a great game. You never gave up. Your dribbling is really improved and everyone is passing really well. It was a pleasure to watch the teamwork.

"You know, you'll have another chance to beat this team in a few weeks."

Gradually, Jennifer's disappointment and distress at losing lessened. That summer—much to her parents' delight—she told them she wanted to dance again. She missed the calm of ballet, the camaraderie, the beauty and the pleasure. She wanted to keep playing soccer too, but maybe not softball.

The Millers' story illustrates how to turn the anxiety of the Pressured

Parent Phenomenon into positive parenting by using the Three-Part Framework, including its first leg: promoting a child's autonomy. The Millers had to struggle tremendously with their own feelings, but eventually they managed to see Jennifer's point of view. Letting her know they understood, they then put the decision in her hands. They supported her as she took responsibility for her own behavior and endured the consequences. They resisted the impulse to say, "I told you so." In other words, they supported her autonomy.

And autonomy is crucial for intrinsic motivation.

WHAT IS AUTONOMY?

Autonomy is the feeling of initiating an action.

When people feel a sense of autonomy, the feeling that what they do derives from them, they're happier. And they perform better, because the enjoyment motivates them to study or practice more, building up their skills.

A good way to understand autonomy is to think about your own experience. You might *have* to learn Excel for work, for example, but if you *choose* to learn it for tracking your family's yearly budget, you're much more likely to enjoy it. I slogged through *A Tale of Two Cities* for eighth-grade English class, but reading it later on my own was a pleasure.

Children—in fact, all human beings—need to feel that what they do is self-initiated. We like to solve our own problems whenever possible. That fact hit my friend Sheila over the head one day when her daughter Katie was five. Bouncing into the car after kindergarten, Katie said that she'd grown tired of climbing the monkey bars at recess, but her friend Ashley had refused to go to the swings.

Sheila knew just what Katie should have done. "Did you tell Ashley you'd go back to the monkey bars with her later?" she asked, an edge of anxiety in her voice. She wanted Katie to get along well with her friends.

Katie turned toward her mother. "Mommy," she said firmly, "I don't want you to *tell* me. I just want you to *listen* to me."

"That made an incredible impression on me," Sheila told me. "She doesn't want me to solve her problems. I don't always succeed, but I just try to take a breath and think, 'I'm not supposed to tell her what to do all the time. I'm supposed to listen.'

"I do a *lot* of listening."

AUTONOMY ISN'T THE EMANCIPATION PROCLAMATION

Many people misunderstand autonomy as "doing whatever you want," perhaps because autonomy in politics means self-government. In psychology, however, autonomy is an entirely different concept. It's a willingness to do something, a sense of volition. It's the opposite of feeling controlled by someone else.

You can feel autonomous when someone else is in charge. That may sound contradictory, but it's not. Here's how it works: if a teacher assigns students to read a chapter book but allows them to choose from several titles, that choice gives the children a sense of autonomy. Helping a child with homework when he *asks* for it, rather than standing over him to make sure he does it, also fosters his autonomous feelings.

So when we support our children's autonomy, we don't hand over power or authority to them. It's not the Emancipation Proclamation—autonomy doesn't mean independence. Nor does it mean "hands-off" parenting, permissiveness, or "letting go." When you allow your child autonomy, you still call most of the shots. The Millers let Jennifer decide whether to stay in ballet, but they kept up their family rules and expectations. They didn't let her choose whether to go to school or help out at night with the dishes. When she started playing team sports, she agreed to the rule that she attend practices regularly and play the entire season. Still in charge, her parents stayed closely involved in their daughter's life and continued to guide her.

Some theorists recoil from the idea of autonomy because they connect it to the American archetype of the "rugged individualist." They understand autonomous people as egocentric and separate, rather than being warmly related to their parents, family, and friends.

But that's not my definition. Quite the opposite: autonomy promotes intimacy. It helps you and your child fulfill your basic human need for connection. At first it may seem paradoxical, but promoting a child's feelings of choice and freedom draws you closer. That's what happened to Michelle Weiler and her daughter Megan, who live in Atlanta. Michelle was upset when, after her freshman year, Megan said she hated high school and wanted to drop out.

"It's stupid," Megan told her mother. "They give you so much work, there's no time to think." Her large school didn't feel like the communities described in a book she'd read on alternative schooling. Even worse, Megan's best friend had moved to another city.

Michelle didn't let her daughter quit school, but she did find two nontraditional programs that she could apply to. Megan dove into the application essays, including one that asked her to describe the perfect school. Her resentment vanished, and she seemed happier.

"She got to write about what she cares about," her mother told me. "Plus, she finally has a sense she's doing something on her own. So she's more willing to push herself. Of course, she brought me her essay to look over at 11:30 the night before she had to mail it.

"But I really enjoyed helping her. I felt close to her again."

EVERYONE HATES FEELING CONTROLLED

True to the Pressured Parent Phenomenon, Michelle's first thought when Megan said she wanted to quit school was a horrified "No! You can't drop out of school!!" She managed to hold her tongue, even if she initially felt dismayed.

Similarly, the Millers' first impulse when Jennifer said she wanted to stop taking ballet was to say, "No!" and make her keep dancing. Rather than supporting Jennifer's autonomy, they initially wanted to impose control.

But children hate feeling controlled just as much as adults do. It's highly unpleasant to feel that your actions are not your own. Resentment kills any remnants of your intrinsic motivation. Instead, you devote your energy to twisting and turning, trying to wriggle free. Think how you'd feel, for example, if your boss threatened, "You better get that done right away or else!" You'd probably want to throw your laptop at him. Children feel similarly angry when we order them around with "Clean your room up right now" or "By the count of three, I want you working on your math!" They'll do almost anything to avoid obeying.

People have such a strong need for freedom that we'll resist control even at great cost to ourselves. It's classic "cutting off your nose to spite your face" behavior. I remembered that recently, when I couldn't help saying to Rebecca, who likes to eat cookies for breakfast, "You really need to eat something healthy. No more sweets for breakfast!"

"Okay, then, I won't eat," she said, running out the door. Her reaction mimicked on a much smaller scale kids who—reacting to extreme control at home—go wild with drinking and drugs at college. It's not so much that they're consciously *choosing* to drink and take drugs, it is more as though they're reacting against that awful feeling of someone else controlling them.

THE PERILS OF PUSHING

"I had to ask a mother to take her children to another teacher," says piano teacher Rosita Mang. "The older daughter came to me terrified of playing, as she was humiliated and mistreated by her previous teacher (a competition-obsessed person). It took me a year for her to talk to me, to smile, to enjoy expressing a feeling through music. Then, as she was getting both technically and musically better and fared well in limited-scope competitions, the mom asked for some of the most difficult piano repertoire and one of the most difficult competitions in the state. I refused. She insisted. I told the girl that she could not be pulled between her mom's ideas and mine and it was better for her that she would find another teacher that would please her mother. So they went back to the previous humiliating teacher.

"The child does not smile any more and has horrific memory lapses. She agonizes on the stage. I am so sorry for her. I tried and I failed. I will always regret that failure."

My friend Carol's father made an even more momentous decision, just to avoid control. While he was growing up in Rhodesia, his mother told him all the time how much she wanted him to become a lawyer. One day, when he was standing in line at the local university to enroll in law school, he thought, "Hey, why should I do what my mother wants me to do?" He'd always liked drawing. So he switched to the line for architecture school instead and ended up graduating from the university with an architecture degree. Unfortunately, he didn't like architecture very much. He never worked as an architect and went into business instead. As time went on, Carol's father was sorry he hadn't become a lawyer. He realized he'd avoided it just to spite his mother. And he was very careful not to influence Carol's choice of career. "Do whatever you like," he told her. "And I'll help you get the education you need."

CONTROLLING VS. IN CONTROL

Before going any further, I have to make an important distinction. While parents shouldn't control their children, I *do* believe that parents should be *in con-*

trol. That means acting as an authority and taking firm charge. It includes making decisions that children are too young to make.

I don't advocate a hands-off policy at any age, including the teen years. Far from it.

Research has shown decisively that children need rules, guidelines, and limits. Children thrive on our expectations and they need responsibilities. When they help clear the table, pack up their backpacks, and attend practice or rehearsals regularly, they develop a sense of responsibility. So parents need to exert authority over children's behavior through rules and regulations.

The point is to implement this structure without using controlling methods that pressure your child to adopt certain feelings, ideas, or behaviors. The best way to avoid such a controlling parenting style while staying "in control" is to encourage your child's autonomy as much as possible—even while you're implementing structure. Research has found that fostering autonomy promotes intrinsic motivation and achievement, while keeping parents and children close. Let's look at that research.

AUTONOMY BOOSTS MOTIVATION AND ACHIEVEMENT

In the preface and again in chapter 4, I mentioned the eyesight-ruining experiment I did as a young graduate student with the mothers and their one-year-olds, and how the mothers controlled their kids' actions, destroying their motivation. But what about the other kids whose mothers *didn't* take over? What happened to them?

To answer that question, let's run this movie by again, looking at it from this new angle. One point I didn't mention before is that I purposely gave the mothers ambiguous instructions. "Sit next to your child," I told them, "while he or she plays with the toy."

Some of the mothers understood those directions as "I have to make sure my child does this right." Their mouths tightened with purpose as they fired directions at their child: "Put the block in—No, no, THERE, THERE!" Those, of course, were the moms who took over and whose babies later lost interest in figuring out how the toys worked.

But the other mothers interpreted my instructions very differently. They thought I wanted them to act as a resource for their children. So they let their babies learn through trial and error, trying one shape in the hole and then another. When the child looked at them for help, these mothers gave it. In other words, they supported their child's autonomy.

So what happened to their children during the next phase of the experiment, when we left them alone with shape sorters and Busy Boxes and asked the mothers to sit across the room in a chair? My instructions to the one-year-olds were clear-cut. "Make it work," I said gently. And that's when the babies whose moms had encouraged their autonomy acted quite differently. They tried harder than the other kids to figure out which shapes fit in which holes and how to make the Busy Box characters pop up. And they spent more time playing with the toys overall.

But the experiment wasn't yet over. Eight months later, when we brought them back into the lab, these toddlers were *still* more persistent—and more competent—than the others at working the toys.

This experiment demonstrated graphically why children whose parents support their autonomy achieve more: their parents' style encourages intrinsic motivation, which triggers the persistence that in turn produces competence.

That's true for older children as well, as Ed Deci showed ten years after my study, when he videotaped a similar experiment with mothers and their five- to seven-year-olds, as they played at building structures with Legos and Lincoln Logs. Afterward, when the children played alone, the same phenomenon occurred: kids whose moms had controlled them played lackadaisically, soon losing interest. But those whose mothers had encouraged and helped them kept on merrily building by themselves.[1] Their intrinsic motivation was clearly responsible, because they also told the researchers they enjoyed playing with the toys more than the other children said they did.

When Teachers Promote Autonomy, Children Do Better in School

While I was immersed in this Busy Box and shape-sorter experiment, Ed also explored another idea. Why not look at whether *teachers* could heat up their students' motivation by supporting their autonomy? So before their school year began, he asked thirty-five elementary schoolteachers to read several vignettes about children who had problems such as losing their temper often or acting listless and unmotivated. Then Ed and his colleagues presented options for handling these situations. Some choices, such as discussions with the child and helping her solve the problem on her own, supported the student's autonomy. Others were controlling, such as offering rewards and comparing the child to other students.

Ed assessed the motivational styles of the 610 students of these teachers in October and again in May. Both times, the children whose teachers encouraged their autonomy showed more intrinsic motivation. They were more curious, more interested in challenges, and more focused on building their competence. They also had stronger feelings of self-worth.[2]

The researchers also scrutinized the effect of the two different teaching styles in six of the classrooms over a much shorter period. Three of the teachers had specified they would choose controlling methods to solve children's problems, and three had indicated they preferred methods that encouraged their students' autonomy. Ed and his colleagues measured the intrinsic motivation and self-worth of *all* the children on the second day of school, and again two months later. The students whose teachers favored methods that would foster autonomy felt more competent and again displayed stronger feelings of self-worth than the other children. They were also more eager to master skills independently.[3]

All that after only two months of teaching! Apparently teachers' styles not only influence children profoundly, but they also influence them quickly.

And Parents?

But what about parents? I thought. No one was looking at how *they* affected children's motivation at school.

To answer that question I went to Dansville. You might remember from chapter 4 the parents from that upstate New York town who told us they wanted their kids to be happy, doing whatever interested them. They lived an hour from the Rochester campus in a rural village of five thousand people that is known for its annual balloon festival and as the place where Clara Barton founded the Red Cross. I drove down to Dansville several times a week for almost a year and interviewed more than a hundred mothers and fathers of third to sixth graders in their homes. I asked a slew of questions about their parenting techniques. How, for example, did they get their kids to do their homework, go to bed on time, and clean their rooms—activities that children don't naturally gravitate to on their own?

For some of the parents, coercion was the name of the game. One mother told me she stood over her son every night to make sure he finished his homework. Others expected their children to obey them without question and used controlling methods like spanking and bribes.

But other parents recognized their children's autonomy. One mother had a rule that if her daughter didn't do her homework she couldn't turn on the TV. But she allowed the little girl to decide when and where she did the homework. Another mother told her son that she'd be making dinner in the kitchen and to let her know whenever he wanted her help. Then I asked the children's teachers how they did in school. The results were even more dramatic than I expected: students whose parents promoted their autonomy scored higher on standardized achievement tests and earned better grades than the children of the controlling parents. They also behaved better in the classroom and acted more responsibly, finishing assignments in class and turning in their homework conscientiously.[4]

Of course, that's not to say that the parents' promotion of autonomy *caused* the children's sense of responsibility. It's also possible that, seeing how responsibly their children acted, the parents felt comfortable allowing them autonomy.

A TWO-WAY STREET

That brings up an important point: our on-the-spot reactions to our children's behavior sometimes make it difficult to nurture a child's autonomy. If your son takes responsibility for his homework, it's not hard to let him decide when and where to do it. Say, for example, you're all going to visit your mother for the weekend. It's pretty easy to let him choose whether he'll do the homework Friday night, or at Grandma's house, or the night you come back, because you know he'll follow through.

But what if your child is lackadaisical? What if he always procrastinates or doesn't seem to care if he does his homework or not? Your likely reflex is to control him. "I want you to do your homework before we leave, while I'm packing. And do your math first because it's the hardest for you. Then you'll have it out of the way." Nurturing his autonomy seems like the last thing you want to do or have time for. But if you can't catch yourself and keep pouring on the control, he'll rebel, trapping the two of you in a downward spiral of irresponsibility, control, and rebellion—more shrugging it off, followed by more control and more rebellion.

To break this cycle, you need instead to encourage your son's autonomy all the more. It feels counterintuitive, but the research is very solid. Children's sense of responsibility grows only when they feel autonomous. So, for example, you could ask him:

- When do you plan to do your homework?
- How much time do you think it will take?
- When do you think would be the best time to do it?

Then you can help him to settle on a plan.

"OK, so you think the best time to do it would be when we get home on Sunday. That sounds good. And you're not sure how much time it will take. So let's say it'll take an hour. I think we can be home by six. If you start at 6:30 you'll be done definitely by eight, when I know you like to watch *The Simpsons*.

"How does that sound?"

This process might not feel comfortable at first, so you might try a little bit at a time until you get used to it and see it working. For example, the first time you try, just ask one question and see where it takes you. It may be difficult to give this method time to work, especially if "not working" means your son isn't doing his homework, but if you can steel yourself for a few days or weeks, you'll find that the end result is worth the wait.

This method not only encourages your child's autonomy but also increases *structure*, which includes your expectations (you *expect* him to do his homework) and guidelines (you're showing him that he needs to make a plan estimating how long his homework will take and setting a time for doing it). We'll discuss implementing structure more in chapter 9.

NAVIGATING THE NITTY-GRITTY: *HOW* YOU HELP WITH HOMEWORK MAKES A DIFFERENCE

The Dansville study revealed the importance of supporting children's autonomy in general, but I still wanted more details. After all, parenting takes place in the nitty-gritty of daily life, and parents need to know how best to navigate it. Specifically, I wanted to explore the everyday job of helping children with their homework. Does your style of helping affect your child's learning? A series of studies answered this question.

Remember the experiment in chapter 4 where parents helped their third graders learn to give directions from a map and write a quatrain? Some of these parents, we found, tended to control their children while working on these homework-like tasks. "Do that one now," they'd say, or point out where to go next. Some read the directions out loud instead of letting the child read them or even gave their third graders the answers.

Others, however, respected their children's autonomy. Instead of firing directions, they gave hints. "That street is too far," one mom told her son when he wrote down the wrong street. "Do you see one closer?" When one girl, giving directions, left out the cross streets, her mother asked, "What other information do you need?"

Later, when her daughter got stuck, she said, "I think there's another place you might look."

These moms also supported their children's autonomy by giving feedback. That means providing information on how their kid was doing by, for example, saying "You're almost there!" and nodding encouragement.

Afterward, when we gave the children similar work to do by themselves, those whose mothers had acted controlling made more mistakes. The lines in their poems didn't rhyme, or they didn't follow the quatrain rhyme scheme. They left out a street when using the map to give directions or gave the directions in the wrong order. It seemed like their mothers' control had kept them from taking in much of the lesson.

But children whose mothers had supported their autonomy did much better. They wrote poems with the right number of lines and using the correct *abab* rhyme scheme. They had grasped the concepts, while the children of the controlling mothers had gained at best a superficial understanding.

We also looked at the creativity of the children's poems, using scales developed by Teresa Amabile, the creativity researcher mentioned in chapter 5. Her scale has proven "reliable," meaning that judges who use it derive similar results. We rated the children's poems, relative to the others, on a five-point scale. What did we find? The children whose mothers had given them hints and encouragement but not taken over wrote the most highly rated, creative poems.

That wasn't all. When I looked at these kids' report card grades in reading and math, I saw that students whose moms had fostered their autonomy in the lab earned higher grades than the others.[5]

It's not easy, when the Pressured Parent Phenomenon has you in its grip, to nonchalantly give your child hints and encouragement. When you're anxious and perhaps tired after a long day, it's hard if not impossible to think of your child's autonomy. Especially if your child is not getting good grades or has a learning disability, it's very tempting to control him. It's *so* much easier to say, "Here, look, do it this way."

But the more you practice, the easier it will get to support your child's autonomy. Now we'll look at some additional specific ways to do just that.

AUTONOMY WARMS YOUR RELATIONSHIP; CONTROL COOLS IT

Children feel close to us when we acknowledge who they are and what they want. An important method for nurturing a child's autonomy is to *look at the situation from your child's point of view—to acknowledge her viewpoint and feelings.*

That's what some of the adults did in one of my studies. We showed elementary school children two videotapes of grown-ups leading them through enjoyable writing and drawing activities. The adult in the first video supported the children's autonomy by recognizing their feelings. "I know you might usually like to draw other things," she conceded, "but for this task we'll draw an animal."

The other grown-up, however, spoke in a controlling way: "You have to draw an animal," she said.

Then we asked the children to tell us which adult they liked working with the best. "The first one!" most of them told us. They also felt warmer and friendlier toward her.[6]

Studies of parents and kids similarly show that supporting children's autonomy fosters warm relationships. Rachel Robb Avery interviewed a diverse group of nearly one hundred fourth to sixth graders in a magnet school. "Describe your mother," she asked, "and describe your father." Then she wrote down the children's answers verbatim.

Next she had the children answer twenty-one questions about their parents, many of them plumbing how much the parents encouraged the children's autonomy. She asked which statement better described their parent:

- "Some mothers talk to their children about behaving so their children will understand what is best for them" (promotes autonomy) or,
- "Other mothers make their children behave because parents know what's best for them" (controlling).

CONTROLLING PARENTING CHILLS RELATIONSHIPS

Leslie Dennis laments how when she became a teenager, her mother's controlling parenting thwarted their closeness. She e-mailed me this story:

> When I was a teenager I was defiant. My parents were so frightened and anxious, especially about my going out with boys, that I stopped telling them a lot of what I did. I think that made my mother even more anxious.
>
> She didn't know what to do with me. So she'd talk to me like this: "You'll clean up your room this afternoon," and "You'll wear a skirt when the relatives come to dinner tonight."
>
> That made me boil. It sounded so mean. I felt like she didn't care about *me* but only about how my room and I *looked* when the family came to visit.
>
> So I kept my room messy and came to dinner in blue jeans.
>
> If my mother had just taken my feelings into account and said, "I know you hate to clean up your room," or "I know jeans are so much more comfortable, especially when it's cold," I think I would have felt much less angry.
>
> But as it was I couldn't stand getting these stern orders. They really drove a wedge of ice between us.

The more the children saw their parents as encouraging their autonomy —explaining the reasons for rules, for example, or allowing them to make certain decisions—the more the children described them as nurturing and close.[7]

Control Heats Up Family Conflict

Control also alienates children from their parents because it heightens family conflict. Who doesn't recognize this upward-spiraling struggle?

"David, stop teasing your brother!"

"Don't hit him!"

"Stop that wrestling!"

"David, he's so much smaller than you! Quit it!"

Understandably, these sibling tussles exasperate you, and so you automatically order the kids to stop. But these commands exacerbate the conflict by making both children feel misunderstood. You all end up angry at each other.

Stopping these cycles means meeting the conflict not with control but with structure and support for autonomy. For example, if your children do a lot of wrestling that drives you crazy (mine did), here's what you might do:

Wait for a calm moment and then start a conversation: "I understand how much fun it is to wrestle on the floor, but it makes me worry that one of you is going to get hurt. Look, you could easily bump your head on that coffee table. It's so close to you. What else do you think you could do when you feel like wrestling?"

David: We could play outside.
Mom: Yes, but it's dark outside.
David: How about the basement?
Mom: Okay—let's put the old mattresses out so no one gets hurt...

Now we'll explore in a more detailed way how to support your child's autonomy with the story of Sam Aguilar, who loved skateboarding and playing video games and didn't do much homework.

ENCOURAGING AUTONOMY:
PUTTING YOUR CHILD IN THE DRIVER'S SEAT

Two of Susan and Bill Aguilar's three children were conscientious students. But nine-year-old son Sam was a different story. Nothing mattered to him except video games and skateboarding. After he brought home a report card with three Cs—two more than in the previous grading period—Bill hit the roof.

Susan felt frustrated. She'd already told Sam how important she and his dad considered school and how proud they'd be if he did better. When Bill offered him $5 for every B he brought home, Sam had worked hard for a week and then forgot about it. The Aguilars had enlisted his older brother Erik to talk to Sam, but that hadn't worked either. Maybe Sam had Attention Deficit Hyperactivity Disorder, one of his teachers suggested, but a psychologist ruled out that diagnosis. All Sam seemed to care about was playing Super Mario Brothers 3 and hanging out at the skate park.

Finally, the Aguilars decided to try a method they had heard about at a PTA workshop. "We've got nothing to lose," Susan sighed.

"OK," said Bill one night after dinner, before Sam could run back to the video game he'd put on pause. "We're having a family conference."

Sam looked surprised. "We have to solve a problem," said Bill. "Can you stay here and talk, say, for five minutes?"

"OK," said Sam tentatively, his eyes flitting between his parents, trying to figure out what they had in mind.

"What do you think made your grades go down this semester?" Susan asked, trying to keep her voice gentle.

"I don't know," Sam muttered, a worried look clouding his face. His torso tilted off his chair at 45 degrees in the direction of his video game console.

"I wonder if changing schools this year has been hard for you," said Susan. "It seems like they have a different way of doing things at this school. Everything is in long projects instead of short assignments."

Susan helped Sam list several other possible reasons for his low grades, including the excitement of the Nintendo he'd received for Christmas and not liking his teacher very much. Social studies was boring, he added.

"I can understand that video games are more exciting for you than social studies," conceded Bill.

"I know it's hard to do good work when you have a teacher who seems too strict and mean," added Susan, remembering Sam's many complaints about Mrs. Coyle.

Finally, they asked Sam to suggest solutions and to give his opinion of their suggestions. Should they set up a specific homework time? Should Sam go to the after-school tutoring club? Did he want his parents to see if he could change teachers?

The following day they had a second conference. If his grades didn't improve, Bill asked Sam, what consequences would seem fair—should he quit Cub Scouts, or would limiting his time on the Nintendo make more sense? Asked for his suggestions, Sam said, "How about taking away *Monday Night Football*?" The Aguilars knew that was his second-favorite TV show, after *The Suite Life of Zack and Cody*.

That weekend, the family settled on a plan. Susan would talk to the school principal about whether Sam and his teacher were a good fit. Sam would do his homework right after dinner, either in his room or at the kitchen table. He could play video games all he wanted before eating, but couldn't go back to them until his homework was finished. If he didn't do his homework any night and failed to make it up, he would miss *Monday Night Football* the following week.

"Whew," Susan thought to herself. "Finally we've got a strategy."

LOOKING AT OTHER CULTURES: IS AUTONOMY A WESTERN PHENOMENON?

Once during a graduate student seminar I was discussing the importance of parents encouraging their children's autonomy when I noticed a befuddled look on the face of one of my students, Juliet Yee.

"Am I being confusing?" I asked.

"No," she answered. "It's just that what you're saying doesn't make sense for Chinese families. My parents were super-strict compared to American families. You'd probably call them controlling.

"For instance, I was never allowed to go on sleepovers. 'You don't sleep at somebody else's house,' my mother said the first time I was invited to a slumber party. So I never asked again. When I wanted jeans and tennis shoes, spaghetti strap tops and shorts, they insisted on buying me pleated skirts, cardigan sweaters, and lace-up shoes. I looked different from everybody else.

"But the interesting thing is, Dr. Grolnick, I never questioned them. You might not believe this, but we never fought about sleepovers or clothes. I knew they loved me and that the family came first for them. I would never have thought they were impinging on my autonomy."

My student's comments about her own upbringing sent me to research parenting practices and beliefs in Chinese culture. Do Chinese American parents downplay their children's autonomy? I wondered. Are they more controlling than parents from other ethnic groups? I found several studies that had concluded just that.[8] They fed right into the prevailing stereotype of Asian Americans as "programmed by their parents to ace math and science," as Daniel Golden puts it in his recent book *The Price of Admission: How America's Ruling Class Buys Its Way Into Elite Colleges—And Who Gets Left Outside the Gates*, which examines among other issues the charge that elite schools have informal quotas for Asian students.[9]

But why did Juliet never question her parents' alleged "control"?

I found the answer to this question in the research of Ruth Chao, a psychologist who teaches at University of California, Riverside.

Chao helped me examine Chinese American parenting practices through the prism of Chinese culture.[10] (I won't generalize about Asian American parenting, since there are at least thirty distinct Asian American ethnic groups.)[11] She explains that, according to Confucian tradition, each member of a family must honor the responsibilities of his or her role. Parents occupy the top of the family hierarchy, and their role is to train children to behave properly, which includes doing well in school. The concept of training, or *chiao sun*, calls for parents to nurture their children carefully and intensively, paying attention to their every need. As the children grow, parents support and encourage them and maintain high standards. These standards aren't considered dominating, however, but protective of vulnerable young people.

Another Chinese parenting notion, *guan*, translates as "to govern," but also as "to care for" or even "to love." So parenting practices that might at first blush seem controlling to European Americans within Chinese culture carry a message of love. That might well explain why Juliet felt her parents' rules were loving and caring, rather than controlling.

A study contrasting the feelings of 125 Korean and European American teenagers bolsters this notion that culture affects how children feel about parenting practices. University of Connecticut psychologist Ronald P. Rohner found that the more controlling the European American teens rated their parents, the less warm they considered them.[12] Korean teens felt the opposite: the more "controlling" their parents, the warmer they rated them.

Such research demonstrates that members of different cultures may experience the same practices differently, arriving at different culturally valued results. "Chinese upbringing grants autonomy gradually," notes Dorothy Chin, a research psychologist at UCLA's Neuropsychiatric Institute and psychology professor at Santa Monica College. Families end up with a feeling "of interdependence among family members, rather than independence of children from their parents."[13]

However, studies do show that when children feel controlled, that does affect them negatively in most if not all cultures.

For example, University of Western Ontario psychologist Xinyin Chen studied 304 second graders in Beijing and their parents. He found that when the parents used highly controlling methods—spanking, harsh criticism, and suppressing their feelings and opinions—their children didn't behave or achieve well in school. Nor did they have many friends. But parents who, on the other hand, gave reasons for rules and encouraged their children's autonomy had children who behaved better, achieved more, and were better liked.[14]

To create this game plan, the Aguilars had employed the three methods recommended at the PTA workshop for giving children feelings of autonomy:

- Taking your child's point of view and acknowledging her feelings.
- Supporting your child's independent problem solving.
- Giving your child choices.

The Aguilars *explored Sam's point of view* and *acknowledged his feelings* (saying things like "What do you think made your grades go down this semester?" "I wonder if changing schools this year has been hard for you," "I know it's hard to do good work when you have a teacher who seems too strict and mean," and "I can understand that video games are more exciting for you than social studies.")

They *supported his independent problem solving* by asking him to suggest solutions and give his opinion of their suggestions. (Should he go to the after-school tutoring club? Did he want his parents to see if he could change teachers?)

And they *gave Sam choices* when they asked him which consequences he wanted if he didn't do his homework. This way the Aguilars could stop nagging him with "Did you do your homework?" Sam could take responsibility, and if he didn't do it, he and his parents knew the consequences—he would miss *Monday Night Football*. In the next chapter we'll look at more ways to encourage your child's autonomy in everyday situations.

CHAPTER 7

THE HOW-TO OF AUTONOMY

In the last chapter, we laid out three ways to promote your child's autonomy:

- Taking your child's point of view and acknowledging her feelings.
- Supporting your child's independent problem solving.
- Giving your child choices.

How exactly can you use these techniques? I know from raising my own children that expert advice often sounds good—but applying it isn't always easy. In this chapter, we'll make these three methods user-friendly. We'll also take a special look at rewards and praise, two practices that look positive but can actually undermine children's autonomy. I call them the "positive poisons."

LOOKING AT IT FROM YOUR CHILD'S POINT OF VIEW

Remember in chapter 4 when I scolded Ben for teasing Zach about his bike helmet? Here's how I could have promoted Zach's autonomy that day.

"Are you okay?" I could have asked Zach, pulling him aside and listening to anything he might say. That would have helped me understand Zach's point of view. I also might have tried to figure out his feelings from his facial expression.

Taking your child's point of view is challenging. The anxiety of the Pressured Parent Phenomenon makes it very hard to put yourself in your child's shoes. In this case, I felt so enraged at Ben that I could scarcely imagine Zach's feelings, although one glance would have shown me his hurt. It was only later that night that I felt calm enough to ask Zach how he felt.

Sometimes in less emotionally charged situations—especially ones that you face often—it's easier to focus on your child's state of mind. Let's say your son isn't doing his homework. You might be able to imagine, "If I were ten years old, what might I prefer doing right now? Would I rather ride my bike outside or read a chapter on coal production?" You are thinking that studying will get him into college and a good job, but *he's* reasoning, "It's going to get dark soon! I want to have some fun *now*. I can do my homework later."

Acknowledgment and Empathy

The morning of the Darth Vader helmet incident, time was short. So I might have simply acknowledged Zach's emotional turmoil—out of Ben's earshot—with "I can see that didn't feel very good. What a way to start your day! Maybe we can talk about it later." What counts is acknowledging your child's feelings. You want to convey "I'm with you."

You may feel worse than your child does, but you wouldn't want to inadvertently fan the flames, especially when there's no time to douse them. Since Zach had to get to his classroom, it's good I didn't ratchet up his feelings by sharing my own with "What a jerk that Ben is!" Nor did I exaggerate his hurt with "You must be devastated."

Recently I visited a kindergarten class whose teacher, Linda Rosenbaum, showed me how a bit of empathy goes a long way. Right before recess, it started to rain.

"We're going to have to stay inside," Ms. Rosenbaum told the children. "Oooooh," the children moaned.

"I know," the teacher said sympathetically.

That's all it took. Linda, who had taught for more than twenty years, understood the students' feelings and acknowledged them with two words, a sad tone of voice, and a cheerful ironic grimace. It felt as though she had applied a balm to the class. The children relaxed and gathered around the toys she put out for them.

So while empathizing may seem daunting, with a little practice you'll master the art of a simple word or two and a matching tone of voice.

You might also express empathy at greater length. Linda could have said, "I know you wanted to go outside and it's very disappointing that you can't. So we'll try to do something fun in here. And tomorrow you'll have a longer recess outside to make up for today."

Similarly, you can say to your son who is itching to ride his bike, "I understand that it's going to get dark soon. But tonight we're going to Aunt Karen's for dinner, so unfortunately, this is the only time to do your science homework."

Just make sure you don't discount your child's feelings. Linda didn't say, "Kids, when it's raining there's really nothing we can do about it." You also don't want to tell your son—even though it's on the tip of your tongue: "Stop complaining and get to it. You have to do your homework, and that's that. Life is not all fun and games.

"I worked hard all day too and I'm tired. Give me a break!"

Better when you're that stressed out to walk away for a moment, try to calm down, and return when you can muster a sympathetic "I understand" sentence, such as "I understand that you want to watch TV, but now it's homework time."

"Mom, It's Not Such a Big Deal"

Showing how strongly parental empathy can affect a child, child psychologist and author Haim Ginott tells this story about Eric, a nine-year-old boy whose class picnic was called off when it started to rain.[1]

That afternoon when Eric came home, his mother saw how angry he was, but she managed to keep from saying some of the words that sprang to her lips, such as "No use crying over rained-out picnics" or "*I* didn't make it rain, so why are you so angry at me?"

She realized that her son was sharing his disappointment with her by showing his anger. Well, he's entitled to his feelings, she thought.

"You seem very disappointed," she told him.

"Yes."

"You wanted very much to go to this picnic."

"I sure did."

"You had everything ready and then the darn rain came."

"Yes!"

After a moment of silence, Eric said, "Oh, well, there will be other days."[2]

This story rang true for me. Sometimes empathy acts like a key opening an emotional lock, and your child's feelings come pouring out. At other times, just feeling understood lightens up your child's gloom, as it did for Eric in Ginott's story.

This kind of empathizing may feel counterintuitive. Your child's whining may be so unpleasant that you think, "Why indulge it?" But keeping emotional company with your child for a minute is often the best way to get rid of the whining because it soothes him. It might even make him happy.

Then he's in a good place to problem solve.

Empathy during a Disagreement

"Mom, me and Tyler want to go to Great Thrills and Chills Adventure Theme Park on Saturday."

"Well, maybe, Jared, but you guys are too young to go by yourselves."

"Mom! Why do you always do that? We're not too young! Steven and Colin go by themselves all the time!"

When you and your child argue, taking his perspective will make him feel understood and in turn open him up to your limits and suggestions. You can start by exploring his thinking:

"Why do you guys want to go alone?"

"Mom, we don't want you there telling us we can't go on this ride because it's dangerous and that one because the line is too long..."

"Well, I can understand that. You want to be free to have a good time, go where you want, and do what you want."

"So," you might continue, "It's not fun with an adult there..."

"We're not babies!"

"That's right, you're almost a teenager."

"We like to do stuff you don't want to do."

"Oh, I see. Like...hanging out at the refreshment stand?"

"No. Like meeting our friends there. Like riding the Super Coaster that makes you sick."

"I see what you mean. Well, that makes sense..."

Now that he feels understood, your son might be open to a compromise. Maybe you can think of a nonintrusive way to go to the theme park with him.

"Hey, what if I just dropped you off at the gate and took my work and sat at the refreshment stand?" you might say. "You guys could check back with me every couple of hours. It's not that I don't trust you. I just worry about gang fights, like the one they had there last summer. If something happened I could get you out of there quickly."

"Well, maybe. I'll see what Tyler says."

SUPPORTING YOUR CHILD'S AUTONOMOUS PROBLEM SOLVING

Another important way to encourage your child's sense of autonomy is to encourage her to take an active role in solving her own problems. I know that when my kids have a problem, a solution often pops into my head and dances to the tip of my tongue. When the Pressured Parent Phenomenon is operating full force, "solving" your child's problems for him is especially tempting, because the stakes seem so high. ("If Emily doesn't make the basketball team, she's going to fall apart. I've *got* to talk to that coach.") Plus, you want to relieve your anxiety ASAP. That's what I tried to do by scolding Ben during the bike helmet incident.

But instead of leaping in and telling your child, "You should do *XYZ*," you can problem solve in a way that supports her autonomy. That means exploring how she sees the problem, what she feels about it, and what ideas she has for solving it.

Here's how I might have done that with Zach the evening of the bike helmet incident:

"Do you want to talk about what happened this morning?" I might have said. "What was that like for you?"

"It was horrible! I hate Ben!"

"Well, yes, I can certainly understand why."

"He's mean to me all the time. You thought it was a big deal this morning, but really what I hate is what he does in the lunchroom. He's always bugging me. I can't eat at the table with Adam and Robert when he's there."

"Have you tried anything to get him to stop?"

"I ignored him. Like you told me once. He didn't care."

"You could ask your teacher to help you out."

"Are you kidding? No way. I'm not asking her."

"Hmm. What else could you do?"

"I could tell him to shut up."

"Yes, you could say you don't like it when he does that. What do you think would happen if you did that?"

"He would probably laugh at me."

"What else could you do?"

"I don't know."

"How about your friends?"

"They hate him too but he doesn't bother them. Except Trevor. He bugs Trevor too. He won't sit at that table either."

"So both of you don't feel comfortable at that table, hmmm?"

"Maybe Trevor and me can sit at that table by the window."

"Sounds like a good idea. Make your own table!"

Notice how, in this imagined dialogue, I helped Zach generate possible solutions (*What else could you do?*) and think them through (*What do you think would happen if you did that?*).

Even when your child asks you to help, it's still better to support his problem solving rather than telling him what to do. You still play an active role, but by following your child's lead, you'll strengthen his problem-solving ability.

If you stay close by when he's working on a problem, ready to coach if he asks, that nourishes his feelings of connectedness too.

THE TEMPTATION TO TAKE OVER

It's hard to turn over responsibility to your children. When mine were in elementary school, I used to ask if they wanted me to check over their homework when they'd finished it. If they said no, I felt like pulling it out of their backpacks anyway. Sometimes after they'd gone to bed, I did sneak a look. It's easy to give lip service but much harder to *feel* convinced that their homework reflects on them, not on me.

Even teachers—who understand this idea very well—struggle when parenting their *own* children. Felecia Branch, a Detroit teacher with three children, remembers the day her daughter Alanna, then ten, was assigned to compare and contrast three Great Lakes Indian tribes, as described in her social studies book. Alanna had left that book at school.

Felecia's first impulse was to write Alanna's teacher a note, explaining the problem and asking if her daughter could hand in her assignment a day late. But when Alanna started crying, Felecia couldn't bear it. She wanted to fix the problem right away. So she found a Web site describing the three tribes. Since the reading level was way above Alanna's, however, her mother sifted through it and printed out the information Alanna needed. By that time, it was 10:30, way past the little girl's bedtime.

"I wish I'd acted on my first instinct and simply written the teacher a note, saying 'We're sorry, but Alanna forgot to bring her book home,'" says Felecia. "Alanna could have spoken with her and asked permission to turn the work in a day later."

That way, she noted, her daughter would have learned about the tribes.[3]

GIVING YOUR CHILD CHOICE: A LITTLE BIT GOES A LONG WAY

The feeling of choice is a hallmark of autonomy. When we choose to take a specific action, that gives us a sense of ownership of that action. It makes us feel that we're behind what we do.

It's amazing how even a tiny degree of choice boosts a child's feelings of autonomy. University of Texas psychologist William B. Swann explored this phenomenon by sitting a group of first through third graders at a table equipped with felt-tipped pens, a stack of white drawing paper, a Slinky, colored bricks, and Tinker Toys.[4]

He let half of the children choose their activity. "You can pick any of these games to play with," he told them. "Why don't you start with the drawing game? But you don't have to. You have a choice of any of these games. Would you like to play the drawing game?" They all accepted his suggestion and started drawing. Swann had given these children the "illusion" of choice, since drawing was attractive to the children and they had no reason not to take his mild suggestion. Why not comply with this nice man who let us choose among these interesting games? they thought. Swann applied this subtle pressure because he wanted *all* children in the study to draw, so that later on he could compare "apples to apples" (that is, compare kids who drew and were given a choice to kids who drew but were given no choice).

He didn't give the other children any choice. "I used to let children choose what game to play," Swann told them, "but I can't do that anymore. Instead I will tell you which game to play. You will be playing the drawing game."

The experimenter then started the drawing game. After five minutes, Swann told all the children that their time was up, but that they didn't have to return to their classrooms. "Why don't you stay here and play some of these games until it's time to go back?" he said. "You can do whatever you like."

Swann sat across the room for the next ten minutes, pretending to ignore the children but in fact discreetly noting down their behavior.

What difference did choice make? Eighty percent of the children who'd initially had the illusion of choice went to the drawing activity first during their free time. Only 20 percent of the kids who were *required* to draw during the first phase did so.

Clearly, compelling children to draw curbed their interest in drawing, while giving them a choice allowed it to blossom.

Of course, you'll give your child choices according to her age and include only choices that are OK with you. Yesterday I was talking to the mother of a preschooler on the phone when she turned away for a minute. "This is not the time for TV—you can eat a banana now or play with your dollies," I heard her tell her daughter. Another appropriate choice for a toddler is "Do you want carrots or celery?" You might give an older child the choice to do his chores before or after dinner. When my kids were younger, my favorite was "Do you want to go to sleep right away, or read for fifteen minutes?" ("No, giving the cat a bath right now is not a choice.")

Children Choose Competence Boosters

When allowed to choose, what *kind* of choices do children make? Do they choose the easiest task? Do they jump wildly from one activity to another? Or does choice paralyze them?

Richard deCharms set up an ingenious study to answer just this question. His result, which always reminds me of Goldilocks's choice of porridge, may surprise you.

DeCharms organized students into teams for a spelling bee game. They received one point for trying an easy word, two for a fairly hard word, and three for a very hard one. The researchers calibrated these words to the ability of each child, as measured in a pretest.

As the children played the game over five weeks, they began to choose the "fairly hard" words more and more. In other words, they increasingly chose words that were neither too easy nor too hard, but "just right" for their learning. Psychologists call this the "optimal challenge" because it leads children to take the natural next step for increasing their competence.[5]

Meaningful Choices

Part of nurturing autonomy is helping children meet their goals and explore their interests. So it's important to give your child choices that take those goals and interests into account. Choice simply for the sake of choice doesn't enhance intrinsic motivation.

That's what Avi Assor and his colleagues at Ben-Gurion University found when they gave questionnaires to 862 Israeli Jewish students ages eight to fourteen.[6] The students indicated which of their school subjects interested them most. They also answered questions about how much choice their teachers gave them and to what extent the teachers "fostered relevance"—explained why studying certain subjects related to their own goals and interests.

Interestingly, the teachers' explanations of relevance mattered far more to the students' feelings of autonomy than did allowing choices. Simply giving students choices, concluded Assor, doesn't foster feelings of autonomy if the students don't see a "connection between any kind of schoolwork and their personal goals and interests."

In other words, to foster a child's autonomy, choices have to be meaningful and interesting. So, for example, if you know your child wants to watch a particular TV program, giving choices about doing homework that take this goal into account will work best. "Do you want to do your homework before or after the football game?" makes sense, but "Do you want to play hockey or basketball?" doesn't, if your child is really dying to play baseball or tennis or perhaps doesn't like sports at all and would rather spend his afternoons drawing.

Misuse of Choice

It goes without saying that you'll give your child *reasonable* choices—not "Would you like to do your homework now or jump off that cliff?"

NOT JUST *ANY* CHOICE WILL DO

Psychologist Idit Katz, also at Ben-Gurion, wondered which mattered *more* to children—choice or relevance?[7] (Both are elements of autonomy.) So she asked a group of seventh graders what subjects interested them. Then, after telling the children that they could later take an extra class, she told one-third of them that they could choose that class. She told the other two-thirds that their parents had chosen a class for them—for half of the kids in a subject that interested them, and for the other half, in one that didn't. Then Katz asked them how much the upcoming extra class excited them and also asked them to create an advertisement for the class. The two groups of children about to take the class that interested them were more intrinsically motivated and put more effort into the advertisement than the children whose parents had chosen a class that didn't interest them. In other words, the kids who had chosen a class that interested them and those whose parents had chosen that class *for* them both had more intrinsic motivation than the other children. So, Katz concluded, choice matters, but pursuing your interests matters more. Therefore, when it comes to autonomy, interest trumps choice.

Similarly, your choices shouldn't mask manipulation. I remember vividly the day the dean of the education school that ran my children's university-affiliated laboratory elementary school told a packed meeting of worried parents that the university needed the school's land to expand its business school. We could choose, he said, between shutting down the elementary school and moving it to a nearby school district.

We parents were furious. What about the "choice" of keeping the school on the campus? We fought back, and in the end that's just what the university did.

Similarly, children will see that offering them a choice among unattractive alternatives actually amounts to control. Real-life situations may demand such forced choosing, but that's unfortunate, not a granting of autonomy.

Language Makes a Big Difference

Language plays a huge role in giving children a feeling of autonomy.

Psychologist Richard Koestner of McGill University showed how words like *have to*, *should*, and *must* wield a surprising amount of emotional power over children.[8] Koestner visited a school and asked first and second graders to paint pictures. Each child sat at a table outfitted with a paintbrush, watercolor paints, one large and one small sheet of paper, and several strips of paper towel. Koestner said to them, "What I'd like is for you to paint a house that you would like to live in. You can make any kind of house you want and you can put anything at all in the picture.... It can be as make-believe as you want it to be."

He had divided the children into three groups. He said nothing more to the first group, thus giving them no limits at all about neatness.

But he added a list of neatness rules for the second group.

"Before you begin," he said, "I want to tell you some things about the way painting is done here. I know that sometimes it's really fun to just slop the paint around," he continued, acknowledging their feelings. Then he gave them information about neatness, including the reasoning behind it: "The material and room need to be kept nice for the other children who will use them," he said. "The smaller sheet is for you to paint on, the larger sheet is a border to be kept clean. Also, the paints need to be kept clean, so the brush is to be washed and wiped in the paper towel before switching colors."

To the children in the third group, however, he gave rules using the controlling words *have to*, *must*, *don't*, and *I want you to*. "Before you begin," he said, "I want to tell you some things that you will *have to* do. You *have to* keep the paints clean. You can paint only on this small sheet of paper. And you *must* wash out your brush and wipe it with a paper towel... in general, *I want you* to be a good boy (girl) and *don't* make a mess with the paints."

After ten minutes, Koestner gave the children two more sheets of paper and told them they could paint or play with some puzzles on a nearby table. Then an assistant timed how much time the children spent painting over the next eight minutes.

Finally, Koestner returned and asked the children how much they had enjoyed the free-choice period.

His findings? The first and second groups painted for about the same amount of time, since the second group had received the neatness rules as information, backed by reasoning, and therefore didn't feel controlled. The children in these first two groups spent *more than twice as much time* painting during the free-choice period as did the kids who'd been told, in controlling language, that they *had* to follow the neatness rules. So the controlling language seriously weakened the intrinsic motivation of the third group.

Koestner also looked at the children's creativity and the quality of their pictures. The children who'd been told the rules in controlling language painted much less creative pictures. They used fewer colors and made fewer "spontaneous elaborations," one of the criteria examined by judges, than kids in the other two groups.

The judges also looked at "organization" and "technical goodness." Especially when it came to these two qualities, Koestner concluded, the "informational" limits had mitigated the negative effect of the rules.

So this study showed that on the one hand, if you give limits as information, kids won't feel controlled. But saying things like *have to, must, don't,* and *I want you to,* on the other hand, has a significant chilling effect on intrinsic motivation, as well as on the creativity and quality of the children's work.

It may astonish you that a few words matter so much to children, but they do. One or two words can determine whether a child feels autonomous or feels controlled. That means you can prevent a great deal of resentment and conflict by avoiding words like *should, have to,* and *must.* They feel coercive to children.

Instead, you can try giving information, as Koestner did when he explained the neatness rules for painting to his second group. That way your child will understand that you're not trying to be pushy and not making up rules simply to give her a hard time. It shows her that the rules have a reason, and they apply to everyone. If you remove the language of control and add reasons, your child is more likely to follow rules willingly, which in turn helps sustain her intrinsic motivation.

Here are some ways to phrase rules using noncontrolling language:

- "Homework needs to be done before playing outside, because that way you can play longer, since your work will be already done."
- "Teeth need to be brushed before bed so you don't get cavities."
- "We need to keep the cat food outside because when we put it inside it attracts ants."

I know some of this phrasing sounds awkward ("needs to be done"). But if you try it, you'll see that it works, because removing "I want you to" and "You have to" strips the feeling of control from your sentences. As you use this noncontrolling language more, it will start to feel less clumsy.

If you want to phrase your suggestions so that your child feels he has a choice, not that you're forcing him to obey, try also:

- "Sometimes people break up their practicing up into segments. They'll do fifteen minutes in the morning and fifteen more at night."
- "Practicing five times a week will make it more likely that you'll make the orchestra."
- "Have you thought about (or considered) putting a title on your essay?"
- "One way to learn that is to look on the Internet. Or the reference librarian might know. Her phone number is on the library Web site."
- "Some cooks like to put a teaspoon of sugar into their biscuit dough."
- "Your aunt used to tape her lines up on her mirror to help her memorize them."

I often ask my children whether they'd like to be reminded about a deadline or chore. That takes the chill of coercion off my words, because they've agreed to my jogging their memories.

WHEN YOUR CHILD PLAYS SPORTS: SUPPORTING AUTONOMY

While myth tells us that behind every great athlete lies a relentlessly pushy parent, the facts more often reveal parents who followed their children's lead and supported their child's autonomy. Summer Sanders remembers pulling her mother and father along after her.

"My parents never saw my talent or my competitive drives as an invitation to impose any ambitions on me…" She says, "Whatever I wanted to do, they were behind me, matching their level of commitment to mine."[9]

A good way to nourish your child's autonomy in sports is to give him a choice of activities. You can take him to the park to watch different games. If he has to train to get in shape, let him choose, if possible, where and when. If he joins a team but doesn't want to go to practice, try to find out why.

Once your child is on a team, if he has a good reason for skipping a practice, explain why it is necessary to call the coach.

TO NOURISH AUTONOMY, REDUCE PRESSURE

Nurturing your child's autonomy in sports is an effective vaccine for preventing conflict and burnout due to the Pressured Parent Phenomenon. One of the best ways to support autonomy is to think of ways to reduce pressure. I've already suggested focusing on whether your child had fun, not whether he won. You can also analyze your goals and make sure you're emphasizing sportsmanship and love of the game rather than dreams of scholarships and professional contracts. Children are attuned to subtle pressure from their parents, so be careful, too, about off-the-cuff comments, such as "I bet Jake gets the MVP award!" This gives your child the message that you'd like *him* to win an award.

The Silent Saturdays Movement

"This is going to be the best game ever!" a ten-year-old boy told his father one Saturday morning as they drove to the boy's soccer game in the East Bay of San Francisco.[10]

Why was this young player so excited? His Jack London Youth Soccer Club was one of many that, concerned about pressure on its young players, has curbed shouting from the sidelines by instituting "Silent Saturdays." Only polite applause is allowed. Even coaches are allowed only to clap courteously.

Silent Saturdays strengthen kids' autonomous feelings about sports because they eliminate controlling comments from the sidelines. While there's nothing wrong with encouraging and cheering, kids want to feel that they own the game, and sidelines without screaming spectators allow them to do so more fully. Children enjoy playing more when there's no adult pressure to perform.

I'm not suggesting, of course, that you drop your involvement with your child's sports. Far from it! But the heightened competition in most youth athletics today brings forth the Pressured Parent Phenomenon with its temptation to push your child. And research shows that children very much resent that pressure. A study of competitive ski racers ages thirteen and under, for example, found that 73 percent considered their parents a source of pressure to compete, and more than a quarter said their parents "forced" them to do so. The youngsters who said their parents pressured them the most were most likely to say they disliked their parents' attitude and behavior.[11]

Now that you know how to support your child's autonomy, it's time to look at some common household methods that may appear positive but in fact will harm your child's intrinsic motivation.

Praise and rewards seem like good motivators—and plenty of experts advise them—but in fact they are subtle forms of control. Along with conditional love, I call them "the positive poisons." They're ways unintentionally to take away your child's autonomy.

AVOID THE POSITIVE POISONS

The spring my oldest daughter was two and a half, we decided it was time for potty training. She was slated to start preschool in the fall, and toilet training was mandatory. But Allison wasn't interested. "Honey, you know if you don't have to wear diapers, it won't smell pooey, and you'll feel all clean and dry!" I told her.

"You know, if you learn to use the potty," my husband tried, "you'll meet lots of new friends to play with at school."

Our words did not move her.

So I did as many parents have done and pediatricians have long advised: I made her a star chart. "Every time you go in the potty," I explained, "Mommy will paste a shiny gold star on this paper. When you get five stars I'll buy you a toy."

Allison seemed interested. I didn't really want to set up a reward system because it didn't fit my ideas about autonomy. But in the back of my head lurked the worry that I was wrong—and that she might *never* get toilet trained. So I forged ahead.

The first day of the new star chart, Allison used the potty twice and earned two bright gold stars. I didn't say anything when she wet her diapers once, but she must have seen my crestfallen expression.

The next day, my grand plan fell apart. Allison didn't use the potty once. I noticed her watching me with fascination every time I smelled or felt her soiled diaper. Once she even giggled. It was as though I had created an exciting game of "How to surprise mommy and watch her make different funny faces."

I stuffed the star chart in the trash. Knowing I had to try another method, I sat down on the couch and put Allison on my lap.

"Honey," I told her, "when you want to give up your diapers and use the potty, you let me know." The next day my daughter used the potty all day long. After a week I stopped putting her in diapers. She never wore them again.

I know that this story sounds too good to be true. But I swear that's exactly the way it happened.

This experience with Allie was a revelation. It illustrated so clearly for me why some psychologists call rewards a form of insidious control—because people want and like them, yet they're manipulative. They're a way of forcing kids to do what we want. That's why Allison rebelled against my star chart: she wanted to use the potty for her own sake, not for mine. She liked the stars, but she didn't like my exertion of power through them.

When the Pressured Parent Phenomenon takes us in its anxious grip, we sometimes feel as desperate as I did when Allison balked at potty training. Our catastrophizing ("If Jared flunks math, he won't take algebra early, he won't get into college, he'll never get a good job..." or, "She'll *never* get potty trained!") makes us grab whatever short-term solution pops into our heads. Why not dangle a cookie for doing homework or for practicing the piano? It works! At least at first. But rewards soon stop working and they can also ruin our long-term goals for our children.

Besides, who wants to trail along carrying a bag of cookies as our children go away to college?

Does this idea that rewards can harm children seem counterintuitive to you? It probably does, because rewards are deeply ingrained in our culture. Perfect attendance merits a certificate, athletes get MVP awards, airplane trips earn frequent flyer miles, and good movies win Oscars. We're especially attached to grades for good schoolwork, as a study by Ann Boggiano illustrates.

She gave parents several scenarios of children reading, behaving aggressively, helping others, and making friends. The researchers asked parents to think about how they could increase the children's enjoyment or interest in the activity or, in the case of fighting, in more peaceful behavior. They could choose from four strategies: rewards, reasoning, punishment, or noninterference. The parents chose rewards for reading, but not for the others. Further, they chose the rewards whether or not the kids were already interested in reading.[12] And they believed that the bigger the reward, the more it would motivate their child academically.

REWARDS SQUELCH INNER PASSION

More often than not, and as counterintuitive as it may seem, rewards feel controlling to children and thus undermine their intrinsic motivation. Studying mainly for the sake of a test score or grade might make a child learn, but it won't boost her interest in learning. Ed Deci showed how this works when he gave college students the enjoyable SOMA puzzles described in chapter 2.[13] He told half the students they'd win money for doing the puzzles but didn't promise any money to the others. After a short period, Deci announced the end of the experiment and left the room briefly, telling the students they could play more with the puzzles or read some magazines. The results were striking: those students promised money for working the puzzles spent far less time playing with them than the others. The reward had ruined their fun. Once they'd been paid, they apparently thought, "Why should I do puzzles for free?"

What about younger children? Wondering about the effect of rewards on the preschool set, Stanford University psychologist Mark Lepper gave three- and four-year-olds Magic Markers and construction paper.[14] He told half the kids that they'd get Good Player Awards—with their name, a red ribbon, and a gold star—for drawing a picture. The other half simply got to play with the materials.

Several days later, both groups came into the lab, and Lepper let them choose their activity. He looked on with a stopwatch. The group who'd received Good Player Awards spent far less time than the other children playing with the markers and construction paper. Lepper's conclusion? The rewards had shifted these kids' attention away from the pleasure of drawing on to the reward. It had squelched their intrinsic motivation, turning their play into work.

REWARDS UNDERMINE PROBLEM SOLVING
AND CONCEPTUAL UNDERSTANDING

In the late 1970s, psychologists Kenneth McGraw and John McCullers did the first of many studies investigating the effect of rewards on the ability to think flexibly. They asked college students to figure out problems that called for pouring a specific amount of water from several different-sized bottles into one jar. They paid half the group for solving each problem but not the other half.

The first nine problems had similar solutions, but the students had to "break set" and invent a new type of solution for the tenth problem. So which group of students did better at thinking out of the box? Those students whom the researchers *didn't* pay solved this last problem faster, apparently thinking more flexibly than the paid students. This study and many that followed show that rewarding people constricts their thinking.[15]

A few years later Rich Ryan and I decided to see if rewards—in this case, the nontangible reward of grades—affected younger students in the same way. We gave ninety-one fifth graders a social studies passage about farming methods from the past to the present, asked them to read it, and then asked them how interesting they found the passage and how pressured they felt reading it.[16] That was mainly a setup for part 2.

For this second part, we gave more complicated instructions. After giving the children a passage about methods of treating illness from prehistoric through modern times, we told one-third of the kids, "After you've finished, *I'm going to ask you some questions about the passage.* It won't really be a test, and you won't be graded on it. *I'm just interested in what children can remember* from reading passages." To another third we said, "I want to see how much you can remember. You should work as hard as you can because *I'll be grading you on the test* to see if you're learning well enough." We told the rest of the kids, "After you are finished, *I'll be asking you some questions* similar to the ones I just asked about the other passage."

After they'd finished reading, we asked the students, "What was the main point of the passage?"

Who did best on this little test? Not the children who knew they'd be graded. They understood the main point of the passage much less well than the others. For example, some of these kids told us the reading mostly discussed witch doctors (who were mentioned). But many of the children who *weren't* told they'd be graded answered correctly that the passage mainly explained how the practice of medicine has changed through the ages.

Two weeks later, we made a surprise visit to their classroom and tested all the students on the material they'd read about treating illness. We got very consistent results: those told that they would be tested forgot the *most* information between the initial testing and the later one.

I bet this finding surprises you. "How could the students promised grades learn *less* well than the others?" you must be thinking. After all, don't grades motivate kids to learn? Well, they motivate kids to learn in a certain way—to pay attention to details that might be on the test, or to help them win an admission, a scholarship, or money—whatever is attached to the grade. But that concentration narrows their focus. It works against the flexibility, openness, and broad perspective needed to understand ideas and solve sophisticated problems. So rewards may help a child to memorize the multiplication table, at least temporarily. But they don't help him grasp and apply complex scientific concepts, understand the meaning of a story, or write creatively.

REWARDS CAN SPOIL CREATIVITY

In this era when economists warn that our country needs abundant creative intellectual talent to thrive, the question of how to encourage creativity takes center stage. Teresa Amabile, the creativity researcher whose work we visited earlier, has investigated extensively the effect of rewards on creativity.

In one experiment she invited a group of seven- to eleven-year-old girls to two weekend "art parties" in the common room of an apartment complex. As the first group of girls entered the room on Saturday, they passed a table of toys that Amabile told them she would raffle off at the end of their party. The girls spent the afternoon playing games and doing enjoyable art projects, including making a collage. The raffle took place at the end of the party.

On Sunday, another group of girls played the same games and did the same art projects as the first group had done the day before. There was one difference, however: as they walked into the common room and saw the table of toys, Amabile told them that judges would award them as prizes to whoever made the "best" collages.

Later, a panel of seven artists judged all the girls' projects. They found that the collages of the first group of girls—who'd had the raffle—were much more varied, complex, and creative than those of the other girls. Apparently the girls in the second group had focused on what the judges might like, rather than on what they would enjoy doing. The rewards had dampened their intrinsic motivation, stifling their creativity.[17]

That's because creativity, Amabile explains, demands an environment allowing you to feel free, pursuing your own goals and trying out new ideas. Your mind has to feel at ease, roaming without fear of penalty or punishment. But rewards rein in that sense of freedom.

Even giving a reward *before* an activity can dampen children's creativity. Amabile let half of a group of children play with a Polaroid camera if they promised to tell a story. Their tales turned out less creative than those of kids who were also allowed to play with the camera but who hadn't made a deal to tell their tale.[18]

When to Use Rewards

Rewards aren't always problematic. At times they're useful and appropriate. They change behavior immediately, if only for the short-term. When my sons used to fight with their carpool mates on the way from school, I offered them all egg rolls from a Chinese takeout if they would calm down. That worked because I wasn't interested in helping this particular set of boys get along over the long term. I just wanted peace and quiet so we wouldn't have an accident. Rewards can also be effective for low-interest activities like memorizing spelling words or washing the car.

Furthermore, rewards do not harm children when they're unexpected. If a child knows ahead of time that good grades will earn him a dinner in a restaurant, that will undermine his intrinsic motivation for learning. But deciding to eat out on the spur of the moment—"What a wonderful report card! Let's celebrate!"—won't.

Rewards that mainly carry the message of a child's growing competence also don't damage kids. Commentators have beaten to death the truism that giving every child a trophy simply for participating on a soccer team doesn't mean much. What they haven't noted is that an "informational" reward—like a certificate attesting that a child has learned to dribble, pass, and shoot the ball—increases a child's desire to keep learning skills. That's because competence in and of itself is motivating.

You can help ward off the feeling of control when your child is up for an award by helping her focus on the information it brings. That's why singing teacher Anne Adams counsels her students to downplay concern about winning or losing competitions and focus instead on the judges' comments.

"It's usually very helpful for young students to get other people's ideas of what's going on technically or musically," she says. "It can be an eye-opening experience."

REWARDS MAY NOT UNDERMINE STRONG INTRINSIC MOTIVATION

In certain cases, extrinsic motivation goes hand in hand with creativity. Prizes that afford more time, freedom, or money to pursue exciting ideas can enhance creativity, points out Teresa Amabile. For example, the MacArthur Foundation's "genius" grants—$500,000 over five years, no strings attached, to people doing creative work—do just that.[19] Scholarships to a computer camp or a prize consisting of a series of painting lessons might also be equally motivating. Recipients often take such rewards as opportunities to do more of what they love. They also see them as evidence of their competence, which motivates them further. In these cases, their passion for their work overrides any other meaning of the prize for them.

IMMUNIZING YOUR CHILD AGAINST THE POSITIVE POISONS

How can parents prevent rewards and prizes, grades and competition from damaging their kids' intrinsic motivation?

Kids are bombarded by these external motivators, but research has shown that encouraging learning for its own sake—pointing out the joys and satisfactions of learning—can inoculate them against the harmful effects of rewards and prizes, grades and competition.

Wellesley College psychologist Beth Hennessey demonstrated how to do this when she showed a group of fourth graders videotapes of two attractive eleven-year-olds talking about how much they enjoy learning.[20] They also told how they put aside thoughts about rewards, grades, and competition.

"I like social studies the best," said one boy in the videotape. "I like learning about how other people live in different parts of the world. It's also fun because you get to do lots of projects and reports. I work hard on my projects, and when I come up with good ideas, I feel good."

The fourth graders then talked with the researcher about their own favorite school subject and why they liked it, as well as about their concerns about report cards, competition, and pleasing their parents. (A control group of children watched a videotape and talked with the researcher about American Sign Language.)

Next Hennessey told half the children that they would get the reward of painting and keeping a T-shirt if they promised first to make up a story to go with a picture book that had no words—an activity she knew these fourth graders enjoyed. The other half of the children also got to paint a T-shirt after telling the story, but simply as a "thing to do."

Then three elementary school teachers rated the creativity of the children's stories. Whether or not they had been promised the shirt painting reward, the kids who had watched the videotapes about intrinsic motivation and sidelining thoughts of rewards told more creative stories than those who had not received the intrinsic motivation training. The *least* creative stories were told by children who had instead seen "control" tapes about sign language and received the shirt painting reward. That's because, explains Hennessey, the reward turned the storytelling into a tool for getting a reward—a means to an end rather than an end in itself.

This study shows that you can immunize your children against the "positive poisons." Ask them what subjects and activities they find exciting and interesting, suggests Hennessey. "You can sit with your child and have a pretty high level conversation about their strengths, the things they're really good at and love to do," she says. "'What brings you great joy and enjoyment?' you could ask. 'What are you doing when the sense of time falls away?'"

Then ask your children how you can help them put on the back burner the grades and rewards that kill their enjoyment and interest.

As Hennessey tells her own kids, "Sometimes it's nice to get a good grade or win a contest, but what's really important is that you know you did your best and enjoyed what you did."

PRAISE: PROCEED WITH CAUTION

This idea may shock you: praise, like rewards, has a dark side.

But what, I hear you asking, could possibly be wrong with praise?

Over the past three decades, child-rearing experts have enthusiastically promoted self-esteem in children, and rightly so. Without a doubt, feeling good about yourself is healthy and motivating. This idea counteracts early twentieth-century advice to treat children as if they were little automatons, sternly molding their behavior through criticism, humiliation, and other negative reinforcements. In 1928, for example, behaviorist psychologist and best-selling author John Watson warned mothers not to love their children "too much." Rather than hugging and kissing them, he advised a hearty morning handshake. How strange that idea seems in the twenty-first century! A few parenting traditionalists still claim that sparing the rod spoils the child, but the overwhelming majority of psychologists today recommend a loving style of parenting, which includes lots of praise.

The Best Kind of Praise

The most effective praise or feedback is informational: it specifies what children have achieved, giving them a feeling of competence.

- "You did a great job with your opening sentence. It really expresses the theme of your story."
- "Those colors are beautiful."
- "That was so kind, the way you helped your friend get up after he fell."

Praising hard work and persistence is a particularly good idea. It reinforces Thomas Edison's point, "Genius is one percent inspiration, ninety-nine percent perspiration." We can do our children a big favor by telling them:

- "Wow, you really worked hard on that PowerPoint! It's so clear, and so interesting."
- "All that time and effort you put into your science project really shows."
- "You kept at that problem until you solved it. That's the way to do it!"

Praise for trying different strategies and for making progress will also facilitate your child's intrinsic motivation.

Keep Control out of Your Praise

The problem is that, even though it's the opposite of what you intend, praise can feel controlling to your child.

It all depends on how you use it. Like rewards, praise strengthens a child's intrinsic motivation when it conveys information about competence. But praise can also carry a message of control that smothers your child's motivation.

What determines the difference between motivating praise and controlling praise? Wisconsin psychologist Audrey Kast looked into this distinction by giving third, fifth, and eighth graders a word search game to play. Afterward she gave some of the kids plain praise: "Good," she said. "You did very well on this game. You were right on almost all the puzzles."[21]

But for the others Kast spiced her praise with control: "Good. Keep it up," she said. Then she added a further bit of control: "I would like you to do even better on the next game."

When Kast asked the children how much they liked the game, the first group said they liked it much more than the second group. In other words, her study showed that praise should express positive feedback without any pressure to do more or improve.

Praise Effort or Product, Not Character

Praising a child's character rather than how hard she's tried or what she's produced risks a similar controlling taint. If you tell your son after he reads to you, "You're a good boy," that teaches him that he has to keep performing well for the sake of his self-worth. That's why, as far back as the 1960s, Haim Ginott cautioned parents to praise with care. If you tell your child she's an angel, Ginott observed, she invariably reacts with "devilish" behavior.[22]

Why is that? Kids want you to think the world of them regardless of what they did today or will do tomorrow. Implying that they have to continue being "good" to remain an "angel" makes them test your love and regard for them.

Praise that is spiked with control feels like pressure to act or be a certain way. That's why many kids react against that pressure by doing the opposite.

KEEP YOUR LOVE UNCONDITIONAL

Ingrid Clarfield once had a ten-year-old student take a master class with pianist Lang Lang before an audience of a thousand people.

"I'm feeling so nervous," he told Clarfield backstage.

"You're really well prepared," she reassured him. But the boy kept staring at the floor, swinging his legs back and forth nervously. A picture of his anxious mother flashed into Clarfield's head.

"No matter how you play, I'll bet your mom will be thrilled," she said. "She'll still love you."

"No, she won't," the boy replied.

Clarfield jumped up and ran up to the auditorium balcony where his mother sat waiting.

"You have to go down there right now and tell your son you'll love him no matter how well he plays," the teacher told her.

"Doesn't he know that?" the mom asked.

"No," said Clarfield.

"I made her walk all the way down there, and she said it," the piano teacher remembers.

"And when she did, I saw her son relax, literally. He stopped swinging his legs and he lifted up his head. He was smiling.

"He played incredibly well. Lang Lang was blown away by his performance."

Linking your love to kids' achievement, as this boy at first thought his mother did, is a particularly damaging way to exert control over children. Parents don't often realize that's what they're doing. But when kids sense that their parents' affection depends on their performance, they suffer from fear and anxiety, sometimes even shame and guilt. Have you ever known a parent who left a child alone, or stopped talking to him because of something the child had done or not done? To a child, it feels like the withdrawal of love. That tactic plays on a child's feelings of dependence and evokes fear of abandonment. Such cruelty might motivate a child to work hard or behave temporarily, but eventually it debilitates him and fills him with fury.

Psychologist Avi Assor and his colleagues at Ben-Gurion University demonstrated this dynamic when they asked college students to check off statements about conditional love that applied to them, such as "As a child, I often felt that my mother/father would give me more affection than usual if I did well in sports." Then Assor measured whether the students felt controlled by their parents or angry at them. The more "conditional love" statements the students checked, the more control they sensed from their parents, and the angrier they felt toward them.[23]

It's not hard to make your child feel unconditionally loved. Before a game or performance starts, tell your child that you think it is great that he is out there playing, regardless of how well he plays. Afterward, whether he won or lost, give him the same message—that you're proud of him.

I've shown how the first leg of the Three-Part Framework, fostering your child's autonomy, brings the two of you closer. In the next chapter, we'll tackle the second leg, involvement. I'll describe how you can involve yourself to the maximum in your child's life, while continuing to promote her autonomy.

LOVE HAS NO PRICE

Piano teacher Rosita Mang prepares parents for piano competitions by explaining, "Pride in your child comes from their accomplishments. Pride comes from goals achieved. Pride comes from the work and the diligence spent in many hours of practice. Pride also comes from winning. But pride cannot conflict with love. They are two different emotions. Love has no price."

CHAPTER 8

STAND BY ME
Maximizing Your Involvement

When Magic Johnson was growing up in Lansing, Michigan, he had two sets of "parents." His mother, a school lunchroom supervisor, took him and his eight brothers and sisters regularly to church. His father, Earvin Johnson Sr., worked the 5 p.m. to 3 a.m. shift on the assembly line at General Motors' Fisher Body plant. He felt so exhausted afterward that he'd sometimes fall asleep while taking a bath. To support the family, he also worked at a nearby Shell station and started up a trash collection business.

After Magic (whose given name was Earvin Jr.) scored forty-eight points in a junior high school game, Earvin Sr. got permission from his foreman to leave work and watch his son play. From then on, he never missed a game. Earvin Sr. had played high school basketball in Mississippi, and Magic tried fiercely to outscore him in one-on-one matches at the neighborhood playground. On Sundays father and son watched the NBA game of the week together.

When Magic was ten, the other set of "parents" entered his life. Magic had a little crush on his young fifth grade teacher Greta Dart, who played kickball with the class at recess. Wanting to form a basketball team, Magic and his classmates persuaded Greta's husband, Jim, to coach them. That spring Greta shocked Magic: she kept him from playing in a Saturday basketball league championship game because he hadn't handed in his homework. As the young basketball player grew from five feet in fifth grade to six foot nine by high school graduation, Greta altered his pants frequently. Jim marked his growth in pencil on the Darts' living room wall and took Magic to high school and college basketball games, hired him to paint and clean his rental properties, and got him a job as batboy in a summer softball league.[1]

"They made sure I had everything I needed," says Johnson. "They sent me to basketball camps, took me to every game they could and really helped me to stay out of trouble."[2]

The kind of support young Magic received from his two sets of "parents" illustrates the second leg of the Three-Part Framework: involvement in your child's life. Involvement means giving your child support—the tangible support of food, clothing, books, and toys, and the emotional support of your understanding and warmth. It means supervising your child's schooling, giving him whatever opportunities you can to pursue his passions, and generally "being there" for him, as both his parents and the Darts were for Magic Johnson.

INVOLVEMENT COMES NATURALLY

When it comes to parents' involvement, there's good news: chances are good you're already highly involved with your children. You probably already devote as much time and energy to your child as you can. You also take an interest in her life—her activities and friends, her problems and successes, her worries and passions.

All these threads of involvement weave the fabric of your relationship with your child. They fulfill your child's need for connection, the second of the three feelings—autonomy is the first—that pave the way for her intrinsic motivation.

So when the Pressured Parent Phenomenon has got you down and you're feeling anxious, intensifying your involvement—through listening and interest, spending time, and providing emotional support—will help to turn your worry into positive parenting. Instead of pressuring or pushing your child, you can step up your connection with him, which will help fuel his inner passion. That in turn will help make him happy and successful.

Involvement in your child's life is nearly a no-brainer. Nature has filled us with affection for our children so that we strive to give them whatever they need. That's why we enjoy buying school supplies or baseball mitts for our children, taking them to the library, and meeting their friends. As I was writing this chapter, my son asked me to read over his application for an internship.

After I told him that it looked good and suggested a specific addition or two, a sense of happy calm came over me. It felt like an oxytocin rush. My sons are both in their twenties now, but they still occasionally ask for my help, and I still love to supply it. Giving children what they need is one of the pleasures of life. I realized this as I looked over his application, enjoying my cheerful feeling of "all's right with the world."

THE FALSE DANGER OF "OVERINVOLVEMENT": YOU CAN'T BE TOO INVOLVED

Do we parents have to steer clear of *over*involvement? The mass media bombard us regularly with parent-blaming articles such as *Time* magazine's February 2005 cover story: "What Teachers Hate about Parents."[3] A spate of stories in 2005–2006 detailed a new familial scourge, "helicopter parents"— those who "hover" over their children. With their predilection for conflict, the media would have us believe that meddling mothers, overprotective fathers, and monster parents are the norm.

Yet here is the second piece of good news about involvement: there's no such thing as too much involvement with our children. You can't support your child too much. There's only one caveat: you simply have to make sure you're respecting her autonomy as well.

In other words, healthy involvement isn't *intrusive*.

A multitude of studies has found that the more support we give our children, the happier they are and the more they achieve. High parental involvement goes hand in hand with high self-esteem. It makes children feel solidly connected to us and more secure.

When we interviewed the parents of elementary school children in Dansville, for example, we found that the more involved mothers were with their children—that is, the more time they spent with their kids and the more they knew about what their children did and what they liked and disliked—the better their children did on report cards and standardized achievement tests, and the fewer learning and behavior problems they had in school. The highly involved parents weren't necessarily at home more than other parents, but when they *were* at home, they made it a point to spend time with their children. They asked how the day had gone at school, knew their child's favorite and least favorite school subjects, and who their friends were.[4]

Other researchers have found that students with involved parents are 30 percent more likely to achieve higher grades and test scores than kids with less-involved parents.[5]

IF YOU MISS THE BAKE SALE, DON'T FEEL GUILTY

Not everyone can serve as class parent. Many of us work long hours, and it's all we can do to make it to a parent-teacher conference or back-to-school night. Some parents don't have time to help with math homework, and others lack the patience. But if these kinds of involvement escape you, don't worry: there are many different ways to take part in your child's schooling, and they all rev up her intrinsic motivation and contribute to her achievement.

A few years after the Dansville study, when education reformers began calling parental involvement decisive for improving American K–12 schools, I scrutinized the different ways parents participate in their children's learning.[6] How did the varied kinds of involvement affect the children's achievement and their desire to learn?

My colleagues and I questioned three hundred sixth through eighth graders, their parents, and their eighteen teachers in a suburban New Jersey school district.[7] We asked the students not only whether their parents went to school meetings and helped them with homework, but also how much their parents knew about what they did in school and about their lives overall. The students rated on a scale from "very true" to "not at all true" statements such as "My mother knows a lot about what happens to me in school" and "My father asks about my school day."

We also asked about school-like activities at home. How often did their parents talk to them about current events? Take them to the theater, movies, or museums? Read with them?

All three kinds of involvement—school, personal, and intellectual—contributed to the children's motivation and school performance. Personal involvement in particular—simply taking an interest in and talking to children about their life at school—helped children take responsibility for their work. Parents attending school events and providing intellectual stimulation at home made the children feel competent and in control of their success in school. These feelings of competence and control over their progress in turn boosted their achievement. This research made a very useful point: it showed us that anything you do to convey, directly or indirectly, the importance of school to your child motivates him to learn and succeed.

Simply showing your child how much you love him and how important he is to you also builds his motivation.

In other words, you have many options and needn't feel guilty about not taking *all* the paths of involvement. That knowledge may also ease any envy or resentment you feel toward parents who can spend a lot of time at school.

> ### INVOLVEMENT IN YOUR CHILD'S SCHOOL LIFE: THEY LISTEN TO WHAT YOU SAY
>
> Children appreciate your opinions about their school life, even if, as they move into the pre-teen and teen years, they may not acknowledge it. My friend Leslie Dennis once explained to her daughter that her science teacher Mrs. Dietrich might have lost her temper and given out detentions one day because she was pregnant and feeling tired.
>
> "Oh, Mom, I don't think so," said Maya, rolling her eyes.
>
> The following week Leslie was driving Maya and some friends to the mall. "Well, Mrs. Dietrich gets angry these days because she's so tired," she heard Maya telling one of her friends in the backseat. "You know you get very, very tired when you're pregnant.
>
> "We have to be patient with her," said Maya wisely.

ASIAN PARENTS' INVOLVEMENT

Some researchers have found that Asian American parents tend not to spend much time at school. Esther Ho Sui-Chu, an education professor at the University of Hong Kong, looked at data from the National Education Longitudinal Study (NELS), a large, long-term national database of children who were in eighth grade in 1988 and were followed up on four times until the year 2000.[8] They found that Asian parents tended to supervise their children's homework more but spent less time at school than European or American parents.[9]

Yet Asian American students on the whole do very well in school. In 1996 psychology professor Laurence Steinberg of Temple University and his colleagues found that, even after they controlled for economic and educational background, Asian and Asian American students performed better on standardized tests of achievement than any other racial group.[10]

Parents are involved in their children's schooling in different ways, which vary according to family background, parents' schedules, and children's needs and preferences. What counts is staying involved in some way that communicates to your children the importance of education. That's what Asian American families tend to do. When combined with the high expectations embedded in many Asian cultures, that involvement tends to produce high-achieving children.

INVOLVEMENT IN YOUR CHILD'S SCHOOLING: THE DETAILS

Involvement in your child's schooling means, first of all, seeing if she's doing her work and finding out if she needs extra help. You probably also want to learn what her grades and test scores mean and whether your child is meeting your state's academic standards.

When your child is in elementary school, involvement means keeping an eye on her progress between report cards and working in partnership with the teacher to make sure she's on track. Teachers like to hear, "What can I do at home to help?"

Your regular communication with a teacher—face-to-face when possible —also raises her expectations. "Teachers have higher expectations of kids whose parents they've gotten to know," explains Anne T. Henderson, a senior fellow with the Community Involvement Program at the Annenberg Institute for School Reform.[11]

You might want to discuss with your child's teacher how he learns best. Does he do well with long independent projects? Does he learn better visually or verbally? With more or less structure? You can use that information as input for the following year's class assignment. You might tell the principal, "Aaron learns best with a teacher who can give him individual attention, so if you could take that into account for next year, I'd be very grateful." Talking to teachers and administrators about "what's best for the child's learning" is a great way to find common ground.

What if your child comes home and says, "I hate my teacher! I don't want to go to school anymore!" or "Whenever anyone acts up in class, I'm always the one that gets blamed!" The first step is to get as much information as you can.

"I'm interested in hearing about what happened," you might say. "Did it happen just this once, or does it happen all the time?" If you decide there really is a problem, you can make an appointment to discuss it with the teacher. Perhaps the two of you will work out a solution together, but if not, you can go to the principal or the counselor or talk to other parents and see if they're having the same experiences.

Some schools welcome your visit more than others. That attitude greatly influences the degree of parents' involvement. Most schools take a "come if we call" stance, points out Henderson. Ideally, however, all schools would create a "culture of partnership" that would make it easy for parents to advocate for their kids.

Advocating for your child also entails looking for enriched programs and advanced classes. Guiding your child through the system means learning about and helping her apply for gifted and talented programs, honors and AP courses, magnet schools, the International Baccalaureate program, or specialized offerings of language immersion or themed instruction in media technology, health sciences, or the arts.

As your child gets older, you can help her learn the rules of the school game by pointing out that she needs to earn certain grades to qualify for an honors class or that she needs to take pre-algebra to qualify the following year for algebra, which is required by most four-year colleges.

"The more parents have information about how the system works, the better their children do," says Henderson.[12]

One way to acquire this information is to join the parent-teacher group or the network of parents active in raising money or supporting the school in other ways. In some schools, the downside is that you'll have to brave some elitism and exclusion in these networks—well described in Rosalind Wiseman's *Queen Bee Moms and Kingpin Dads: Dealing with the Parents, Teachers, Coaches, and Counselors Who Can Make—or Break—Your Child's Future*.[13]

And that increased contact with parents may also bring on bouts of the Pressured Parent Phenomenon. If that happens, create your own network with a few savvy parents who won't drive you nuts.

Gifted and Talented Programs

Often created to keep middle-class students in public schools, gifted and talented programs offer a high-quality curriculum enriched by field trips, art and drama offerings, and special projects. They frequently provide superior pedagogy, emphasizing hands-on and creative learning experiences.

In some schools, 60 percent of children attend a gifted program, while in other schools that number plunges to only 10 percent.[14] Unfortunately, many financially strapped districts have recently cut back or eliminated their gifted programs. But schools that still have programs are increasingly admitting students based on their interest and class performance, rather than on test scores. And in at least one district, parents are working to extend the benefits of the gifted program to all students. In Montgomery County, Maryland, where about 40 percent of the students are identified as "gifted and talented," Evie Frankl remembers a decisive moment during a back-to-school night in 1999, the fall that her daughter entered fourth grade.[15]

When the bell rang for the parents to go to their children's math and science class, "All the parents of color went in one direction and all the white parents went in another direction," recalls Frankl.

"I asked, 'What's going on?' and they said, 'This is where we regroup for gifted and talented.'"

Not long after, Frankl joined other parents and several teachers to create the Montgomery County Education Forum (MCEF), with the goal of opening up the enriched curriculum of the gifted and talented program to *all* children. "Every child should benefit from the high expectations and instruction in 'higher order thinking skills'" of such programs, says Frankl, who calls tracking an "engine of inequality."*

Under the banner of "no labels, no limits," MCEF joined in coalition with the NAACP, the local teachers' union, two Latino-based organizations, and several other groups. In 2005 they succeeded in persuading their school district to set up two elementary-school pilot programs that, rather than separating out gifted and talented students, give all students accelerated and enriched instruction. As I was writing this book, they had elected a majority of supporters to the local board of education and awaited the board's review of the gifted and talented policy.

Finding out about the gifted and talented program in your district is important for your child. If she doesn't qualify, you might want to work to change admission requirements so that all children who are interested and willing to do the work can join. You might even want to try to expand this enriched option to the entire district, as MCEF is doing. But even if you don't have the time or inclination for such intense participation, learning about what programs are available is crucial for helping your child navigate the increasingly complex journey from preschool to college graduation.

---

*"Tracking," also called "ability grouping," means placing students in different curriculum sequences according to their ability or achievement.

IT TAKES A VILLAGE: A MODEL OF EXCELLENT INVOLVEMENT

Most involvement with your child takes place within your own family, but parents can also band together to promote an activity or solve a problem. That's what a group of African American parents at Eagle Ridge Middle School in Ashburn, Virginia, did when their sixth-grade sons started shying away from honors classes, doubting their ability to do advanced math and science and yielding to a peer message that honors or AP classes aren't "cool."

The parents formed Club 2012, named after the year their boys would graduate from high school. The club seeks to infuse the youngsters with a sense of self-worth and purpose and the ability to articulate goals for themselves, says Gabrielle D. Carpenter, founder of Club 2012. The group also intends to ensure that their sons will enter college on time.[16]

The parents take the boys on field trips, teach them etiquette, and organize community service projects. The students also hold "rap sessions" with their fathers and do homework together twice a week supervised by a volunteer parent tutor. The strongly supportive middle school principal attends the parents' monthly meetings. Parents also hope the club will make the boys comfortable in a multiethnic academic environment, raise standardized test scores, and build strong relationships between the parents and schoolteachers and administrators. They have formed a nonprofit group and plan to hold a conference to help others replicate their club. "Parents have to take an active role in moving this forward and it takes a lot of time," says Carpenter, a high school guidance counselor with a son in the club.

The most important aim of Club 2012, says Carpenter, is to give each boy the self-image of being "a cool, smart kid" who automatically takes high-level courses.

"The goal is to create this positive peer group in middle school, so that when parents' influence becomes less important, they'll look around and see kids they've been with since sixth grade who are taking the higher level AP and honors courses. There will be other black boys with them because it will have become the norm to do so and not be seen as 'uncool.'"

SHOULD INVOLVEMENT SLACK OFF AS YOUR CHILD GROWS OLDER?

As your child gets older, the form of your involvement will change slightly. You may go to school less often. But you can still keep open the lines of communication with teachers and principals and keep track of what's going on with your child. I found out just how important that participation remains when I studied children's transition from sixth to seventh grade.

That move from elementary to junior high or middle school is notoriously difficult. For some children it's treacherous. Emerging from the nurturing cocoon of one teacher and one classroom, they begin changing classes during the day and relating to their teachers less personally. Schools are often larger and more bureaucratic, and students are more regimented. Work is more challenging, and teachers grade much more strictly than do elementary school teachers, who often award good marks simply for effort. And the social life of early adolescence is more complex. Suddenly, deciding which lunch table to sit at can provoke your child's tears.

Faced with these big changes, some children's grades drop, and their self-esteem crumbles. But others fare just fine. Which children are vulnerable? I wondered. Could parents' involvement ease children through this difficult transition?

To answer this question I selected from a larger study of 209 children and their mothers and teachers a sample of 60 families whose children entered seventh grade over the course of the study. To gauge the extent of the parents' involvement, I asked them and their children questions twice—in the spring of the child's sixth-grade year, and a year later. Questions included:

- How often did the parents attend school activities and teacher conferences?
- How often did they talk about current events to their children or take them to the library?
- Did the parents know when report cards would come out, what their children were doing in school, and the names of their classmates?

I also examined whether parents encouraged their children's autonomy. Finally, I asked the teachers about the students' grades and behavior.

Many of the children's reading and math grades *did* drop in seventh grade, but not everyone's. Parent participation in school events and conferences didn't seem to prevent problems, but the reading grades of children whose mothers were involved in their school lives personally and intellectually did not fall. This kind of involvement—knowing what was going on in their children's lives, having books around the house, and discussing ideas and events with them—made the biggest difference in students' achievement and behavior.[17] The self-esteem of the kids whose parents supported them in these two ways did not slump. Involvement didn't seem to bolster students' math grades, however, perhaps because parents tend to help more with reading than with math.

When we measured the parents' support for their children's autonomy in both sixth and seventh grades, we found that it was just as important as their involvement. The more parents were involved with their children, the better their grades, while the more they encouraged their children's autonomy in sixth grade, the fewer behavior and learning problems they had in seventh. In fact, when parents paid *increased* attention to their children's autonomy over the transition, their children held onto their feelings of self-worth and of knowing how to succeed. But these feelings tended to decline in children whose parents—possibly panicking—increased their control in seventh grade. Their children tended to agree with statements such as "My mother is always telling me what to do" or "My father insists I do things his way."

I think that this strong effect of parents' encouragement of autonomy emerged because of the new requirements of junior high or middle school. As children say good-bye to the simplicity of the earlier grades and face teachers with more "grown-up" expectations, they have to organize their homework for themselves, often juggling it with new extracurricular activities such as choir or community service. Children whose parents told them just exactly what to do and how to do it in elementary school may have found it harder to organize their work under these new requirements. They may have had trouble handing in assignments on time and studying systematically. Furthermore, these kids were more likely to act up in class—possibly their reaction to feeling controlled by their parents.

How does parental involvement affect children's emotional well-being? In another study, I found that seventh through eleventh graders whose parents were both highly involved and highly supportive of their autonomy had the least depression and anxiety as well as the fewest social and behavior problems of all the students studied.[18] This formula of involvement plus autonomy nurturing, I concluded, also fosters emotional health.

INVOLVEMENT CRUCIAL FOR STUDENTS OF ALL AGES AND ECONOMIC BACKGROUNDS

But how about *older* teenagers? They are moving toward independence. Doesn't involvement matter less for them?

To answer this question, psychologist and author Larry Steinberg of Temple University studied 6,400 high school students in Wisconsin and California.[19] They came from every kind of socioeconomic and ethnic background, from one- and two-parent, divorced, and blended families, and from urban, suburban, and rural communities. The teenagers answered two sets of questions twice, a year apart. The first set focused on parents' involvement: could the teenagers count on their parents to help if they had a problem? Steinberg asked them. Did their parents attend school programs and pay attention to their academic progress? Did they watch the teenagers in sports or other activities or help them pick courses? How often did the families do something that was fun together?

The students reported their GPAs, their time spent on homework, and how often they focused in the classroom, or whether they tended to daydream.

During the year between the two surveys, those students whose parents were more involved with them earned higher GPAs than the kids of less-involved parents.

Steinberg also asked the students whether their parents encouraged autonomy: Did their parents let them make some decisions? Help them think through and solve their own problems? "How often," he asked, "do your parents answer your arguments by saying something like 'You'll know better when you grow up'?"

The grades of students whose parents were involved, while *also* encouraging their autonomy, zoomed highest of all. In other words, parental involvement with a democratic style is more powerful than just plain involvement.

"*How* parents express their involvement and encouragement," explains Steinberg, "is as important as whether they do."

This study also counters the stereotypical notion, adds Steinberg, that teenagers are impervious to their parents' influence.

Although you might think that involvement matters more for low-income teens, who face more barriers in life than their wealthy counterparts, this study strongly suggests that parental support that encourages autonomy has a potent effect on all students.*

---

*Steinberg did find that African American teenagers' achievement did not reflect the fact that their parents scored among the highest in involved and democratic parenting. While calling for more research on parenting practices in various ethnic groups, Steinberg notes that another of his studies found that African American students are especially influenced by their peers, which could explain the difference in findings.

INVOLVEMENT IN YOUR CHILD'S SPORTS

What sort of involvement helps children enjoy and excel in sports?

When children are young, our involvement in their sports is indispensable. We sign them up, often pay a fee, equip them with shoes and shin guards, and take them to practices and games.

You might think that our involvement should taper off as our children grow. Surprisingly, however, research has shown that parental involvement is crucial for keeping kids playing. As I mentioned in chapter 2, kids steadily drop out of organized sports starting at age ten, with about 75 percent dropping out by age eighteen. Others estimate that in many organized sports, 80 to 90 percent of the participants drop out by age fifteen. Girls are especially vulnerable to quitting.

In her study titled "Hugs or Shrugs?" the late Barbara A. Brown, of the University of Western Ontario faculty of physical education, asked whether parental involvement contributes to this high attrition rate.[20] She posed a series of questions to 376 Canadian girls ages thirteen to nineteen, who played sports in school and in the community. The questions included:

- "How much do your parents encourage and support you?"
- "How much do they approve of teenage girls playing sports?"
- "Do your parents play sports themselves?"

The more parents encouraged and supported their daughters, Brown found, the longer the girls kept participating in sports. And each of the three forms of parental involvement proved important to the girls' sticking with their sport. In fact, the study showed that parents' support increased as the girls grew older.

Can parents get too involved? A University of New Hampshire kinesiologist, Heather Barber, studied parents who coached their children's teams, which of course required a very high degree of participation. She wanted to find out how their coaching affected their children's desire to play and their competitive anxiety. Barber gave questionnaires to thirty-six kids whose parents coached their teams and twenty-six kids whose parents didn't. The young athletes were nine to fourteen years old, and nearly two-thirds were boys.[21] Then Barber measured the children's anxiety about competing and their motivation to play. When parents coached, she thought both would be higher.

Barber was wrong. There were no differences between the two groups. Children felt the same desire to play and the same anxiety about winning and losing, regardless of whether their parents coached the team or not. So high involvement—such as coaching your child's team—doesn't present a problem, even when children grow older. As always, the caveat is to support without intruding or controlling.

ANOTHER REASON NOT TO FEEL GUILTY: PARENTS TODAY SPEND MORE TIME WITH THEIR CHILDREN THAN IN PAST GENERATIONS

Many working parents feel guilty for not spending enough time with their kids. But a recent large study revealed that both mothers and fathers spend more time with their children than they did forty years ago.[22]

A team of sociologists led by Suzanne Bianchi of the University of Maryland examined time diaries of twelve hundred parents, who told interviewers how they'd spent the previous day.

Bianchi and her colleagues found that in 2000, married mothers spent 12.9 hours a week caring for their children, up from 10.6 hours in 1965. Single mothers spent almost as much, 11.8 hours a week, compared to 7.5 hours in 1965.

Married fathers' involvement jumped from three hours a week in 1965 to seven in 2000.

Furthermore, the additional time with kids isn't spent shuttling them in cars or even dressing and feeding them. "Quality time"—spent reading to and playing with kids—has gone up.

How could parents spend *more* time with our kids, when so many women now work outside the home? One of the main reasons is that we're . . . messier. Or, depending on your point of view, less perfectionist. Married mothers are doing a lot less housework. Their time spent cooking and cleaning plunged from thirty-two hours a week in 1965 to only nineteen hours in 2000. (Single mothers' housework stayed the same at seventeen hours, although it rose and fell over those thirty-five years.) In addition, parents are having fewer children and can spend more time and money on each one. And they're having children later in life, when they want to devote more time to them.

Mothers' leisure time has also suffered, perhaps explaining why so many women feel so time-crunched. Whatever leisure time parents do have, however, they tend to spend with their children, taking them along to restaurants and on vacations more than in past generations.

Why Do Parents Still Feel Guilty?

There's still plenty of guilt to go around, says Bianchi, who notes that the cultural ideal of mothers as eternally self-sacrificing and devoted to their children twenty-four/seven is still going strong.

"Just because mothers are spending more time in the workforce doesn't mean that they have shed this notion that you should be ever-present, always there for your children," she explains.[23]

In addition, notions of "intensive parenting" are proliferating. More and more people, says Bianchi, feel that "you need to invest lots of time with your children if they're going to have the opportunities you want them to have and turn out the way you want them to."

The requirements for good mothering, she believes, have ratcheted upward at the same time as women's career options are expanding.

Interestingly, the researchers found that dads feel guiltier than mothers. "It's like the more time you spend at work, the more you have a heightened sense that you're not spending enough time," explains Bianchi.

Interestingly, the increased time parents are spending with their children occurs when only about 30 percent of American children live in families with a working dad and a stay-at-home mother, compared to 60 percent in 1965. In other words, fewer children live in Ozzie and Harriet families. But parents today spend more quality time with children than Ozzie and Harriet did.

Staying Tuned In: Watching Out for Burnout

Ranked in the boys' singles fourteen-and-under United States Tennis Association/mid-Atlantic section, Matt Davidson had been playing tennis five or six days a week since he was eight. A high school freshman, he'd recently achieved his goal of reaching the top ten ranking in the region.

But late one September night, as his mother Joyce was unloading the dishwasher, he came into the kitchen. "I don't want to go to tennis tomorrow," he told his mom as he opened the freezer and took out an ice cream sandwich. "I'm not having fun anymore."

Joyce straightened up and turned around, surprised. "I want to try out for the school play instead," said Matt. "Auditions are next week. I want to sign up." Matt had just started high school, and the theater program, unlike tennis, was, of course, coed.

Joyce's heart dropped to the bottom of her stomach. She told me, "All that time he's spent playing! I thought. 'He's so good!'

"I wanted to blurt out, 'If you stop playing you'll fall off the USTA chart! And if you don't play any tournaments for three months you won't be able to make sectionals!'

"But I held my tongue."

Joyce's husband, Stewart, was upset too. He worried that Matt would lose interest in tennis. And Joyce was afraid that the tennis coach, who'd gone out of his way for their son, would be angry. At the very least, they told Matt, he had to talk to his coach before he quit.

Matt's coach came over to the house.

"OK, if you definitely want to try out for the play, I'll support you," he said. "You might want to think about doing some running or weight training at the same time, though. You don't want to get out of shape.

"You know," he added, "I could tell you weren't happy. Tennis has got to be fun, or it's not worth it.

"Just remember, you've got a gift. You don't want to throw that away. Down the road it will open doors for you."

Matt got a part in the play and attended rehearsals every afternoon after school, even though he only had a few lines. But several of his friends also had parts or worked backstage. He was invited to theater program parties, and the experience made him feel part of the high school. He played tennis only on the weekends.

In February, Matt said, "Oh, my gosh, tennis season is coming soon! I have to get ready—how many times a week can I go?!"

He plunged back in, happier and more enthusiastic than before his time off.

"Taking a break was totally the right thing to do," laughed Joyce when she told me the end of the story. "He was burned out. I'm glad we didn't push him through those three months.

"Emotionally we *really* didn't want him to quit," says Joyce. "But it wasn't our decision."

Whether it's sports or community service, after-school science lab or Scouts, children have to follow their own rhythm of interest and intensity. You can remind them of their responsibilities and commitment to others, but their need to take a break is real. If you stay involved with your kid, he'll tell you when he's burned out. Despite the anxiety and disappointment you may feel, it's important to let *him* decide if and when to take a break.

HELPING YOUR CHILD WITH A SCIENCE FAIR OR OTHER BIG PROJECT

Not long ago I interviewed dozens of families about involvement in their children's schooling. The school science fair had just ended, and the parents couldn't stop talking about it. It was as though my questions had opened a spout in their veins so their complaints could gush out. Voices striking high notes of stress, they grumbled about battling with their children over the directions, what to focus on, and who would do what. They couldn't gripe enough.

I took a tour through the fair, and sure enough, I saw the signs of intense parent participation if not outright ownership; some of the projects looked like they came straight from NASA or the Centers for Disease Control.

Science fairs are a prime breeding ground for the Pressured Parent Phenomenon. What could be more competitive than this public display of students' work, for which judges will award prizes? More intense than daily homework, science projects are virtually impossible to complete without a parent's help.

Science fairs also subject parents to a social expectation of high participation. (So do assignments such as sculpturing an animal in its habitat and making shadow boxes and panoramas to illustrate a storybook. A really spiffy project means trips to the crafts store to get little figures, animals, and trees. It also means watching over that dangerous glue gun.) The non-level playing field can intimidate, since some parents know more about science or have more time to help their children than others. We're under extreme pressure to make our children— and us—look good. It's as though a sloppy project indicts the entire family for criminal neglect. How could science fairs *not* send our hardwiring haywire?

Since large project assignments show no signs of abating, let's look at how to turn this angst-producing task into a good experience for you and your child. How can you participate without trampling on his autonomy?

You can use the three techniques for promoting autonomy outlined in chapter 6.

Start by *taking your child's point of view and acknowledging his feelings*. When Zach showed me two single-spaced pages of instructions for his sixth-grade science fair, he looked intimidated.

"Oh, gosh, so much to do!" I said. "This must seem so overwhelming! Such a big, long project!" He looked up at me expectantly.

"Don't worry. We'll do it one step at a time."

That night I asked Zach, "How would you like to work together?" I gave him *choices*. Did he want to do it mostly himself and come to me when he had problems or questions? Did he want the two of us to make a plan that he would carry out? Or did he want us to do the entire project side by side?

He said he wanted us to start all the steps together and that he would try to finish each one himself.

"Okay," I said. "First let's choose a project. What would you like to find out about? Any questions you would like to answer?" Zach wasn't sure, so we went to the Web sites of the San Francisco Exploratorium, the Franklin Institute, and several other science museums to look for project ideas.

"Maybe we can find a project connected to football, baseball cards, or movies," I said, naming his interests. That train of thought started to *give him more choices*: we talked about experimenting with our cats to see which food they liked better, or how to coax Heathcliff, the skittish one, to sit on your lap. Or maybe, Zach mentioned, he could figure out different ways to throw a football in a spiral. "I got it," he said, "I want to know how a movie camera works."

After a while, we found some directions for making a camera obscura, a box that focuses light through a pinhole onto its back wall, projecting an upside-down image of the view outside.

The next day I had Zach read me the instructions that the teacher had sent home for the project.

"Okay, what will be your hypothesis?" I asked him. We talked about that for a few minutes.

The directions from the Exploratorium said to get a big cardboard box.

"Where do you think we could find a big box?" I asked, hoping to *support his autonomous problem solving*.

He looked befuddled. But after a minute he said, "I know—behind the store on Pico Boulevard where they sell refrigerators!" He and his friend dragged a box up the street and into our backyard. I continued asking questions.

"How could we make the pinhole?" Zach remembered we had an ice pick and ran to get it. "Make sure you carry it without running!" I shouted after him. "And with the point facing down!" That Saturday I took Zach to buy some light-sensitive photographic paper from a camera store.

After Zach told me what other families were doing, I tried fending off the anxiety from the competition—for both his sake and my own—by empha-sizing the goal of learning from the experiment.

"Let's not think about winning or losing," I said. "This project is for learning. It can teach us about the scientific method and..." (I glanced at the directions) "about ummm, light refraction, and even how the eye works.

"Plus a little chemistry," I added, "when the light changes the chemical on the photographic paper."

We had hassles. It was hard for me to let Zach cut out the hole and trim the edges of the cardboard box because it looked so roughly hewn. I could have cut it so neatly! And he made the pinhole too big the first time, so he had to tape it over and make another. I tried to banish from my head thoughts such as "It's going to look really messy. Everyone else's will be so spiffy—especially that kid whose father works at Lockheed! What will his teacher think? And the judges? And the other parents?!"

I'm not exactly a marvel of patience. A few times I almost blew my cool but managed to walk away before losing it. Every so often I felt like taking over and telling Zach what to do or doing it myself, and I had to check those reflexes. But the project must have succeeded overall, because recently when I asked Zach what he remembered about the project, he said, "The biggest chal-lenge was making sure it was dark inside the box." Then he added, "I had such a feeling of exhilaration when it worked!"

When Your Child Takes to the Stage

For parents of children who enjoy drama and musical comedy, involvement presents particular challenges. Competition is usually fierce, and since stage productions can be quite elaborate, the theater program usually needs all the help it can get.

Given all the competition, and the chances that your child will lose out and feel hurt, it's tempting to spend time and money helping out, with the hopes of tipping the casting scale in her direction.

"Parents start quietly lobbying about their children's talents from the get-go," says Cynthia Notley, a physical therapist and mother of three in Fremont, California. "They show up for raising money, sewing costumes—that sort of thing.

"But I couldn't do that as a working mom, nor would I want to."

On the drama teacher's suggestion, Cynthia's daughter Lauren began taking singing lessons from a particular coach her freshman year. Over the next three years Lauren "paid her dues," attending rehearsals faithfully and painting sets while older students won the starring roles in the annual school production.

In her junior year, Lauren sang three lines in *The Pajama Game*. The audience applauded her wildly.

Lauren began her senior year anticipating a major part—finally. The drama teacher chose *Grease*, and Lauren, who had never taken dance, got a small character role with no singing. A dancer without acting experience snagged the lead role of Sandy.

Cynthia was livid. "To see your kid so disappointed—it's like someone punched you in the stomach," she says.

"My maternal instincts were to go in and complain about this teacher in charge and about how my daughter had been taking lessons from someone whom she'd suggested, and then she had been so ignored.

"I asked Lauren what she thought I should do, and she said, 'Don't do anything.' So I didn't. But I did want to go in and tell this teacher how she had ruined my child's last year of high school."

Lauren is having a wonderful time in college, her mother told me recently. She sings in the school's madrigal ensemble and has developed an interest in filmmaking.

"I'm glad I didn't interfere," reflects Cynthia. "I did see kids who got roles because their parents went in and raised Cain. If theater had really been Lauren's be-all and end-all—if she really and truly wanted to go on the stage, maybe she would have asked me to go in and talk to someone and maybe I would have done so.

"But it's turned out for the best. Lauren loves to sing, she benefited from the lessons, and now she's found a professional goal that really and truly interests her. What more can a parent ask?"

PREPARING FOR A MUSIC COMPETITION

Making progress in music often takes a long time, and parents' encouragement makes "all the difference in the world between someone succeeding or not," says Jane Magrath, director of piano pedagogy at the University of Oklahoma School of Music.[24]

Eminent music teachers devote a fair amount of time to coaching their pupils' parents psychologically. Princeton, New Jersey, piano teacher Ingrid Clarfield, whose pupils have won many prizes, recently told me how she helps parents combine intense involvement with respect for their children's autonomy as they prepare for competitions.

"I tell them to respect each child's individual, personal needs before, during, and after the competition—not to do as *they* would want, but as the *child* would want," she explains.[25]

Before the Twenty-first International Young Artists Piano Competition in 2006, Clarfield knew that the mother of ten-year-old Raymond Zhang would be nervous the day of his performance and would want him to practice that morning. She also knew the boy was a finicky eater on competition days.

Clarfield counseled his mother not to push him.

"If Raymond wants to practice fifteen minutes the day of the competition," the teacher told her, "respect that. If he wants to eat a peanut butter and jelly sandwich, let him."

When the young performer woke at 6 a.m. and asked to go to the practice room, his mother took him. She didn't flinch when he refused to eat anything but a Chinese bun for breakfast.

Raymond played Prelude in G-sharp Minor, op. 32, no. 12, by Rachmaninoff, and Shadow Puppet, by Li-Ly Chang. He won first prize for his age group and an award for outstanding performance of a Chinese piece.

As I write, Raymond's intrinsic motivation remains alive and well. "I still love to play the piano," he told me by e-mail. "I find it fun, and relaxing. I like to learn the new songs and pieces."

TIPS FOR POLISHING UP YOUR INVOLVEMENT[26]

It's not always easy, especially with older children, to know what's going on in their lives. Here are some suggestions for ways to boost your personal involvement with your child.

At Home

Try to put your chores and work out of your mind and focus on your child when she needs you and when you're doing something together. Be there mentally, not just physically, advises Larry Steinberg.[27]

Introduce your child to your hobbies—hiking, jazz, knitting, or cooking.

Give your child a choice of activities for just the two of you: a bicycle ride, lunch out, a swim at the Y.

Ask your child to introduce you to her hobbies. Force yourself to focus on his video games or on how cars work, and see if you can get interested.

With a younger child, play with the blocks or dolls or simply watch. Find it boring? Listen to the stories he is making up. Check out her block-building skills. You might, says Steinberg, be impressed with them.

Let her "try for herself"—do it her own way. Don't teach unless she asks you to.

If your child participates in sports or the arts, and there's a fund-raiser, volunteer. Nothing bonds you together more than washing a car or serving pancakes together.

At School

If "How was school today?" doesn't get you anywhere, try specific questions, such as:

- What did you learn in school today? Did you learn anything interesting?
- What's your favorite time in the school day?
- What did you do at recess?
- Who do you like to play with? Why?
- What did you do in math today?
- Who did you sit with at lunch?
- Was your teacher back after her illness?

Popular Media

With an older child, play the video game that he likes. Warning: the noise might be almost unbearable. The action is quick, and you'll find the games very challenging—especially when your fingers are less nimble than your child's.

Watch movies with him, read the same book or comic book he's reading, or listen to the music that he listens to—even if it doesn't interest you. Watch TV together—especially shows that you think might bring up interesting topics. It is a great chance to share your views.

You can also ask your child to tell you why he likes a certain game, movie, book, TV show, or song. What are the themes that he enjoys? That can lead to interesting conversations. For example, teenagers often watch or read about boys not being understood by authority figures. He might tell you which adults he thinks don't understand him, and why.

More Ways to Find Out What's Going On in Your Child's Life

Welcome your child's friends to hang out at your house. Put a basketball hoop in the driveway, snacks in the kitchen, and invite them to eat with the family.

When driving a carpool of kids, listen to what they're saying in the back-seat—but don't let your child know.

Sit down and listen to your young musician. Encourage her: say things like "I really like this piece," "Would you play that for me?" or "It sounds like you're really starting to feel the music when you're playing."

What are her favorite sports? Which athletes does she admire? Celebrities? Why?

Helping with Homework[28]

With an elementary school child, ask if she has homework and if she needs help, and make sure she finishes it.

Check over her work occasionally. If she's made careless mistakes, have her go over it again.

If she doesn't understand the assignment, either explain it or let the teacher know she needs help.

If she has a book report due, make a trip to the library together and discuss what she might learn from different books or why she might enjoy them. You might want to pick up some extra books for fun.

With middle school–age children, ask what homework they have and check if they've done it. Look at the homework occasionally to see what she's learning. "Offer your assistance from time to time," says Steinberg, "but don't insist that she take it."

Suggest that she and her friends form a study group together at your house. Be sure there is an adult at home.

Once children are in high school, get involved in homework only if your child asks you to. When I was growing up, that meant my mother "quizzing" me on memorizations such as Latin vocabulary words, brainstorming with me to find a term paper topic, and taking me to a specialized public library.

If your child is having problems with a teacher or a subject, help him problem solve.

Ask him questions until you understand the problem thoroughly:

"What's the matter honey? What happened today?"

"Mr. Rhoades moved me again."

"Why?"

"He says we're too noisy."

Listen without interrupting. Check that you understand what he means: "Oh, I see, Mr. Rhoades thinks that you're talking with your friends too much, so he moved your seat?"

Empathize: "Oh, you must be very disappointed not to be able to sit with Alex and Jorge anymore."

"What do you think you could do to get to sit with them again?"

Your conversation, in addition to showing empathy, is helping your child see that his behavior isn't working for him and that he can choose to change his behavior.

HELPING WITH MUSIC COMPETITIONS

There's a lot of psychological support you can give your child if he enters music competitions. You can suggest that he:

- Make winning a secondary goal.
- Take judges' comments as interesting and informative, although sometimes they're way off track.
- See what else he can learn from the experience—even if it's only "how to sing when you're not feeling your best, psychologically" or "how to use the extra energy of your nervousness."[29]
- Understand that judging among the top contenders is often arbitrary and that the runners-up often have a better career than the winners (see

the chapter 5 section on creativity), who tend to be technically correct but not adventurous.

- Try to enjoy making music and expressing his feelings.

WHAT'S GOING ON? HOW TO GET MORE INVOLVED IN YOUR CHILD'S ATHLETIC LIFE

"Who are the people, for example, to whom you go for advice? Not to the hard, practical ones who can tell you exactly what to do, but to the listeners; that is, the kindest, least censorious, least bossy people that you know. It is because by pouring out your problem to them, you then know what to do about it yourself."

—Brenda Ueland from her essay
"Tell Me More: On the Fine Art of Listening"[30]

Positive Coaching Alliance executive director Jim Thompson advises parents who want to increase their involvement in their children's athletic lives to take on a "Tell-Me-More" attitude. That label comes from the essay "Tell Me More: On the Fine Art of Listening" by Brenda Ueland, a journalist and writing teacher who hosted an early twentieth-century radio show during which she responded to listeners' personal problems.

Adopting a "Tell-Me-More" attitude means letting your child know that you really hear what she has to say. Think of your conversation, Thompson advises, as an Olympic event with judges.

"A conversation that rates a nine or a ten is one in which the child does more talking and the parent more listening," he explains.[31]

Timing is all-important. When something happens to my child, I am always bursting to talk with her about it, to make sure she's okay, and to soothe any emotional wounds. But that may not be the right time. The raw emotion after a tough game may make it impossible for a child to talk. She has to let it settle, return to familiar surroundings, and even wait for her body to calm down. Don't worry if your child clams up. Wait until that night or the next day—whenever she's ready. And let her talk first.

Many children, but especially boys, like to talk while shooting hoops, playing cards, or doing a jigsaw puzzle. Important conversations also take place in the car. Sitting in a parallel position rather than face-to-face somehow makes it easier for children to confide. Don't worry, advises Thompson, if a conversation is short. That may be enough for your child![32]

OVERSCHEDULING: NOT TO WORRY

It's fashionable to criticize parents, especially affluent ones, for "overscheduling" their children—forcing them to run without respite from one extracurricular activity to the next. One recent book even chastised parents for trying to give their children opportunities they never had.[33]

Of course, children need time for free play and relaxing, for dreaming, for hobbies, and for friendships. We have to pay attention to their happiness and try to minimize the stress in their lives. We shouldn't pressure children with the specter of college admissions to get on a competitive treadmill. Clearly, nonstop activity benefits no one. But let's not throw the enrichment baby out with the anxious bathwater.

Giving children whatever opportunities we can afford—Tae Kwon Do, cello lessons, baseball camp, or a computer course—are signs of healthy parental involvement in children's lives—as long as children enjoy those activities.

That's what Yale University psychologist Joseph L. Mahoney concluded after a comprehensive review of relevant studies, which included a survey of 2,908 nationally representative American children five to eighteen years old.[34] Young people who participate in after-school activities, he found—even the 3 to 6 percent who spend as many as twenty hours a week on them—are psychologically healthier than those who don't. In fact, the researchers discovered, the more kids participate in activities, the better their well-being.

There's also strong evidence that kids who participate in organized activities do better academically than those who don't. Furthermore, they smoke and use drugs less and have better relationships with their parents.

As one psychologist commented after reviewing the Mahoney report, "Generally the soccer moms have it right and organize after-school activities that benefit their children."[35] I would add that it's not just the soccer moms; it's moms and dads everywhere who manage to introduce their kids to hobbies, sports, music, dance, and drama.

The problem in America, says Mahoney, isn't that middle-class kids have too many activities but that less privileged kids don't have enough. American youths average about five hours a week in extracurricular activities, but 40 percent of American youngsters don't participate in *any* organized out-of-school programs.

Of course, parents need to pay attention to children's autonomy and let them choose their after-school activities, not force them to take piano lessons or play Little League if they don't want to.

But when Mahoney synthesized the results of more than a dozen studies, he found that young people from nine to nineteen years old cite enjoyment and excitement, building skills, and making friends as their most common reasons for participating in out-of-school activities. Few mentioned pressure from their parents or building up their résumés. In other words, when it comes to extracurriculars, intrinsic motivation rules the day. Parents' instincts to give their children the chance to learn new skills and to experience the joy of athletics and the arts are right on the mark.

Recently, on a visit to New York City, I spoke to a tall seventeen-year-old at a ballet studio, her head with its small dancer's bun bending over one knee as she unlaced her toe shoes after an advanced class. In addition to dancing and attending an academically demanding school, she told me that she worked after school for two hours three times a week with a mentor in a biochemistry laboratory at the local university.

"Do you enjoy being so busy?" I asked.

"My mother says, 'Don't you want to slow down—to have some down time?'" she answered. "But I told her, 'I love everything that I'm doing!'"

She flashed a huge smile as she packed her toe shoes in her duffle bag. *How lucky some children are, I thought, to have so many interesting activities in their lives and so many caring adults to guide them.*

CHAPTER 9

"WHAT DO YOU EXPECT?"
Channeling Anxiety into
Rules, Guidelines, and Information

One windy autumn afternoon as I watched my daughter play hockey, I began chatting at half-time with Pam, a mother standing next to me. Our daughters were young teenagers, and we started talking about how hard we found it to decide what to let them do on their own. We live in a small town, and she told me that after her daughter Molly had turned eleven she let her ride her bike to the park, to her friends' houses, and into town.

"I made a few rules though," she said. "She had to wear her helmet to protect her head if she fell, and she had to ride on the sidewalk to protect her from cars. I also told her she couldn't ride to town alone, that if she always rode with a friend they could watch out for each other."

One Saturday afternoon, Molly and several friends decided to ride to town to get ice cream at the drugstore. Her friend Lindsey took a spill and skinned her thigh so badly she couldn't ride home.

"I was very proud of Molly," said Pam, "because when the girls talked about how to handle the situation, she remembered the rule about not riding alone. They had her friend Vanessa stay with Lindsey while she and her other friend Kim rode their bikes to get help."

Later Molly told her mother, "Lindsey was really glad that Vanessa stayed with her while we went to get help."

I liked this story because it showed how kids internalize our rules and use them to stay safe. I'm sure your child has rules like this too. But what do these rules have to do with the Pressured Parent Phenomenon?

Rules, and their underlying rationale, are an important component of the structure that parents can provide for their children. This structure gives children a feeling of competence. And competence, as you remember, is the third of the three feelings that foster your child's intrinsic motivation.

That's why structure provides the final leg of the Three-Part Framework, which you can draw on when you're caught up in the Pressured Parent Phenomenon. Faced with the escalating competition in our children's world, you can turn to structure to head off your anxiety. Reminding yourself that structure builds her feelings of competence will help counter the impulse to push and pressure your child. And nothing motivates children (adults too) more than feelings of competence. (Think about it: don't you enjoy doing what you're good at?) The spike in feelings of competence that structure gives your child will nourish her intrinsic motivation. That will not only prevent her from slacking off, but it will also help her be the best she can be.

Besides rules, structure encompasses information, expectations, and guidelines, as well as consequences and feedback. These methods put parent and child on the same wavelength. And they'll position your child to make good choices. Since he knows the consequences of his actions, he'll stop and think before deciding what to do next.

STRUCTURE CREATES FEELINGS OF COMPETENCE

Psychologists have long stressed that children need rules and supervision to keep them safe and secure. That's very true. Structure is the way parents exert their authority and keep children from getting into trouble.

But children need structure for a second important reason: because it teaches them that their actions matter. Structure provides clear consequences that make the child's environment predictable. It shows children that they have an impact on the world, which in turn gives them a basic feeling of competence.

The structure that Pam set up around riding bikes helped Molly feel competent, because when there was an accident, the rule told her what to do—not to leave her injured friend alone—and why. As a result she felt responsible and effective.

ORDER OR CHAOS?

Father: What this family needs is discipline. When people start riding horses up the front steps, that's going too far!

Irene: I didn't ride the horse, but if I did, who broke those windows on Fifth Avenue? [Insinuating her sister Cornelia is the culprit.]

Father: I don't care who rode the horse or broke the windows but this family has got to settle down!

This dialogue from the Depression-era screwball comedy *My Man Godfrey* illustrates the chaos that ensues when a loving moneybags of a father, Alexander Bullock, leaves all authority to his flighty wife. No one has given his daughters, Irene and Cornelia, limits. So who ends up bringing order to the Bullock household? A butler, the kind of employee known for the strict rules of propriety and the discreet competence he brings to the job. (Of course, since this is a romantic comedy, he also falls in love with Irene, and they marry. And he turns out to be a millionaire in disguise.) None of us have butlers suddenly appearing on the scene to bring a sense of order to our children, but the movie speaks nonetheless to the idea that if we don't give children structure—horses or no horses—our home lives will be chaotic.

My research in Dansville illustrated this point very well.[1] The families I interviewed ran the gamut from highly structured to extremely loose. Some parents had clear rules and expectations for their children about when to do homework, when to go to bed, and when to clean their rooms. They had consequences for not fulfilling responsibilities. A child could say to herself, "If I don't do my homework, I'm not going to get to play outside tomorrow" or "If I don't clean my room, I won't get to watch any TV tonight."

Other homes had little or no structure. In one, for example, the parents had no rules, either stated or understood, about when to do homework or when to go to sleep. Family life was so chaotic that their daughter rarely got her homework started before it was way past a reasonable bedtime. She didn't do very well in school.

But most families fell on a continuum between the two extremes of high structure and none at all.

How did these differences in structure affect children's feelings of competence? To find out, I asked the children questions such as:

- "When you get a good grade in school, why does that happen?"
- "When you do well in sports, why does that happen?"
- "In general, when good or bad things happen, why is that?"

The children chose from such answers as "Because I try hard," "Because I'm good at sports/math," or "I don't know why."

The more the parents had created a clear and consistent structure, we found, the more their children felt that they had control over their successes and failures. They had learned how the world works. "If I really try hard in school," they thought, "then I'll do well." The sense of clear expectations and predictable consequences for their actions at home carried over into their academic and extracurricular lives.

But the kids from unstructured homes tended to feel helpless and ineffectual. They were at a loss for how to succeed. When asked why good or bad things happened, they answered, "I don't know why." Their haphazard home lives gave them a sense that the world outside was haphazard too, and that made them feel powerless.

AUTONOMY MAKES ALL THE DIFFERENCE

Structure Doesn't Equal Control

Does structure seem like control to you? Does it seem as though I'm contradicting myself by calling for *structure* when I've spent so much time emphasizing children's *autonomy*?

At first glance, structure might seem controlling. The word itself conjures up images of steel girders and concrete walls holding people in. "Structure" might also make you think of reward-punishment systems used to pressure children to change their behavior.

The kind of structure I'm discussing, however, is firm but comfortable, adapted to each child. It's like a material that provides support without leaving red welt marks on the skin. Think cotton with 10 percent spandex and how comfortable that material feels, since it changes to fit your shape. Just as you can weave cloth with or without spandex, you can create structure that respects your child's autonomy or doesn't. It's all in the way you do it.

Let's take a look at how to create structure in a style that encourages your child's autonomy. That way you'll avoid power struggles that result from your child's resistance and anger.

"WHEN THE LITTLE HAND IS ON THE FIVE": TWO DIFFERENT WAYS TO SET UP STRUCTURE

Structure with Control

Let's say you want your child to come inside from playing at 5 p.m. You could try it this way:

"You *must* come in by five o'clock. You *should* look at your watch and when the little hand is on the five, that's when you *have to* come in. Do you understand?"

If your child has resisted coming in on time before, you could add a threat: "If you don't come in on time, I'm going to make you come in earlier tomorrow." Or you could pressure him: "I really want you to pay attention to your watch and not fool around." Finally, you could remind him that you'll be watching: "I'm going to be in the kitchen, waiting for you at five."

As I'm sure you've guessed, the examples above illustrate ways to lace structure with control.

Structure with Autonomy

On the other hand, you could encourage your child's autonomy, starting by *empathizing.* "I know that you hate to come in, especially when it's still daylight outside. I know you'd much rather keep playing."

Then you could give *reasons for the rule.* "But it's important for you to come in when it starts getting dark. Cars can't see the kids playing outside at dusk. And it's time for you to help set the table and wash your hands for dinner."

You can *give information.* "When the little hand is on the five" (or, if the watch is digital, "When the watch face reads 5:00"), "then it's time to come in."

"Would you like a reminder?" you might ask. If your child says yes: "Okay, I'll give you one right around 5 p.m."

If your son has been coming in late despite reminders, you might also let him know that if you have to prompt him more than twice, he'll have to come in the following day at four p.m.

HOW TO CHANNEL THE PRESSURED PARENT PHENOMENON INTO STRUCTURE

When the Pressured Parent Phenomenon has you in its grip, and you're feeling anxious because your child has an important test that day or an audition, you can siphon your nervous energy off into setting up structure.

Here's an example of how to set up structure. Let's say that your child, who has already tried and quit piano and violin, decides she wants to take up the guitar. You're wary of putting out the money yet again for an instrument and lessons, but you wonder if now that she's a little bit older, she might stick with the new instrument. Maybe she's found some new motivation listening to a friend who plays guitar, you think, or listening to music on her CD Walkman or iPod.

Let Your Child Have Input into the Structure

How can you create a structure that will encourage her to practice this time around? And how can you do so without venting your frustration from the violin and piano debacles?

When it comes to fundamental decisions such as whether she attends school or gets an annual checkup, your child has no say. But for less vital decisions like this one, you can create a structure that you both agree on. If you let your child play a role in making rules—if you allow her the autonomy of deciding some of the specifics—she'll buy into them much easier.

Let's say you decide to borrow or rent a guitar this time around. You could start by asking questions. "I think it probably makes sense to keep renting and paying for lessons only if you practice," you might say, to start the conversation about structure. "What do you think?"

If your daughter agrees, ask her how many days she thinks she'd like to practice. Keep talking until you agree on the number of practice days and how long each session should be. You could add *information.* "You'll be surprised at how far you can go if you practice every day."

Give her choices about where to practice and for how long. (As always, try to stay away from using words like *should, must,* and *have to.*) Say things like: "Would you like to practice in your room or in the living room?" or "Do you think twenty minutes is a good practice time, or half an hour?"

You'll probably have to negotiate. "Okay," you might say at the end of this discussion, "how about if we say you practice in the living room for twenty minutes, every day except Saturday?"

This process won't unfold smoothly. Your daughter might, for example, say, "I don't like to practice when you're still at work. I like it when you listen. Laura's mother always listens when she practices."

You could say you understand and that perhaps you felt the same way when you took piano lessons as a child. Maybe she'd agree to record her practicing to play for you later or to do her homework earlier so she can practice when you're home at night.

If you don't like sitting with her while she practices or if you are pressed for time, maybe you could compromise and agree to listen once or twice a week.

When she starts to practice, don't forget to give encouraging *feedback*: "You probably don't realize how much you've progressed in the past two weeks, but when I was listening yesterday I heard a big difference. You're really getting good!"

This kind of structure heads off the impulse to try to overpower your child with screaming or other tactics when you're worrying about him slacking off. The rules and consequences you've agreed upon can head off that yelling because they're invented precisely to keep your child on track. Instead of screaming, all you need to do is rely on the structure that you've already set up. At first you may be afraid to do so, since forcing your child feels better at first—you get immediate results. So to help calm your fears about giving up control and taking the slower route of structure, remember that structure builds your child's competence, feeding his intrinsic motivation, which in turn will help him be the best he can be.

More Examples of Letting Your Child Participate in Setting Up Structure

- Let your child decide when and how he'll clean his room.
- Instead of decreeing, "You're going to bed at nine p.m. because I said so," sit down and talk about why your child wants to stay up later and what makes sense to you. Then negotiate.
- Discuss when your child would like to start her homework, where she'd like to do it, and what consequences are reasonable for not doing it.

Setting up structure takes a lot of time. It's not easy. But it pays off, because structure teaches a child to take responsibility for her own actions. It also prevents conflict and, by setting up a clear understanding between parent and child, opens up the lines of communication.

FLEXIBILITY IN STRUCTURE: YOU'RE NOT A WIMP IF YOU NEGOTIATE

In the example above, I mentioned that you would probably have to negotiate while setting up the structure. Maybe your daughter wanted to practice for fifteen minutes a day, you suggested thirty minutes, and you ended up agreeing on twenty minutes.

I used to feel wimpy "giving in" to my children. We all know kids whose parents say they're born lawyers. Zach was one of those kids who liked to argue, and I used to worry that I negotiated with him too much.

"Can I have another piece of chocolate cake?" he would say.

"No, you've already had two."

"Just a little piece."

"No. I'm afraid you'll get sick to your stomach. You already had a big bowl of ice cream."

"How about one bite?"

And on and on. Eventually I would say something like, "Okay, you can have half a piece more, but that's all." It was tiring, and I always felt I had done the "wrong thing" by not sticking to my guns.

It wasn't until I started learning more about motivational psychology that I realized negotiating with Zach wasn't so bad after all. I never gave in on questions of principle, and, as it turns out, rigidity isn't a good parenting tactic.

While predictable consequences help children recognize the effect of their actions, your flexibility helps them too. This may seem contradictory, but life is complicated and learning how to discuss and change agreements is a good skill for a child to acquire.

You're always the ultimate authority, but if your child makes a good point, giving in to it doesn't weaken that authority. I'm not suggesting that if your child breaks a rule for which you've agreed on a consequence you should go back on that. But even toddlers benefit when you negotiate with them.

Negotiating, the research shows, teaches kids both to express themselves and to see someone else's point of view. Kids who learn how to give and take get along better with other children. But they can't learn this complex social skill from other kids. They have to learn it from their parents. Studies show that when parents sometimes negotiate with their children, rather than using their power to push their own agenda, it helps their kids in turn manage better with their friends.[2]

CONSEQUENCES

Structure includes consequences. When setting them up, it's important to ask three questions:

- Do the consequences flow from the broken rule?
- Can you tolerate them?
- Does your child accept them?

Let's say your children won't stop poking and teasing each other in the backseat of the car. You can explain that their fighting drives you crazy and that distracting you could cause an accident.

"So I'm going to make a rule: no fighting in the backseat. Would you agree to that rule?"

"But Corey always starts it."

"We're going to have consequences for both of you, no matter who starts it. What do you think should happen if you fight in the backseat? What do you think would be a good consequence?"

"I don't know."

If child doesn't suggest suitable consequences, try giving them some to choose from:

- "I'll pull over to the side of the road until you stop." (You have to be willing to risk being late.) Or
- "We'll turn around and go home," or
- "I will stop and put one of you in the front seat," or
- "You won't get to choose the music on the radio. I'll choose," or
- "You can't watch your favorite TV show that day/that week."

Only offer consequences that you can stand—don't suggest pulling over to the side of the road if you can't be late, and don't propose taking away their favorite TV show if you treasure that time to relax.

(This same template can be used for boys who won't stop pulling the cat's tail, girls who leave their clothes all over the floor, etc.)

LIMITS

In *My Man Godfrey*, the movie I mentioned near the beginning of this chapter, the spoiled Bullock daughters, Irene and Cornelia, obviously needed structure. In particular they needed the common form of structure called limits. Limits are rules that tell how far your child can go. They set boundaries. When your son knows he's not supposed to jump up and down on the couch, eat cereal in his bedroom, or keep his Legos scattered over the living room floor— and that if he does, you'll ask him not to or even apply consequences—that gives him information about expected responses to his behavior.

Some parents have trouble setting limits. I know I often did. This difficulty may stem from fear that our children will be angry at us for saying no. Or it may come from our childhood, because our parents set too-stringent limits on us or none at all. Setting limits on a very persistent child is particularly hard, especially when you're tired. And sometimes, in the midst of a battle, it's difficult to believe that your child will welcome limits or gain competence from them.

To make setting limits easier, here's a tip from child psychologist Haim Ginott.[3] Ginott suggested avoiding harshness and power struggles by couching limits in the third-person. Rather than "I [first-person] told you [second-person] not to jump on the couch!" Ginott recommended, "Couches are not for jumping on." It's a clumsy way to talk—it sounds as though you're making a royal proclamation or translating from the Latin—but getting out of the "I" versus "you" format lessens your child's feeling that you are controlling him. It prevents him from feeling that you're all-powerful and he's powerless, posing the situation more as a natural law of the universe. It's a strategy for no screaming, no struggle—just the facts, ma'am.

Ginott suggested bringing the tension down still another notch by then acknowledging your child's feelings and, when possible, suggesting an alternative: "I know jumping on the couch is fun. If you want to keep jumping, you can jump around on the leaves in the front yard." (Or, if you don't have a yard, "You can jump on the beanbag in the living room.")

Choice within Limits

A good way to set limits while acknowledging your child's autonomy is to give your child choices within limits. That helps avoid whining and complaining and other annoying symptoms of a power struggle:

"I'm going to sit here on the bench while you play," you might say. "You can play anywhere that I can see you. Do you want to go climb on the monkey bars or dig in the sandbox? Or maybe take your truck over there on the pathway?" Or, "Dad's taking a nap, so you can play whatever game doesn't make too much noise. Putting on the TV might wake him up, but you can bring out your blocks, or play with your cars, or I can read you a story. Which would you like?" Or, "Sure, you and Cecilia can go over to the mini mall. It's too dangerous to ride your bikes on that street, but you can walk, or I'll drive you."

FEEDBACK

In the example I gave at the beginning of the chapter about helping your child stick to the guitar, the structure included this feedback: "You probably don't realize how much you've progressed in the past two weeks, but when I was listening yesterday I heard a big difference. You're really improving!"

Feedback is a crucial component of structure. It contributes directly to children's feelings of competence. And that feeds their intrinsic motivation, since feeling competent encourages us to strive even more. On the other hand, we simply don't do well when we feel incompetent. Compliments like "I liked the way you organized your closet" will go a long way. (This is the sort of informational feedback mentioned in chapter 7.)

In several experiments, psychologist Robert J. Vallerand of the Université of Québec at Montréal showed how well feedback works when he had students balance on a machine called a stabilometer, a game they enjoyed.[4] After they had tried four times, he gave the children either positive feedback (e.g., "It looks like you have a natural ability to balance and it shows in your performance") or negative feedback ("This is an easy task, but your improvement is quite slow. Try to perform as well as you can"). Those who received the positive feedback later had more intrinsic motivation because it made them feel more competent. Negative feedback had the opposite effect.

Negative feedback can help, however, if it doesn't imply incompetence and gives helpful tips. For example, a comment such as "That sounds like a train squeaking on the rails" won't encourage your child to keep practicing her singing. But giving her helpful information along with the negative feedback will: "That doesn't sound quite right—I remember Leticia suggested inhaling quickly and exhaling slowly? Would you want to try that?" Even "It doesn't sound like you're there yet—keep trying, I think you'll get it if you try it a couple more times" works better. Feedback with information for improvement gives your child the hope of reaching competence.

Children often need help in breaking down an assignment or job into manageable chunks. If you then give them feedback whenever they complete a segment, they'll feel empowered.

When Zach took a tough history course and felt discouraged, I helped him go paragraph by paragraph, summarizing the meaning of each one as he went along. At first I gave him feedback for his summaries. "That's right, now you've got it," I said. "Yes, good work!"

Similarly, if your child has to write a report, she might like you to help her break it down into research, outlining, and then writing. Each time she completes a section, give her feedback. That will provide her with feelings of competence that in turn will spur her on to take up the next part. If she has not done a good job, gently point out what she still needs to do. Eventually she'll start breaking her work down into chunks and giving positive feedback to herself.

And breaking it down into doable chunks has given her an important strategy she'll use throughout her life.

SPOKEN AND UNSPOKEN

When I was growing up, my parents never said, "We expect you to go to college." Yet there was no question in my mind that they wanted me to. I knew that they were saving money for my tuition, and they probably made remarks like "When you go to college, you choose a major, and then you take lots of courses in that one subject." Neither of my grandmothers had gone beyond the eighth grade, but both my parents had gone to college, and my mother went back to school for a master's degree when her youngest entered kindergarten. So even though they didn't explicitly state it, I gathered their expectation very easily from their conversation and behavior. When the time came to sign up for college prep courses in high school, I did so automatically. That's how it goes in many families: expectations are implicit. So are many rules and consequences.

"We don't have a rule about when I'm supposed to be home, but if I don't call and say where I'm going after school, I know my parents will be upset and angry," a preteen boy once told me. "If I'd forget to call more than once, I'm sure they'd ground me." Many families make structure explicit only when they need to solve a problem. This is perfectly fine. It may be a sign of harmony in the family. Checking on habits and expectations occasionally might be worthwhile, however. ("You'll call me if you leave Robert's house, right?") Keeping communication open is always a good idea.

DIFFERENT KIDS, DIFFERENT REACTIONS TO STRUCTURE

While teaching a course on motivation, I asked my students to write papers about how they'd experienced structure in their own lives. One student, Sarah, had gone to boarding school. She wrote about the school's long list of rules—dress code, curfew, study hall hours, and compulsory sports.

"I hated these rules!" Sarah wrote. "They felt so controlling!" Later we talked in my office, and I asked her if everyone disliked the rules as much as she had. Her look of surprise told me that she hadn't thought about this possibility.

"Actually," she said after a minute, "my best friend there *liked* the rules."

"Really!" I said.

"She was very social," said Sarah. "She'd say, 'It's fun in the dorms after curfew! We're all together there, and it's really cool.' The structure didn't seem to faze her a bit."

This wasn't the first time I realized that different children experience structure very differently. Some kids like it, but others are more control-sensitive. Your high-strung daughter may do everything she can to ignore rules or break them, while your mellow son slides along smoothly, in harmony with every limit.

A third child may have mixed feelings, chafing at the structure while realizing it's good for him, like a young law student I spoke to recently. When he was in elementary school, Luis said, his mother always had him show her his homework after he'd finished.

"How did that feel to you?" I asked. "Did you resent it?"

"No—I needed it," he answered, with a wry smile. "If she hadn't been there to look at it, I would have been distracted by every little thing that came along. I had to finish my homework before I could play, so this way I got to play."

Since children are so different, it's important to fashion structure to fit your child's personality. For example, if your child bristles at any kind of restraint, it's worth weighing the importance of each rule and expectation. Then pick your battles.

Furthermore, it's doubly important to give a prickly child some say in making the rules—as the mother mentioned earlier did when helping her child stick to the guitar. The same goes for involving him in setting up consequences, as the mom did when her kids wouldn't stop poking and teasing each other in the car. And if your child is sensitive, giving her meaningful rationales for the rules will take off much of the sting.

INTERNALIZATION

When structure boosts your child's feelings of competence, that promotes his intrinsic motivation, but it can also foster its motivational cousin, internalization. Internalization takes place, as I explained in chapter 5, when children adopt their parents' values and goals and behave accordingly. If, when you set up structure, you encourage your child's autonomy by explaining the reasons for the rules and guidelines, he can then adopt that logic as his own.

Of course, those reasons have to add up to your child. "You need to read twenty minutes a day so you'll do well on your SATs," makes less sense to a ten-year-old than "The more you read, the better you'll read, and the more you'll enjoy it." Structure allows your child to take responsibility and do for himself the jobs you'd like him to do—everything from cleaning up his room to doing his math, from taking out the garbage to practicing his trombone. As your child gets older, he'll start doing his homework and chores around the house on his own, thinking to himself, "learning is really important" and "I like it when the kitchen is clean."

The story about Molly at the beginning of this chapter is a good example of internalization. When an accident happened, she pulled out the rule about never riding alone and applied it to the new and potentially scary situation.

Helping your child wake up on time also illustrates how structure leads to internalization. At first you wake up your son in the morning. As he gets older, if you agree on a structure and let him know the reasons for getting up on time, he'll internalize them and start waking himself up. For example, you might explain that school starts at 8:15, which means that he has to leave the house by 7:45.

You might clarify why that's the latest he can leave: "If you leave at 7:45, that means you'll be to school at 8:10, and that will give you five minutes to put your knapsack and your jacket away and get into the classroom on time."

When you set up the structure, you might discuss what time he needs to wake up, whether he'd like you to wake him or whether he'll use an alarm clock, and what the consequences will be if he oversleeps.

DO DANGEROUS NEIGHBORHOODS CALL FOR MORE CONTROL?

Do parents who live on a block with drug dealers on the corner and gangs running the streets have the luxury of encouraging their children's autonomy? In neighborhoods where errant gunshots kill children playing in their front yards, maybe blind obedience to limits and structure saves children's lives. Perhaps parents in dangerous neighborhoods need to throw autonomy out the window and clamp down on their children to protect them.

And what about children in high schools where drinking, drugs, and early sexual experience run rampant? Shouldn't parents protect them, too, with strict control? Isn't that how those "tough love" programs we hear about succeed?

Experts who favor stepping up control to protect children from dangerous environments like to cite a study by psychologists Alfred and Clara Baldwin, who began following a group of children when their mothers were pregnant with them.[5] When the children were ages twelve to fourteen, the Baldwins interviewed their parents about their rules and regulations and the values they held for their children. How *restrictive* were the parents? For example, did their children have to let them know where they were at all times? And how *democratic* were the adults—did they consult their children when they set rules? And did they explain why the rules were important?

Taking the parents' answers, the Baldwins then looked at how their different rules and styles affected their children's competence, as measured by their IQ and school achievement. The more restrictive the parents in the low-income group, they found, the more competent their children. But for the middle-class families, it was completely different. The more restrictive the parents, the *less* competent their kids. So you might reasonably conclude that in dangerous environments, more control is a good idea.

But if you examine the Baldwins' study closely, that's not in fact what it showed. They measured restrictiveness by the number of rules in the home. So having more rules seems important when you live in difficult circumstances. But if you look at the parents' *style*, a different picture emerges. In *both* the middle- and lower-income families, children whose parents developed their rules more democratically and explained their importance had higher IQs and did better in school than the other children. Furthermore, the parents of these more competent children said that they valued their children's sense of responsibility much more than obedience.

In other words, children who live in risky neighborhoods or go to drug-ridden schools need more structure—but they need autonomy just as much as children who live in or go to school in safer environments.

One mother in the Baldwins' study illustrated the need for structure to protect children when she walked her child to school each day and picked her up every afternoon.

"Why can't I walk myself to school and home, like my friends do?" the little girl asked. "Don't you trust me?"

"I trust you," the mother answered, acknowledging the child's autonomy. "It's those weirdos in this neighborhood I don't trust."

That made sense to the little girl.

While structure makes children feel competent, *how* parents set up and enforce those rules and regulations is very important. When there's little room for the children's autonomy, the children are less competent. But when the parents are democratic and respect the child's autonomy, their kids feel much more competent.

That idea extends to schools as well. Unsafe schools need more structure—locked doors, security guards, and rules for the hallways and for leaving school. But students should also have autonomy in the form of input into the rules and their consequences, especially when administrators are trying to solve a particular problem.

No matter where they live or what their circumstances, setting up structure democratically and explaining why it's necessary helps make children mature and responsible. Giving kids input into the rules and a role in solving problems builds their competence. Such qualities are crucial for all children, no matter where they live.

CHAPTER 10

CALMING DOWN
"That All Sounds Very Nice,
But How Can I Use These Techniques
When I'm Feeling So *Anxious?*"

"That all sounds very nice," I can hear you saying, "but it's *so* hard to resist the urge to pressure my child. How can I apply the Three-Part Framework when the competition he faces fills me with anxiety? I always want to solve my child's problems *now!*"

You're right. Parenting is hard. It's easy to give parenting advice, but carrying it out is another matter entirely. As my friend Sylvie e-mailed me recently, "Even if I understand the theory, it is sometimes so difficult to put it in everyday life." When you're really worried, how can you possibly calm down enough to encourage your child's autonomy and set up structure while remaining close and supportive?

Turning your anxiety into positive parenting is so much easier said than done. But you *can* do it. Let's look at the challenges to applying the Three-Part Framework and see how you can overcome them, one by one.

CHALLENGE 1: "IT'S HARD BECAUSE WHEN I'M FEELING
ALL KEYED UP, ALL I WANT TO DO IS SCREAM."

The Pressured Parent Phenomenon has a strong physiological component. As your child opens the acceptance or rejection letter from the performing arts magnet program that he's been dying to get into, your blood pressure rises, your stomach ties up in a knot, and your palms start to sweat. All you can think about is whether he got in, not the best way to deal with it if he didn't.

How can you counter this physiological upheaval and, rather than screaming or crying, turn your anxious energy into wise parenting?

Calming Down Physically

Have you ever noticed your mind chasing itself in circles as you try to solve a problem? The same thoughts cycle and recycle through your mind, like cartoons of Tom endlessly chasing Jerry. Then you give up, take a break, and walk to the kitchen for a cup of coffee—and the solution floats into your mind. While I was writing this book, I often struggled in vain to express an idea, and then, as I drove to the YMCA for a swim, the words I needed popped into my head.

Mind and body work together. Each influences the other. Just as certain thoughts tense up your body, relaxing your body changes those thoughts. That's why physical exercise as well as relaxed breathing, meditation, and other forms of relaxation are crucial to calming down. Both exercise and relaxation soothe the physical effects of the fight-or-flight mechanism. They can short-circuit your cycle of ruminating worry and help you put problems into a realistic perspective. Then you'll be ready to patiently give your child hints and support as he's doing his social studies project—rather than doing it for him.

Similarly, when your child opens that envelope with its admission or rejection, instead of focusing on the fears that emanate from your frantic body, your mind will be free to congratulate him or help him think of a backup strategy. (If, while expecting that letter, you've spent a tranquil moment thinking about how you'll support and encourage him, then you'll *really* be prepared.)

Physical Exercise

How can you create such tranquil moments? When competition hits your hardwiring and produces the human stress response, your muscles tighten and your heart beats wildly. Exercising soothes you because it gives those muscles something to do. It slows your heart rate, so that you start breathing more normally, which will calm you down.

But *how* you exercise is very personal. You have to find an activity that you enjoy. For some people that's yoga, for others it's working out at the gym, jogging, or dancing, and for still others it's pulling up weeds or simply taking a walk around the block.

"It's a matter of getting to know yourself and experimenting a bit," says Christine A. Padesky, a psychologist and cofounder of the Center for Cognitive Therapy in Huntington Beach, California.[1]

Relaxed Breathing

Exercise relaxes you because it makes you breathe more efficiently. When you breathe normally, your chest expands and contracts and the diaphragm moves only a little. But when you exercise, your diaphragm moves up and down several inches, opening up the chest cavity and creating a large space for your lungs to fill with oxygen. You can achieve a similar effect through *relaxed breathing*. While slowly inhaling and exhaling, try concentrating on using the abdominal rather than the chest muscles. This method moves the diaphragm and allows your lungs to exchange oxygen and carbon dioxide most efficiently. "Relaxed breathing" takes practice, but once learned, it can calm you down relatively quickly. It's the polar opposite of breathing during stress, which is led by the chest muscles.[2]

Progressive Muscle Relaxation

Since stress clenches your muscles, learning to relax them is another good path to calming down the anxiety of the Pressured Parent Phenomenon. Originally developed by American physician Edmund Jacobson in the 1920s, muscle relaxation techniques teach you to focus on muscle groups, briefly tense them, and then let them go limp.[3] Once you've mastered this method, you can also use it throughout your day to relax the muscles—perhaps in your jaw or back or neck—that may have tightened in response to stress. If this kind of relaxation interests you, there are many Web sites, books, CDs, and tapes that will show you how to go about it.

The jam-packed lives that many of us lead can make it hard to carve out time for exercise and relaxation. But if you know you're going to spend time with your child going over homework or listening to her practice for an audition, you might plan to take a brisk walk or use some muscle relaxation techniques beforehand. If you're going to have a conversation about rules and structure, plan it on the day that you manage to get some exercise. Those endorphins work wonders!

CHALLENGE 2: "IT'S HARD BECAUSE I FEEL ALONE. NO ONE ELSE SHARES MY WORRY."

During my research, which included many interviews, I learned an important feature of the Pressured Parent Phenomenon: we parents seldom share our anxious and concerned feelings. They remain private. We may even feel guilty about them, as though only "uptight," overbearing parents have such worries, much less talk about them. Yet they're nearly universal.

So what can you do? Why not try sharing these feelings with a friend? You may be surprised to learn that not only do other parents feel the same way you do, but they also feel exceedingly relieved to talk about their concerns.

Laughing

It helps to laugh with a partner or friend about worrying. My friend Leslie and I have a running joke about the intensity of our angst. Even though we realize that agonizing only makes a situation worse, we joke ironically that it has a preventative function.

"I'm putting in lots of worrying because I know it helps so much!" I tell her. "I'll do some for you too," she answers helpfully, since she's such a good friend.

"Yeah, we really need to write book on *The Power of Negative Thinking,*" she'll add.

Then we both laugh—which is great, because laughter relaxes your body almost as much as exercise.

Whatever Works

Of course, exercise and humor aren't the only ways to relax. Some people meditate or imagine beautiful, peaceful scenes. Others watch television or talk. You might like sitting in the backyard or on the front stoop for awhile, knitting, or taking a nap—whatever calms you down physically. Experiment and see what works for you.

CHALLENGE 3: "IT'S HARD BECAUSE MY MIND JUMPS TO THE WORST POSSIBLE SCENARIO."

Anxiety over our children's welfare is like a supersonic train heading toward imagined catastrophe. Let's say you're worried because your child got a C in seventh-grade history.[4]

Your brain races inexorably toward disaster: "Olivia's not as bright as I thought! She needs to settle down and study or she won't get into AP history in high school. She'll lose her friends—they'll *all* take AP classes. If she doesn't get into AP history in high school she won't get into a good college, and then won't get a good job. She'll marry another C student and they'll have kids who get Cs. They won't earn any money—we'll have to support them!"

You know it's irrational, but you can't help imagining the worst. Since our human stress response tells us that our child's whole future is at stake, we envision catastrophe to fit the ensuing physiology. As Padesky explains, "We take one negative event and then project it out, telling the entire life story of our child."

Sometimes, instead of imagining catastrophe, your worry will seem vague. All you know is that your child's C in history brings you high anxiety. In that case, give yourself time to identify the specific fears provoking it.

Saying Hello and Good-bye to Anxious Thoughts

But say you've walked a fast mile and you still fear catastrophe. And muscle relaxation hasn't brought you to that important calm place where you can start applying the Three-Part Framework. You're still too prone to releasing your tension by screaming at your child.

The next tactic to try is stopping the runaway train. Talking to someone you trust can bring your specific fears to the surface. Maybe that person will tell you, as my husband often says to me, "Don't rush to any conclusions."

By the way, don't bother flagellating yourself with self-criticism such as "I know I'm being ridiculous, blowing it out of proportion." That will only make you feel worse. Remember instead that your reaction is normal and natural, a product of your protective evolutionary hardwiring.

Gather Evidence and Cut Your Worry Down to Size

Next, start looking for evidence that contradicts your conclusions. What could *really* happen to your child? Ask yourself, "What has happened to other kids in similar circumstances?"

Do your best to step back and take another look at that C, shaving it down to size. Maybe your friend's daughter floundered in seventh grade too. But she started to pull her grades up two years later. In tenth grade she joined the debating team and became very interested in US history. She went to a small liberal arts college that she really enjoyed. She did not turn to drugs or drop out of school. She went to law school and now works downtown as a public defender.

You might also try thinking about similar problems you've already worked through. Remember how your heart dropped to the bottom of your stomach when Olivia wasn't reading in first grade? You took her to a tutor, and she caught on right away. What other problems has your daughter had? How did you help her solve them?

Or, remember when your older son Gabe's math grade dropped in ninth grade? After you talked over the problem with him and the two of you made an action plan, he started going to his teacher at lunchtime for help and studied occasionally with a friend who was good in math. His grade went back up.

Maybe Gabe didn't do well in middle school at all but caught fire—as many kids do—at about age sixteen. He began studying seriously in his junior year of high school. He may even have gone to community college, transferred to the state university, and then went to graduate school. We've all seen many such "late bloomers."

What, in fact, is the worst that can happen? you can ask yourself. Will that C in seventh-grade history keep Olivia out of college? (No, only grades starting in ninth grade "count.") Will she lose friends? (No, children don't usually make friends based on grades.) "Okay, the worst that can happen is that Olivia will continue to get Cs in seventh-grade history." Although if you work with her—ferreting out a problem she may have, helping her solve it, stoking her interest by discussing history with her, perhaps getting a tutor—she'll likely improve.

Things Change and Nothing Remains the Same

Sometimes we heighten our anxiety by projecting a problem into the future as though nothing will change between now and then. We label a temporary trait or situation permanent. We underestimate the available help and forget about our ability—and our children's—to cope with problems.

For example, you might worry that a child who has trouble making friends will be lonely and isolated as an adult. This thought negates the possibility that he'll make more friends when he gets older or goes to a school with a different mix of kids. It misses the point that with help, he could develop needed social skills such as making eye contact and small talk or joining in with a group that's playing.

You might even overgeneralize, "He doesn't get along with other kids and he never will."

But things change. A child who's lonely at age twelve may find birds of a feather in the high school chess or drama club. That's what happened to Mark Hoffman.

"In middle school Mark was small and socially awkward," remembers his mother, Marcia, who lives in a suburb of Chicago. "He was very verbal and musical, but not sports-oriented.

"He'd grown up with a group of macho Little League-kinda guys whose fathers played catch with them and whose mothers drove a station wagon and were the team moms. In our family we're technology and theater geeks.

"In ninth grade Mark decided to join the drama program at school. Seniors in the program could write and direct plays, and that spring a senior chose Mark to act in her one-act drama. Thrilled and appreciative, he spent every spare minute rehearsing.

"Next year, the very ambitious drama teacher staged a production of *Nicholas Nickleby*. It was four hours long and all the kids played multiple roles. Mark had four parts. One was really creepy and he really got into it and impressed everybody. He *loved* the drama program. For the first time he made friends at school. He really found his niche."

Build Up Resilience to Cope with Setbacks and Problems

Even though we'd prefer that our children never face any problems, certain positive human qualities—such as compassion and resilience—develop out of hardship. All children inevitably encounter failure and defeats. As they try to cope with them, they develop empathy, flexibility, and other strengths. That's a dynamic that you seldom think about while you're feeling anxious about the competition your child faces. In ancient times, losing out to a predator meant death, but today losing a competition isn't fatal—far from it: overcoming failure can develop indispensable strengths.

"When you're a young therapist," says Padesky, "you feel so deeply for every difficulty people are going through. 'Oh, this is awful!' you think. 'I want to spare them from this!'

"After twenty years you begin to see that good things can come out of tough experiences, and that what you want to do is help people develop strengths from facing them."

That's what happened to Mark, who learned kindness from the way he broke out of his initial isolation. When as a senior he got *his* chance to stage a play, he wrote a piece about an aging former Hollywood star musing on her glory years. He gave the small part of the housekeeper to a freshman with no acting experience.

"I was so grateful to the girl who had given me my first chance, and I remembered how terrific I felt when she told me I had the part," he told his mother. "I wanted to pass that chance on to someone else."

Parents can play a strong role in helping children to build up their resilience by treating disappointments as chances for their children to learn. Thank goodness we have these opportunities to model calmness and putting events into perspective while our kids are still at home! Setbacks also let us show them how to consider alternative pathways and how to make good decisions.

Gaining from Adversity

When Leslie Dennis's daughter Maya was in fifth grade, she had a teacher, Mrs. Tyson, who had never taught before. The teacher didn't seem to have much sense of the curriculum and what the children had already learned. She relied a lot on rote learning and repetition. Meanwhile, the other fifth-grade teachers were doing fabulous projects, including an end-of-the-year play.

"At first that situation really worried me," remembers Leslie. "'If she doesn't learn all she needs to in fifth grade,' I thought, 'how will she keep up in middle school?'"

Maya asked Mrs. Tyson if her class could do a play too.

"Well, I hadn't planned on one, but if you want to work on it, go ahead," the teacher answered.

So that's what Maya did. She wrote a script based on her favorite book, *Stuart Little*, and organized her classmates to perform it.

In addition to organizing the play, Maya decided to raise money for families who had lost their homes to fire in a nearby town. She became the first student in her school to launch a bottle-recycling drive. "It was a great time!" remembers Leslie, who helped Maya by reading drafts of the script and delivering the bottles and cans to a recycling center. "Who would have thought this year that at first seemed so disastrous would lead to such a good experience?" says Leslie. "I was really happy that Maya learned to take initiative. She developed leadership skills too."

As for the academics, Leslie went in and talked to Mrs. Tyson and explained that Maya had already learned much of what they were now working on. The teacher agreed to give Maya some extra work and to find out more about the previous year's curriculum. While that didn't solve every problem, it did prevent Maya from falling behind in middle school.

When your child faces a problem, as Maya did, you may feel angry and helpless. You'll probably worry, as Leslie did. But if you can take the long view and remember what your son—or you, your friends, or relatives—learned from working through other crises, that will free you up to support your child's healthy problem solving. As Maya did, he'll end up strengthening other skills too.

WHEN TO INTERVENE

This is not to say that solving such problems is easy. Children are a tremendous source of fun and joy, but raising them is often very difficult. When your child has a problem, and it's not the kind that works itself out, it's frequently important to intervene and help solve it. You can't be afraid to communicate with your child, her teachers, her coaches, and other adults who know her. Seeking help, finding out what's wrong, and making an action plan to cope with the difficulty pays off in the long run.

One of my favorite tales about parents who did just that is the story of Noah Brenner, a young man who was about to graduate from college when I interviewed him.

Dyslexic and diagnosed with ADHD, Noah scored below average on some of his standardized tests when he was in elementary school. He could add and subtract in his head, but he had trouble with both paper and pencil tasks and with reading.

"I was always anxious about him doing well in school," remembers his mother, Rachel. "It was sort of that in-the-gut, stomach-turning feeling."

A third-grade teacher herself, Rachel sat with Noah while he did his homework. Her husband, Tom, helped when she couldn't. "Noah liked the support," she remembers. "I didn't do the work for him, but I was there if he had a question." Rachel couldn't decipher the spelling words from the scramble Noah had copied down from the blackboard, so she would call another parent for the list. She invented *Jeopardy!* games for his spelling words. And she put a lot of effort into helping him feel good about himself, especially since he earned mediocre grades while most of his friends did very well in school.

"I let him know that I thought he had good ideas, by listening to what he had to say and carrying on a conversation with him about it," says Rachel. "I tried to shore up his weak points like spelling and focused more on his strengths, like the content of his writing." Concerned that Noah would label himself "disabled," Rachel and Tom decided not to ask for accommodations for his learning disability. (Of course, many parents choose otherwise, and that works out well for their children.) Noah went to an educational therapist for a while, but his schoolwork was so demanding he didn't have time to do the exercises she recommended to strengthen his skills.

When Noah was in fourth grade, a new principal started a program for gifted students. One day the principal announced over the public address system, "All students in the gifted program—please report to the library." Noah's friends all got up and left the classroom. He was crushed.

"I'm just as smart as they are," Noah told Rachel that night. "How come I'm not in the gifted program?"

"You can take a test," Rachel said. Sure enough, Noah tested "gifted with learning disabilities" and was assigned to the gifted cluster the following year.

Yet learning remained a struggle. "His idea of a book report was the thinnest book he could find," Rachel sighs.

But she resisted the urge to pressure him.

"It was a relaxed upbringing," Noah remembers, "like 'make sure you've done your homework,' but it was never forced down my throat. They never said, 'You have to do this for us.'" He understood his parents expected him eventually to go to college, but he agreed with that goal.

When Noah began middle school, his mother's angst intensified. "Now it's going to be even worse!" Rachel thought. "His basic math skills were real strong, but his English skills weren't," she remembers. "I was worried." That summer before he began middle school, she and Tom considered putting him on medication for his ADHD, but the doctor said not to do so until school started.

And to their relief, he seemed to do fine that fall, so they never started the medication. He began doing his homework by himself, as best he could.

Nonetheless, in high school, Noah didn't study. "I'd read a paragraph and get a headache," he recalls. "I couldn't really read." One night Rachel read him an entire chapter from his biology textbook. He would pay attention in class, take notes, and go over them before a test. But he always found an excuse to miss multiple-choice history tests, knowing that the makeup exam was an essay, much easier for him. Then, during his senior year in a humanities magnet school—which emphasized critical thinking—lightning struck. Noah became extremely interested in the ideas of the philosopher Richard Rorty, who believes truth doesn't exist independent of the human mind and of the language we use to describe the external world. "What about the Holocaust?" Noah asked. "How do you rectify that, if there is no truth?"

"I got very, very excited," remembers Noah. "It was the first time I was excited going to class." He transferred his enthusiasm to contemporary American history, reading on his own Howard Zinn's *A People's History of the United States: 1492 to Present* and *Guns, Germs, and Steel* by Jared Diamond.

And then came the only time Rachel remembers pressuring Noah about academic responsibilities: when he applied to college. "I was a bit crazed," says Rachel. "It was, 'Would you work on it? Would you *please* turn it in?' I felt like I was pushing and he was pushing back. He'd say, 'It's okay, I can file them at the last minute.'"

Noah had managed to do well enough to be admitted to the University of California. At college he majored in history and political science, using the compensatory skills he had developed in high school. "I can listen to a lecture and remember a lot of things that most people can't," he says. When he had an assignment expected to take a week, he started a week and a half before the deadline. "He just really became a student," says Rachel. Special tinted glasses that stabilized words on the page for him helped too. And for the first time, he signed up for "accommodations" for learning disabled students, receiving time-and-a-half for in-class exams and for his Graduate Record Exam (GRE).

For his senior honors thesis, Noah wrote about private citizens helping to enforce federal wartime legislation during World War I. In the spring of 2007, Noah graduated magna cum laude from the University of California, obtaining his history degree with highest honors.

CALMING DOWN, STEP BY STEP

Psychotherapist Dee Shepherd-Look often helps patients replace their protective anxieties with positive thinking.[5] Here's how she would travel that road with a parent who worries because her child is not in the popular clique in school:

Step 1: Stop the Runaway Train

Identify the danger you fear:

"My child is with the unpopular girls, so she'll be unpopular. Plus, she probably feels alone, abandoned, and unhappy. And she won't do well in life because she won't network with the right people."

Step 2: Turn the Mountain into a Molehill

Evaluate the danger—is it really as bad as you think? Try to separate exaggerated dangers from real ones.

One way to do so: check out what your *child* is feeling. "Wait a minute—she's not lonely or unhappy," you might find out. "She truly likes these kids she hangs out with." Then you remember, "It's true. I hear her giggling with them all the time."

Then see if you have any ideas not supported by evidence: "Are these kids outcasts? Are they misfits? No—they get good grades. They're into music. They're just not in the top social rung. These are really good kids, nice kids."

Perhaps look inside yourself:

"I'm not *her*. I'm putting my childhood experience onto her. *I* was the lonely, unhappy one. *I* was the one who felt bad because my parents couldn't afford expensive clothes."

Step 3: Look for the Silver Lining

Shepherd-Look advises parents to change "negative trigger thoughts" into "positive opposing thoughts," such as:

"My kid doesn't have the pressure these popular, preppy kids have. I don't have to worry or fight with her about how much money I can spend on her clothes. She's not superficial."

"The kids she hangs out with are loyal to each other. They don't torture anyone with cliquishness."

Step 4: Things Change and Nothing Remains the Same

"Just because she is in one crowd in seventh grade doesn't mean she won't make different friends later on. Now that I think about it, *I* made new friends in ninth grade. Her friends may seem nerdy at this age, but these are the kids who will be interesting when they're older, who likely will achieve academically and in life."

Step 5: Concentrate on Long-Term Goals

Long-term goals: "What do I really want for my daughter? I want her to have friends and to enjoy them, to be friendly and kind. Is there any way I can help her acquire these skills?"

CHALLENGE 4: "TOO OFTEN I GET CAUGHT UP IN WORRYING ABOUT LITTLE COMPETITIONS MY CHILD FACES AND I CAN'T MOVE ON."

Life is full of small competitions our children face daily: the spelling test, the team tryout, the recital, or the audition. It's natural to focus on them because they're right there confronting us. Research shows, however, that focusing excessively on short-term goals makes us feel pressured and anxious. One way to pull yourself out of anxiety is to think about your long-term goals for your child. So you might want to ask your parents or friends with adult children what mattered the most in their children's lives as they grew up. What experiences helped their kids learn and mature into healthy, happy adults? It's highly unlikely that they'll say, "Oh, if only Lily had won that tennis championship, or earned an A in pre-algebra, or snagged the lead in *Bye Bye Birdie*, she'd be so much happier now!" Their perspective will help calm you down, as you realize that what counts for your child aren't the grades and test scores he compiles in elementary or middle school as much as the skills he's acquiring and the way he's learning to take responsibility.

SHORT-TERM GOALS POUR ON PRESSURE; LONG-TERM GOALS LET YOU RELAX

Psychologists George Manderlink, then of Columbia University, and Judith Harackiewicz, of the University of Wisconsin, investigated how short-term goals make people feel pressured.[6] They gave word games they knew were interesting and enjoyable to a group of college students. The goal of the games was to make as many words as possible from a matrix of letters arranged four-by-four, using contiguous letters only. Each student would do eleven such puzzles.

The researchers gave some of the students *a short-term goal for each puzzle*, right before they began to work on it. Then they gave other students *a long-term goal for all eleven puzzles combined*. The puzzles were easy enough for most of the participants to meet their goals.

After the students had finished the eleven puzzles, Manderlink and Harackiewicz measured their intrinsic motivation—how much they had enjoyed the games. Those in the long-term group, they found, had enjoyed themselves much more than those in the short-term group. Focusing on short-term goals, the researchers found, damages intrinsic motivation because it makes people feel pressured and controlled.

Not only will focusing on your long-term goals for your child relieve the pressure you feel, but, once you step back and think about it, you'll also realize that they matter more to you than today's standardized test or tomorrow's basketball game. You probably want your child to learn to:

- work hard;
- take responsibility;
- build her self-confidence;
- advance her intellectual interests; and
- gain the academic, athletic, artistic, and social skills she needs to succeed in life.

You probably also want her to get along well with others and to be happy. You may want her to develop her creativity and talents. Perhaps you'd like her to strengthen her religious faith, her sense of ethics, or her desire to make contributions to the world. Those are some of the long-term goals that may lie behind your short-term concerns of where your daughter goes to preschool and whether she's first or sixth flute in the school orchestra.

If you focus on your child's academic skill development, for example, that will help you concentrate on her progress in learning. When she brings home a test, the two of you can use the mistakes she's made as signals telling her what she needs to learn next. This will divert both of you from worrying about those mistakes.

Concentrating on long-term goals as much as you can will help you "move on" from the little worries of today. It will give you the mind-set that you need for the Three-Part Framework, which will in turn promote those long-term goals.

Take the example of fostering your child's moral development. How do kids build character? Researchers have come up with answers that may surprise you. Psychologist Lawrence J. Walker of the University of British Columbia looked at this question by first assessing the moral reasoning of eighty children in grades one, four, seven, and ten, using a measure of moral reasoning that places children in one of several successive stages of moral development.[7] Next he videotaped them and their parents discussing both a hypothetical moral dilemma and one that the child had faced in real life, usually involving friendships, theft, fighting, or cheating. Finally, he analyzed the family's discussions.

Walker found that parents had different ways of talking with their children. Some discussed the issue in a "questioning and clarifying" style, eliciting the child's opinion, asking clarifying questions, and paraphrasing the child's answers. Then the parents checked the child's understanding by asking further questions.

Other parents, however, tended to lecture—challenging the child's logic, criticizing her opinions, and presenting their own views.

Two years later, Walker again measured the children's moral reasoning. Those whose parents had used the "questioning and clarifying" style had advanced further in their moral reasoning than the other children. That method, of course, nurtures children's autonomy because it encourages them to express their opinions. And parents' questioning and paraphrasing helped them understand their child's point of view.

A Story about Developing Moral Values

When Cynthia Notley's son, Kevin, was a junior in high school, he ran for class president. Since he'd always been a comedian, he gave a funny speech and did very well in the first ballot. When it came time for the runoff, however, Kevin started thinking hard about his own motives. Did he really want to carry out the duties of class president, including planning the prom and senior day? No, he just wanted to continue entertaining his class, which he could do in plays and talent shows. "Class president" would have looked nice on his transcript, and may have boosted his ego, but deep down he knew the responsibilities didn't interest him and that he wouldn't serve the class well in that post.

Cynthia had to struggle with herself. "Wow, I'd never thought of him as class officer material!" she told me, delight swelling in her voice. She remembered how much she'd respected and even envied class officers in her own high school. "They were always smart and popular," she remembered, "and usually good athletes too. Wouldn't it be terrific if Kevin were class president?" she remembers thinking.

But Cynthia managed to keep this ego-involvement at bay when she and Kevin weighed the decision. "I mostly listened and said 'yes' to his reasoning," she recalls. "I validated his good ideas with 'That sounds right' or 'Yes, I see what you mean.'" I asked him one or two questions.

Kevin also talked to a teacher he was close to. Finally he decided to drop out of the race. That way he could feel true to himself and maintain his integrity. Kevin's principal praised him for making a mature choice. Cynthia felt happy that he had thought it through so responsibly.

"In the long run that was the right thing to do," she now says, looking back. Kevin went on to major in theater in college and now lives in New York, working for an Internet company during the day and acting at night.

One of the most important parenting jobs we do is helping children sift through the dilemmas of daily life to make decisions that reflect our family's values, as Cynthia did in this case, with the help of Kevin's teacher. By focusing on Kevin's developing responsibility, Cynthia avoided the anxiety of worrying about the short-term gain of Kevin's winning an election for a post that didn't fit his goals and personality. By exploring his point of view, she helped him make a sound decision.

Focusing, as Cynthia did, on a long-term goal for your child will help you find your way through the minefield of competition in his life.

Long-Term Goals and Sports: Helping Your Child Build Skills, Honor the Game, and Learn Life Lessons

When your child plays sports, you can stay calm by focusing on helping her build skills, honor the game, and learn life lessons.[8] Thinking about these three long-term goals will help you put winning and losing in the background. Your child's healthy psychological growth and the formation of her character are far more important.

Honor the Game

You may remember when a *Sports Illustrated* reporter in 2001 unearthed the birth certificate of a star Little League pitcher from the Bronx and found out that the "12-year-old star" was really a 14-year-old ringer. Talking about such incidents with your child encourages her to respect both the letter and the spirit of the sport.

Unfortunately, you'll have plenty of real-time chances to discuss such rule bending, especially if your child is male. A survey of 5,275 high school athletes conducted in 2005 and 2006 by the Josephson Institute of Ethics, a nonprofit institute in Los Angeles, found that 43 percent of boys and 22 percent of girls thought it was fine for a coach to teach basketball players how to illegally hold and push. Forty-one percent of the boys and one-fourth of the girls saw nothing wrong with using a stolen playbook sent by an anonymous supporter before a big game. Thirty-seven percent of the boys and 20 percent of girls thought it proper for a coach to instruct a football player how to fake an injury.[9]

Besides criticizing these kinds of cheating, you can also model honoring the game by cheering good plays and effort by both teams and supporting the referee even when you disagree with his call. Jim Thompson, executive director of the Positive Coaching Alliance, also suggests mentioning it to other parents when the officials make good calls.[10] That helps create a culture of respect for the game and for the referees—who often do a difficult job for little or no pay.

Building Skills

Focusing on your child's skill building will also help calm your anxiety by taking the spotlight off winning and losing. She can't go back and replay a game she's lost, but she can always improve by practicing her athletic skills. You can support that effort by asking her questions such as:

- "What did you learn from the game?"
- "What worked well?"
- "What would you like to work on before the next game?"

After a game, you can also give your child specific, truthful praise for practicing new skills, such as:

- "That was a nice screen you set up for Emily's three-point shot."

And for working hard:

- "You really put out good effort."
- "As long as you try hard, that's what counts."

Teaching Life Lessons

Sports provide a great way for children to learn about improving through consistent work, valuing dedication and persistence, and bouncing back from mistakes.

"Parents shouldn't give advice on the three-step drop for quarterbacks, but focus on what lessons you take away from the sport that will help you be successful later in life," says Thompson. The Positive Coaching Alliance recommends that adults stress the "ELM tree method: Effort, Learning, and Mistakes are OK."[11]

Many sports give players repeated opportunities, often seconds apart, to fix a mistake. So when your son's shot clanks off the rim, you can shorten your cringing time by remembering that "things change and nothing remains the same." Will he go up for the rebound? Shoot a follow-up? When he misses a kick in soccer, watch to see if he goes after it to try again.

Team sports also provide a chance for your child to learn the value of cooperation. Focusing on helping her learn about teamwork can push into the background worries about her innate "athletic ability" and whether she can win one of the very few athletic scholarships to college.

CHALLENGE 5: "IT'S HARD TO REMAIN CALM BECAUSE THERE ARE SO MANY STUDENTS APPLYING TO THE TOP COLLEGES."

How high are the stakes, really—does going to a top-tier college make a big difference in a child's life?

Perhaps looking at one young woman's journey will help minimize your worrying.

Erin's Story

Erin Wexler of San Francisco really, really wanted to go to Wesleyan University. An accomplished dancer who edited her school's literary magazine and presided over the ecology club, Erin was deferred for early admission by the Middletown, Connecticut, school in December of her senior year. Wesleyan—which once branded itself the "Independent Ivy"—said it would probably accept her if she raised her SAT scores, although she had no time to take a prep course before the next test.

Her parents canceled a holiday trip to visit her grandparents in Oregon so Erin could fill out applications to other schools. She signed up for AP Statistics second semester because Wesleyan had said she was weak in math.

"I went to my school's college counselor and said, 'Please, please push for me at Wesleyan,'" remembers Erin. "I wanted it so badly. I had such high hopes."

In April, Erin was rejected by Wesleyan, Princeton, the University of Chicago, and Tufts, and she was waitlisted at Brown (where her father had wanted her to go). She was accepted by Reed, Hampshire, and Bard. Brown finally rejected her in June. Meanwhile, her friends were getting into Penn, Duke, and Yale.

"I cried a lot," remembers Wexler. "In May every day I was crying and saying 'Bard or Reed—I don't like either of them. I can't tell the difference. What am I going to do with my life?'"

Her parents and teachers did all they could to make Erin feel better. One day her mother came into her room with a dictionary and said—pointing to the definition of the word *bard*—"I know you didn't get to go where you wanted, but look, *bard* means, it's like, Shakespeare!" she said, and the two of them fell on Erin's bed laughing.

"I really appreciated that," remembers Erin.

Erin had toured Bard during reading week when the campus was dead. But she chose it anyway so she could stay on the East Coast with most of her friends.

"I ended up at my 'safety' school," she says.

Although Bard has since become "trendy" and exceedingly hard to get into, no one Erin knew in San Francisco had ever heard of it. Over and over again, she had to explain that she was going to go to "a small liberal arts school in upstate New York."

As she began her freshman year at Bard, Erin labored under a cloud of bitterness and rejection, as though she'd failed at something monumental in her life, as though the Wesleyan admissions committee had found some fundamental flaw in her intellect or personality. "I felt like they had stamped 'REJECTED' on my forehead," she remembers.

But by the middle of the first semester, Erin realized Bard was growing on her. By May she realized that she loved it. "I have such phenomenal professors," she said when I spoke to her then. "The one-on-one attention has accelerated my growth in writing and analytical skills. Now I think if I hadn't gone here, I never would've met this person, taken this class. I have friends who've dropped out of more prestigious schools. If I'd have gone to one of the big schools I applied to, I'd be in lecture classes even senior year. The biggest class I've ever had at Bard is seventeen, and my smallest class was four. It's amazing here. I'm very happy."

"Where you end up is where you're supposed to end up," she advises high school students. "Don't worry about fancy name schools. The name doesn't matter.

"Kids have to understand that they will be happy as long as they find the right place for them. It's the place you're at, the environment and education, not the name on the diploma."

CHALLENGE 6: "IT'S HARD BECAUSE PEOPLE AROUND ME KEEP FANNING THE FLAMES."

One day after school your child plays at his friend's house. When you go to pick her up, the friend's mother pelts you with anxious questions: "What is Jessie doing over spring break?" "Does she have a tutor?" "What is she doing this summer?"

"Oh, my gosh," you think, panic-stricken. "I haven't even planned what we're having for dinner, let alone what Jessie is doing this summer."

You can't miss the obsessive chatter of other parents who are even more concerned than you are about a child's ability to make it in our increasingly competitive world. If you don't hear it from the parents of your children's friends, you'll catch it on the sidelines of a softball game from a frenetic father discussing his daughter's SAT tutoring before launching into a description of parents' weekend at the world-renowned Ivy institution that his older child is attending.

Such competitive anxiety makes you feel as though your child is threatened, that you aren't doing all you should, and that if you don't take steps right away, your child might have to settle for the local Typewriter Repair Training Institute. In reality, another parent's frenzied worldview means nothing for your daughter—but his anxiety-tinged, competitive tone of voice is catching.

Mirror Neurons

It's not weak-mindedness or lack of self-esteem on your part that lets other parents spiral your mind into worry. Anxiety is highly contagious. In fact, all feelings are contagious. Have you ever known someone who made you feel cheerful whenever you talked to him or her? Cheerfulness and anxiety are both "catching," many neuroscientists believe, because of a recently discovered class of brain cells that fire when we see others taking action or feeling an emotion. These "mirror neurons" are found in certain areas of the brain, including the premotor cortex, the posterior parietal lobe, the superior temporal sulcus, and the insula.[12]

Mirror neurons swing into action when, for example, you see a tennis player hit a ball. They simulate that action in your brain, even though you're not actually moving. The same cells activated in the tennis player's brain stir in yours. That copy in your brain of that other person's action makes you understand what they're doing. Likewise, when you see sadness in another person's face, you, too, may feel sad.

Scientists believe that evolution has selected for these "mirror neurons" because understanding the actions, intentions, and feelings of others helped our ancestors survive. They also help human babies learn by imitating other people. That's why even newborns sometimes will stick out their tongues in response to an adult doing the same to them.[13] But when it comes to the Pressured Parent Phenomenon, it's important to remember that the anxiety your mirror neurons "catch" from another parent is rooted in that person's fears, rather than in a real danger to your child.

Fending Off Contagion

Here are some other suggestions for mentally washing your hands after contact with anxiety in others:

- Take a deep breath and let it out slowly, counting. If you're on the sidelines of a game, take a brisk walk around the field.
- Employ empathy. Remember that a frantic father's need to feel "one up" comes from his own fear and possibly also from his low self-esteem. So, employ empathy: "All this college preparation is anxiety-provoking, don't you think?" you might say, or at least think.
- Vent to a sympathetic partner or friend. "This guy's driving me crazy!"
- Think about the dictatorial approach you'd have to use to get your child to do everything the other child is doing and how that would harm your child and your relationship with him.
- Turn the anxiety aroused by other parents' frenzy into positive energy. For example, decide that you're going to read the same book your daughter is reading for the enjoyment of talking to her about it.
- If all else fails, imagine the way the frantic acquaintance controls his or her child. Consider inviting the child over for a relaxing Saturday afternoon of playing cards or baking chocolate chip cookies.
- You can also simply stay away from parents who are very anxious. That's what my friend Sheila did when her daughter Katie was applying for a middle school magnet program.

"I know people who talked constantly about the magnet school application to everyone they knew," Sheila explains. "That was something I really tried to avoid, because every time I had a conversation like that, it raised my anxiety level."

Keeping Up with the Joneses

You might also want to remember that what meets one family's needs may not work for yours. Just as some families buy different kinds of cereals or cars, they may also give different kinds of support to their children. Your family's style is unique. Your neighbor's child may do very well with a tutor in the afternoon while yours thrives writing comic books or climbing trees in the backyard. One child can love sleep-away computer camp, and another can be perfectly happy spending the summer at home reading, babysitting, and playing with friends.

CHALLENGE 7: "IT'S HARD BECAUSE MY CHILD'S WORRY IS CONTAGIOUS."

Children catch competitive anxieties at the school lunch table and bring them home. At the same time as he picks up a valuable study tip from his friends or hears about a terrific science teacher whom he may get in middle school, your son may also pick up another child's competitive anxiety. There's a thin but important line between peers encouraging his desire to go to college and peers who start him worrying in fifth grade about getting into an Ivy League school.

ACT AS AN ANTIDOTE TO YOUR CHILD'S ANXIETY

To avoid ramping up the Pressured Parent Phenomenon, you can provide your child with a soothing antidote. When Leslie Dennis's daughter Maya was eleven, she started worrying about what college she was going to get into. Leslie said, "You don't have to worry about that. You can always go to the nearby state university. All you need to think about now is learning.

"When the time comes, you'll have plenty of good colleges to choose from," she told Maya.

As your child gets older, it may feel like swimming upstream to stop him from piling up an impossibly heavy schedule of AP classes or juggling too many activities—music, sports, community service, clubs, and internships—in the race for admission to a top college. If he's cheerful and enjoys what he's doing, fine. But if he's frenetic and grumpy, you can calm him down by stating your opinions clearly:

- "Colleges want you to take a challenging program, but they're not going to reject you for taking two AP courses rather than three."
- "There are lots of good schools out there. There are plenty of places where you'll fit in, have a good time, and learn a lot."
- "What counts is that you work hard and figure out what you're interested in."
- "Working intensely on three subjects is better than learning superficially about five."

One of the most important antidotes parents can give their children is to de-link their self-esteem from admission to a "top" college. You can explain to your child as often as necessary that, even if it looks merit-based, the system in fact is not fair. Many factors other than merit enter into admission and rejection decisions. Thousands of kids who have worked hard and done very well are rejected by schools where they would succeed. Sometimes kids whose parents went to a certain school receive preference as so-called legacy admissions. The system increasingly resembles a lottery in which playing by the rules no longer guarantees a student will win the game.

"You have to understand—they're not rejecting *you*," says Erin Wexler, who, as you saw a few pages back, ended up loving her "safety" school. "There are so many people applying. For a long time I thought, 'They didn't like me.' That's not it at all. It really is a total crapshoot.... Although it helps if your grandfather is on the board of trustees.... You can't take it personally. I did and that screwed me up for a long time."

CHALLENGE 8: "IT'S HARD BECAUSE WHEN I *DON'T* PRESSURE MY CHILD, I CAN'T SEE RESULTS RIGHT AWAY. IT'S AS IF I HAVE TO HAVE FAITH THAT HE'LL SUCCEED."

When intense competition is making you anxious, and you want to do something NOW, it can be hard to have faith in your child's potential to develop her own motivation, which may still be emerging. It's difficult to turn responsibility over to your child, especially with the mass media bombarding us with controlling suggestions such as paying kids to study or practice. It's so much easier simply to *tell* your child what to do. I know what it's like to feel impatient and slip into pressuring your kids—remember how I put up a star chart for Allie's toilet training and considered timing her swimming with a stopwatch, even though both actions went against everything I knew about the value of intrinsic motivation? I didn't know for sure that she would work on her swimming without my pushing her. She did—but it took a year before I could say, "Yes, that was the right thing to do. That worked out well." As Noah Brenner's mom said to me, "As a parent I don't think you're ever one hundred percent sure you're doing the right thing." Sometimes we have to patiently wait for results and just try to enjoy the journey.

The research I've presented, however, gives us good reason to expect a happy outcome. I've certainly found with my own children that encouraging their autonomy while providing structure and support has allowed their inner passions to flourish.

Taking Positive Action to Solve Problems: Using the Three-Part Framework

So whenever you feel the Pressured Parent Phenomenon coming on—whenever your heart starts to race, your muscles tense up, and you're edgy with anxiety—whenever you feel as though your child's life is at stake over a grade or a test or admission, over making a sports team, or winning a role in a drama production, or snaring the first violin chair in the orchestra—whenever panic tempts you to pressure and control your child, remember the Three-Part Framework. Stepping up your involvement and setting up a structure with your child while at the same time encouraging her autonomy may not be easy at first. But the more you do it, the easier it will become, and the better you'll feel about it.

As you get used to encouraging your child's autonomy and staying close without intruding, you'll get the hang of it. After you talk with him a few times about rules and guidelines and discuss why they are important, you'll see it all come together. The Three-Part Framework will keep you close to your child as he grows increasingly competent, responsible, and intrinsically motivated. And the Pressured Parent Phenomenon will soon fade away, leaving in its wake a calm parent and a happy, successful child.

A FAMILY SUCCESS STORY

Steve Burrows played the private school admissions game to the hilt.

"I read all the books about it. I signed Mark up for the Secondary School Aptitude Test (SSAT) prep course, and I pushed him to take up trombone and soccer," the father remembers. "This kid was going to Choate or Greenwich Country Day School, and there was no question about it."

Mark got all As in fourth and fifth grades and scored in the ninety-ninth percentile on his standardized tests. He played in the school orchestra and was a top scorer on his club soccer team. Beginning in his fifth grade year, the Burrows took him to visit and interview at six private schools.

That spring, Mark was suspended for three days for throwing a pen at a teacher.

"I was devastated," recalls his father. Eventually the principal agreed to write a letter for Mark's applications saying that he was an exemplary student who'd had no other discipline problems.

Mark was turned down at four schools and waitlisted at two. Had it not been for the suspension, one admissions counselor told his parents, Mark would have been admitted.

"I was devastated because this was my superstar kid, and I was living vicariously through him," remembers Burrows. "I was so wrapped up in it!"

Mark went to the local public middle school. He loved it. He made great friends, served as president of the student council, and in high school fell in love with a special science research course. Now at college, he is majoring in neurobiology. "This story has a happy ending," chuckles his father.

"The lesson I learned is that it's not worth the craziness. The bottom line for me is—it doesn't make any difference where they go because ultimately it's the kid who's going to determine what he or she does and how successful he or she is.

"As I look back on it I didn't think so at the time, but when Mark got suspended it was very fortuitous, because I don't think he would've been so happy at private school."

Not surprisingly, Burrows and his wife Joan decided to treat their younger son's school career differently. Always a very serious student, when he was in eighth grade Jed heard from a soccer friend that one of the local private schools taught courses in Japanese language and culture. He begged his parents to send him there. They helped him apply, and he was accepted. With Mark in college, the Burrows were able to get a scholarship for Jed. He's now thriving in the private school.

"I've come full circle," says Burrows. "We acted in the exact opposite way with Jed than we had with Mark. We really wanted him to get into private school because that's what he wanted. We followed his lead."

ENDNOTES

WENDY'S PREFACE

1. Eleanor J. Gibson and Richard D. Walk, "The 'Visual Cliff,'" *Scientific American* 202 (1960): 64–71.

2. Arlene Walker-Andrews and Wendy S. Grolnick, "Discrimination of Vocal Expressions by Young Infants," *Infant Behavior and Development* 61 (1983): 491–98.

3. James F. Sorce, Robert M. Emde, Joseph J. Campos, and Mary D. Klinnert, "Maternal Emotional Signaling: Its Effects on the Visual Cliff Behavior of One-Year-Olds," *Developmental Psychology* 21 (1985): 195–200.

4. Edward L. Deci, "Effects of Externally Mediated Rewards in Intrinsic Motivation," *Journal of Personality and Social Psychology* 18 (1971): 105–15.

5. Wendy S. Grolnick, Ann Frodi, and Lisa J. Bridges, "Maternal Control Style and the Mastery Motivation of One-Year Olds," *Infant Mental Health Journal* 5 (1985): 15–23.

6. Alice Miller, *Prisoners of Childhood: The Drama of the Gifted Child and the Search for the True Self* (New York: Basic Books, 1981).

CHAPTER I

1. Rick Wolff, *Good Sports* (Champaign, IL: Sports Publishing, 1997), p. 19. In this excellent book, Wolff warns parents not to live through their children. ("Rule 6: This

Is Your Kid's Life—Not Yours! Sorry to have to say this, but . . . you have to face up to the stark reality that your childhood is over and that you really don't want to live it again through your kids.")

2. Margaret Talbot, "A Stepford for Our Times," *Atlantic Monthly*, December 2003, http://www.theatlantic.com/doc/200312/talbot (accessed May 10, 2007).

3. Judith Warner, "The Nation: Kids Gone Wild," *New York Times*, November 27, 2005. Warner quotes Dan Kindlon, a Harvard University child psychologist and author of *Too Much of a Good Thing: Raising Children of Character in an Indulgent Age.* "'We use kids like Prozac,' he said. 'People don't necessarily feel great about their spouse or their job but the kids are the bright spot in their day. They don't want to muck up that one moment by getting yelled at. They don't want to hurt. They don't want to feel bad. They want to get satisfaction from their kids. They're so precious to us—maybe more than to any generation previously. What gets thrown out the window is limits. It's a lot easier to pick their towel up off the floor than to get them away from the PlayStation to do it.'"

4. Robert J. Samuelson, "Prestige Panic: Too Many Parents Are Pushing Kids to Get an Elite Degree Even Though It's No Guarantee of Success in Later Life," *Newsweek*, August 21–28, 2006, http://www.msnbc.msn.com/id/14325089/site/newsweek/ (accessed April 27, 2007).

5. Cristina Nehring, review of "Mating in Captivity: Reconciling the Erotic and the Domestic," by Esther Perel. "Of Sex and Marriage," *Atlantic Monthly*, December 2006, http://www.theatlantic.com/doc/200612/nehring-sex (accessed May 10, 2007).

6. Alice Miller, *Prisoners of Childhood: The Drama of the Gifted Child and the Search for the True Self* (New York: Basic Books, 1981).

7. Salvador Minuchin, *Families and Family Therapy* (Oxford, England: Harvard University Press, 1974).

8. Three incidents of parental rage turning violent: one father kills another over youth ice hockey incident, http://archives.cnn.com/2002/LAW/01/25/hockey.death .verdict/index.html (accessed May 16, 2007); one father drugged son's tennis opponents, http://www.timesonline.co.uk/tol/sport/football/european_football/article 739174.ece (accessed May 16, 2007); Wanda Holloway attempts to murder daughter's cheerleading rival, http://www.texnews.com/texas97/mom030197.html (accessed May 16, 2007).

9. Redshirting is defined as "to keep (a college or school athlete) out of varsity competition for one year in order to extend the athlete's period of eligibility. [From the red jerseys worn by such athletes to distinguish them from the regular players]." Dictionary.com, the *American Heritage Dictionary of the English Language*, 4th ed. (Houghton Mifflin Company, 2004), http://dictionary.reference.com/browse/redshirting (accessed May 10, 2007). In some school districts, as many as half the kids start kinder-

garten a year late, and several studies have estimated the national number of red shirts at 6 to 9 percent.

CHAPTER 2

1. Chuck Darrah, interview by Kathy Seal, September 6, 2006.

2. US Census Bureau, "Historical Income Tables-Families," http://www .census.gov/hhes/www/income/histinc/f09ar.html (accessed April 29, 2007).

3. The number of high school graduates in 2002 whose parents made more than $100,000 was 383,101. The projected number of high school graduates in 2007 whose parents would make more than $100,000 was 430,010. "Knocking at the College Door: Projections of High School Graduates by State, Income, and Race/Ethnicity, 1988–2018," Western Interstate Commission for Higher Education (Boulder, CO: WICHE Publications, December 2003), p. 147.

4. Among families with children, the average number of children (under age eighteen) per family decreased from 2.4 in 1965 to 1.9 in 2005, according to US Census data. See http://www.census.gov/population/socdemo/hh-fam/fm3.xls (accessed April 28, 2007).

5. Annette Lareau, *Unequal Childhoods: Class, Race, and Family Life* (Berkeley: University of California Press, 2003), pp. 1–13.

6. Sam Dillon, "A Great Year for Ivy League Colleges, But Not So Good for Applicants to Them," *New York Times*, April 4, 2007. Also, Stuart Silverstein, "Seniors Hedge College Bets, but Now It's Time to Choose," *Los Angeles Times*, April 24, 2005.

7. A study of two hundred multinational corporations for the Ewing Marion Kauffman Foundation by Marie Thursby, PhD, professor of strategic management, Georgia Tech College of Management, and Jerry Thursby, chair of the department of economics, Emory University, found that 38 percent of two hundred multinational corporations surveyed in 2005 said they would do more of their research and development work abroad. See http://www.kauffman.org/pdf/thursby_final_1206.pdf (accessed April 19, 2007). See also Steve Lohr, "Outsourcing Is Climbing Skills Ladder," *New York Times*, February 16, 2006.

8. Peter C. Whybrow, *American Mania* (New York: W. W. Norton and Co., 2005), p. 43.

9. Deborah Stipek, *Motivation to Learn: From Theory to Practice*, 3rd ed. (Needham Heights, MA: Allyn and Bacon, 1998), p. 84.

10. http://www.kumon.com/juniorkumon/default.asp (accessed April 29, 2007); Carla Rivera, "Tutors Prepare Them—for Preschool and Kindergarten," *Los Angeles Times*, September 24, 2006.

11. Stipek, *Motivation to Learn,* p. 82.

12. John Nicholls and Arlen Miller, "Reasoning about the Ability of Self and Others: A Developmental Study," *Child Development* 55 (1984): 1990–99.

13. Diane Ruble, Ann Boggiano, Nina S. Feldman, and Judith H. Loebl, "Developmental Analysis of the Role of Social Comparison in Self-evaluation," *Developmental Psychology* 16, no. 2 (March 1980): 105–15.

14. Alfie Kohn, *The Case against Competition* (New York: Houghton Mifflin, 1992), pp. 25–26.

15. SEC filing on the Internet at http://www.sec.gov/litigation/complaints/comp18111b.htm (accessed April 29, 2007). See also http://www.pbs.org/wgbh/pages/frontline/shows/wallstreet/wcom/92memo.html: "In the course of New York State Attorney General Eliot Spitzer's investigation into Salomon Smith Barney and Citigroup, Citigroup CEO Sandy Weill admitted to having asked Salomon Smith Barney telecom analyst Jack Grubman to take another look at his 'neutral' rating on AT&T stock. Grubman sent Weill the memo below in November 1999, shortly before he upgraded his recommendation on AT&T's stock from 'neutral' to 'buy.' In the memo, Grubman reports back on a 'good' meeting with AT&T CEO Michael Armstrong. He then switches gears and asks for Weill's help in gaining admission for his children into the exclusive 92nd Street Y preschool. Grubman's children were later admitted and Citigroup gave a $1 million donation to the school. In an e-mail to a social friend in January 2002, Grubman wrote: 'You know everyone thinks I upgraded [AT&T] to get lead for [AT&T Wireless]. Nope. I used Sandy to get my kids in 92nd St Y pre-school (which is harder than Harvard) and Sandy needed Armstrong's vote on our board to nuke Reed in showdown. Once the coast was clear for both of us (i.e. Sandy clear victor and my kids confirmed) I went back to my normal negative self on [AT&T]. Armstrong never knew that we both (Sandy and I) played him like a fiddle.' However, both Weill and Grubman deny that there was a quid pro quo or that Grubman changed the rating to obtain banking business for Salomon in AT&T's spinoff of its wireless division or to help Weill in his boardroom battles with then Citigroup co-CEO John Reed. Grubman disavowed the e-mail after it was leaked to the press, and said that he had been showing off to impress a friend. In his investigation, New York State Attorney General Eliot Spitzer declined to press criminal charges against either man."

16. Susan Saulny, "In Baby Boomlet, Preschool Derby Is the Fiercest Yet," *New York Times,* March 3, 2006.

17. David F. Labaree, *How to Succeed in School without Really Learning: The Credentials Race in American Education* (New Haven, CT: Yale University Press, 1997).

18. "U.S. Trends in Team Sports," 2006 ed., survey by the Sporting Goods Manufacturers Association. See http://www.SGMA.com. Also, Mike May, SGMA, interview by Kathy Seal, October 4, 2006.

19. Jon C. Hellstedt, Daniel S. Rooks, David G. Watson, and Virginia M. Kimball, *On the Sidelines: Decisions, Skills, and Training in Youth Sports* (Amherst, MA: Human Resource Development, 1988).

20. Rick Wolff hosts a radio talk show called "The Sports Edge" on WFAN out of New York on Sunday mornings from 8 to 9 a.m. See http://www.wfan.com/pages/119362.php?contentType=4andcontentId=234694 (accessed April 29, 2007).

21. Rick Wolff, *Good Sports* (Champaign, IL: Sports Publishing, 1997), p. 12.

22. R. Martens, *Joy and Sadness in Children's Sports* (Champaign, IL: Human Kinetics Publishers, 1978), p. 184. Cited in Wolff, *Good Sports*, p. 11.

23. Terry Orlick, *Winning through Cooperation: Competitive Insanity, Cooperative Alternatives* (Washington, DC: Acropolis Books, 1978).

24. Jim Perry, Positive Coaching Alliance, speech at parent workshop and interview by Kathy Seal, La Cienega Park, Los Angeles, December 15, 2005.

25. Jennifer Alsever, "A New Competitive Sport: Grooming the Child Athlete," *New York Times*, June 25, 2006.

26. Jim Thompson, Positive Coaching Alliance, e-mail message to Kathy Seal, May 10, 2007.

27. Shari Roan, "Narrowing the Field," *Los Angeles Times*, October 2, 2006.

28. Mike West, e-mail message to Kathy Seal, April 30, 2007.

29. Rosita Mang, interview by Kathy Seal, September 8, 2006, and in e-mail messages to Seal, September 2006–April 2007.

30. Edward L. Deci, Gregory Betley, James Kahle, Linda Abrams, and Joseph Porac, "When Trying to Win: Competition and Intrinsic Motivation," *Personality and Social Psychology Bulletin* 7 (1981): 79–83.

31. Margaret M. Clifford, "Effect of Competition as a Motivational Technique in the Classroom," *American Educational Research Journal* 9 (1972): 123–37, as cited in Alfie Kohn, *No Contest: The Case against Competition* (Boston: Houghton Mifflin, 1986), p. 47.

32. Carole Ames, Russell Ames, and Donald W. Felker, "Effects of Competitive Reward Structure and Valence of Outcome on Children's Achievement Attributions," *Journal of Educational Psychology* 69 (1977): 1–8. Also, Carole Ames interview by Kathy Seal, November 6, 2006.

33. Martha E. Ewing and Vern Seefeldt, "Participation and Attrition Patterns in American Agency-Sponsored and Interscholastic Sports—An Executive Summary," study funded by the Athletic Footwear Council, Sporting Goods Manufacturer's Association, 1988.

34. Leonard M. Wankel and Philip Kreisel, "An Investigation of Factors Influencing Sport Enjoyment across Sport and Age Groups," paper presented at the North American Society for the Psychology of Sport and Physical Activity conference, College Park, MD, April 1982. D. L. Gill, J. Gross, and S. Huddleston, "Participation

Motivation in Youth Sports," *International Journal of Sports Psychology* 14 (1983): 1–4. Heather Barber, Holly Sukhi, and Sally A. White, "The Influence of Parent-Coaches on Participant Motivation and Competitive Anxiety in Youth Sport Participants," *Journal of Sport Behavior* 22 (1999): 162–76. Also, *USA Today* / NBC poll as reported in Mike Dodd, "Children Say Having Fun Is #1," *USA Today*, September 13, 1990.

35. Jim Perry, speech at La Cienega Park and interview by Kathy Seal.

36. Johnmarshall Reeve and Edward L. Deci, "Elements of the Competitive Situation that Affect Intrinsic Motivation," *Personality and Social Psychology Bulletin* 22 (1996): 24–33.

37. Linda Stump, interview by Kathy Seal, September 4, 2006.

38. Jim Perry, speech at La Cienega Park.

39. Kohn, *No Contest*, p. 26.

40. Josephson Institute of Ethics, "What Are Your Children Learning? The Impact of High School Sports on the Values and Ethics of High School Athletes," released February 2007, summarizes a written survey administered in 2005 and 2006 to 5,275 high school athletes. See http://www.josephsoninstitute.org/ and http://www .josephsoninstitute.org/sports_survey/2006/ (accessed April 29, 2007).

41. Josephson Institute of Ethics, "2006 Josephson Institute Report Card on the Ethics of American Youth," released in October 2006, summarizes a written survey of thirty-five thousand high school students from a cross-section of public, private, religious, and nonreligious schools from across the United States. See http://www .josephsoninstitute.org/reportcard/.

42. Dee Shepherd-Look, interview by Kathy Seal, January 12, 2005.

43. Bruce Poch, interview by Kathy Seal, June 6, 2006.

44. "News from the Schools," *Economist.com*, September 25, 2006, http://www .economist.com/business/globalexecutive/displaystory.cfm?story_id=E1_SRSSSRD (accessed April 29, 2007).

45. Ingrid Clarfield, interview by Kathy Seal, September 3, 2006.

46. David W. Johnson and Roger T. Johnson, "Toward a Cooperative Effort," *Educational Leadership* 46 (1989): 80–81.

47. Stipek, *Motivation to Learn*, pp. 112–13.

48. Kohn, *No Contest*, p. 216, citing Kipling D. Williams and Steven J. Karau, "Social Loafing and Social Compensation: The Effects of Expectation of Co-Worker Performance," *Journal of Personality and Social Psychology* 61 (1991): 570–81.

49. Kohn, *No Contest*, pp. 221–22, 225–26.

50. Http://www.jigsaw.org/ (accessed April 29, 2007).

51. Http://www.ucsc.edu/oncampus/currents/98-99/05-03/aronson.htm (accessed April 29, 2007).

52. Kohn, *No Contest*, p. 51, citing David and Roger Johnson, "The Socialization

and Achievement Crisis: Are Cooperative Learning Experiences the Solution?" Leonard Bickman, ed., *Applied Social Psychology Annual 4* (Beverly Hills, CA: Sage, 1983), p. 122.

53. See http://www.fpsp.org/ (accessed September 29, 2006). Also, Marianne Solomon, executive director, Future Problem Solving Program International, e-mail message to Kathy Seal, October 2, 2006.

54. Http://www.usfirst.org/robotics/ (accessed September 29, 2006).

55. Claudia Dreifus, "He Turned His Nobel into a Prize for Women," interview with Paul Greengard, Nobel winner in physiology or medicine, *New York Times*, September 26, 2006.

56. Kohn, *No Contest*, p. 52, citing Robert L Helmreich, William Beane, G. William Lucker, and Janet T. Spence, "Achievement Motivation and Scientific Attainment," *Personality and Social Psychology Bulletin* 4 (1978): 222–26.

CHAPTER 3

1. Edward O. Wilson, *Naturalist* (Washington, DC: Island Press, 1994), pp. 5–15.

2. Edward O. Wilson, *Sociobiology: The New Synthesis*, 25th anniversary ed. (Cambridge, MA: Belknap Press of Harvard University Press, 2000), p. 336. Hemiptera are insects whose mouthparts have evolved into a jointed proboscis that can pierce tissues and suck out liquid, usually sap from a plant.

3. The r in r-selected and K in K-selected come from standard ecological algebra, in which r is used to represent the (rapid) growth rate of the population and K is its carrying capacity. From http://en.wikipedia.org/wiki/R-selected (accessed May 10, 2007).

4. Wilson, *Sociobiology*, p. 337.

5. Ibid., p. 336.

6. Http://www.edge.org/3rd_culture/trivers04/trivers04_index.html (accessed April 30, 2007).

7. Robert Wright, *The Moral Animal: Evolutionary Psychology and Everyday Life* (New York: Vintage Books, 1994), pp. 41–42.

8. Tess T. Dawber and Leon Kuczynski, "The Question of Ownness: The Influence of Relationship Context on Parental Socialization Strategies," *Journal of Social and Personal Relationships* 16 (1999): 475–93.

9. Tracey Shors, interview by Kathy Seal, November 6, 2006.

10. Quoted in Wright, *Moral Animal*, p. 123. Wright references Paul H. Barrett et al., eds., *Charles Darwin's Notebooks, 1836–1844* (Ithaca, NY: Cornell University Press, 1987), p. 619.

11. Wilson, *Sociobiology*, p. 351: "True paternal care is difficult to separate from allopaternal care, and in most instances there is no reason to expect the males themselves to know the difference. Yet variation in the form of male care among the primate species strongly suggests that a clear distinction between paternal and allopaternal behavior exists. In species characterized by the presence of a single male in the troop or at least one or a very few dominant males likely to be father, the males tend to show an almost maternal solitude toward infants."

12. Ibid.

13. Wright, *Moral Animal*, p. 57. "We are, as they say in the zoology literature, high in MPI. We're not so high that male parental investment typically rivals female parental investment, but we're a lot higher than the average primate."

14. Ibid., p. 58.

15. Robert Trivers, "Parental Investment and Sexual Selection," in *Sexual Selection and the Descent of Man*, ed. Bernard Campbell (Chicago: Aldine de Gruyter, 1972).

16. Erik D. Thiessen, Emily A. Hill, and Jenny R. Saffran, "Infant Directed Speech Facilitates Word Segmentation," *INFANCY* 7, no. 1 (2005): 53–71. Also see http://www.medicalnewstoday.com/medicalnews.php?newsid=21329 (accessed May 11, 2007): "Adults may feel silly when they talk to babies, but those babies will learn to speak sooner if adults talk to them like infants instead of like other adults, according to a study by Carnegie Mellon University."

17. Andreas Bartels and Semir Zeki, "The Neural Correlates of Maternal and Romantic Love," *NeuroImage* 21 (2004): 1155–66. Available online at http://www.sciencedirect.com.

18. Bartels and Zeki, "Neural Correlates," p. 1155.

19. Matt Richtel, "School Cellphone Bans Topple (You Can't Suspend Everyone)," *New York Times*, September 29, 2004. "Hundreds of U.S. high schools have eased bans on student cell phones, giving in to parent demands for access to children and other pressures."

20. "Mom Confessions: Baby Smarts, Bragging, and More," *Parenting* magazine poll, September 2006, 102–103.

21. Randolph M. Nesse, "The Smoke Detector Principle: Natural Selection and the Regulation of Defensive Responses," *Annals of the New York Academy of Sciences* 935 (2001): 75–85.

22. Glenn Weisfeld, "The Benefits of Nausea," letter to the *New York Times*, October 31, 2006.

23. Nesse, "Smoke Detector Principle," pp. 77–78.

24. Ibid., p. 80.

25. Ibid., pp. 82–83.

26. Wilson, "Problems without Borders," *Vanity Fair*, May 2007, 164. "In rising to

power beginning with the invention of agriculture a scant 10 millennia ago, we carried along with us the huge baggage of ancient primate instincts. We live in Star Wars civilizations ruled by Stone Age emotions, medieval institutions and gold-like technology."

CHAPTER 4

1. Wendy S. Grolnick, Ann Frodi, and Lisa J. Bridges, "Maternal Control Style and the Mastery Motivation of One-Year Olds," *Infant Mental Health Journal* 5 (1985).

2. Alfie Kohn, "Only for *My* Kid: How Privileged Parents Undermine School Reform," *Phi Delta Kappan* (April 1998): 569–77, http://www.alfiekohn.org/teaching/ofmk.htm.

3. Wendy S. Grolnick, Laura Weiss, Lee McKenzie, and Jeffrey Wrightman, "Contextual, Cognitive, and Adolescent Factors Associated with Parenting in Adolescence," *Journal of Youth and Adolescence* 25 (1996): 33–54.

4. Suzanne T. Gurland and Wendy S. Grolnick, "Perceived Threat, Controlling Parenting, and Children's Achievement Orientations," *Motivation and Emotion* 29 (2003): 103–21.

5. John E. Bates, "The Concept of Difficult Temperament," *Merrill-Palmer Quarterly* 26 (1980): 299–319.

6. Grolnick et al., "Contextual, Cognitive, and Adolescent Factors."

7. Wendy S. Grolnick, Carrie E. Price, Krista L. Beiswenger, and Christine C. Sauck, "Evaluative Pressure in Parents: Effects of Situation, Maternal, and Child Characteristics on Autonomy-Supportive versus Controlling Behavior," *Developmental Psychology* 43 (2007): 991–1002.

8. Jesse Green, "The Making of an Ice Princess," *New York Times Magazine*, December 18, 2005, http://select.nytimes.com/search/restricted/article?res=F70D15FA35550C7B8DDDAB0994DD404482 (accessed May 11, 2007).

9. William James, *Principles of Psychology* (1890), http://psychclassics.yorku.ca/James/Principles/index.htm (accessed May 14, 2007).

10. Jennifer Crocker and Lora E. Park, "The Costly Pursuit of Self-esteem," *Psychological Bulletin* 130 (2004): 392–414.

11. Wendy S. Grolnick, Suzanne T. Gurland, Wendy DeCourcey, and Karen Jacob, "Antecedents and Consequences of Mothers' Autonomy Support: An Experimental Investigation," *Developmental Psychology* 38 (2002): 143–55.

12. Leo Rosten, *The Joys of Yiddish* (New York: McGraw-Hill, 1968), p. 257.

CHAPTER 5

1. Robert White, "Motivation Reconsidered: The Concept of Competence," *Psychological Review* 66 (1959): 297–333.

2. Harry F. Harlow, Margaret K. Harlow, and Donald R. Meyer, "Learning Motivated by a Manipulation Drive," *Journal of Experimental Psychology* 40 (1950): 228–34.

3. Clark Hull, *Principles of Behavior* (New York: Appleton-Century-Crofts, 1943).

4. Henry Nissen, "A Study of Exploratory Behavior in the White Rat by Means of the Obstruction Method," *Journal of Genetic Psychology* 37 (1930): 361–76.

5. Carol Tavris, "Deconstructing Harry," *American Scientist Online* (March–April 2003), http://www.americanscientist.org/template/BookReviewTypeDetail/assetid/17181;jsessionid=baa9 (accessed May 11, 2007). Review of Deborah Blum's *Love at Goon Park: Harry Harlow and the Science of Affection*, a biography of Harlow (New York: Perseus Publishing, 2002).

6. Harlow et al., "Learning Motivated by a Manipulation Drive."

7. Ibid.

8. Edward L. Deci, *Intrinsic Motivation* (New York: Plenum, 1975).

9. Edward L. Deci and R. M. Ryan, *Intrinsic Motivation and Self-Determination in Human Behavior* (New York: Plenum, 1985).

10. Richard Ryan, James P. Connell, and Robert W. Plant, "Emotions in Nondirected Text Learning," *Learning and Individual Differences* 2 (1990): 1–17.

11. Adele E. Gottfried, "Academic Intrinsic Motivation in Elementary and Junior High School Students," *Journal of Educational Psychology* 77 (1985): 631–45.

12. John G. Nicholls, "Achievement Motivation: Concepts of Ability, Subjective Experience, Task Choice, and Performance," *Psychological Review* 91 (1984): 328–46; and John G. Nicholls, Michael Patashnick, and Susan B. Nolen, "Adolescents' Theories of Education," *Journal of Educational Psychology* 77 (1985): 683–92, as cited in Martin V. Covington, *Making the Grade: A Self-Worth Perspective on Motivation and School Reform* (New York: Cambridge University Press, 1992), p. 157.

13. Carol Dweck, *Self Theories: Their Role in Motivation, Personality, and Development* (New York: Psychology Press, 1999).

14. Richard deCharms, "From Pawns to Origins: Toward Self-Motivation," in *Psychology and Educational Practice*, ed. G. Lesser (Glenview, IL: Scott, Foresman and Co., 1968), pp. 380–407. Also, Margaret W. Cohen, Andrea M. Emrich, and Richard deCharms, "Training Teachers to Enhance Personal Causation in Students," *Interchange* 7, no. 1 (1976–77).

15. DeCharms, "From Pawns to Origins"; and Cohen et al., "Training Teachers."

16. Antonio Damasio, e-mail message to Kathy Seal, March 9, 2007.

17. Sandra Blakeslee, "A Small Part of the Brain, and Its Profound Effects," *New*

York Times, February 6, 2007, http://select.nytimes.com/search/restricted/article?res =F30612FB385B0C758CDDAB0894DF404482 (accessed May 11, 2007).

18. Harvey Araton, "When Dreams Come True," *New York Times*, December 8, 2006, http://select.nytimes.com/search/restricted/article?res=F20C13F83C550C7B 8CDDAB0994DE404482 (accessed May 11, 2007).

19. Summer Sanders, *Champions Are Raised, Not Born: How My Parents Made Me a Success* (New York: Delacorte, 1999), pp. 5–6.

20. Pelletier conducted this study over two years. Luc G. Pelletier, Michelle Fortier, Robert J. Vallerand, Kim M. Tuson, Nathalie M. Brière, and Marc R. Blais, "Toward a New Measure of Intrinsic Motivation, Extrinsic Motivation, and Amotivation in Sports: The Sport Motivation Sale (SMS)," *Journal of Sport and Exercise Psychology* 17 (1996): 35–54.

21. Krista L. Beiswenger and Wendy S. Grolnick, "Interpersonal and Intrapersonal Factors Associated with Adolescents' Autonomy in After-School Activities," unpublished manuscript, Clark University, Worcester, MA, 2007.

22. Jeremy P. Hunter and Mihaly Csikszentmihalyi, "The Positive Psychology of Interested Adolescents," *Journal of Youth and Adolescence* 32, no. 1 (2003): 27–35.

23. Ibid., pp. 28–29.

24. Gough Creative Personality Scale for the Adjective Checklist (Gough, 1979).

25. Kirton Adaption-Innovation Inventory (KAI).

26. Teresa M. Amabile, Karl G. Hill, Beth A. Hennessey, and Elizabeth M. Tighe, "The Work Preference Inventory: Assessing Intrinsic and Extrinsic Motivational Orientations," *Journal of Personality and Social Psychology* 66, no. 5 (1994): 950–67.

27. Frank Barron, "Putting Creativity to Work," in *The Nature of Creativity*, ed. Robert J. Sternberg (New York: Cambridge University Press, 1988), pp. 76–98; and Donald W. MacKinnon, "The Nature and Nurture of Creative Talent," *American Psychologist* 17 (1962): 484–95, cited in Mary Ann Collins and Teresa M. Amabile, "Motivation and Creativity" in *Handbook of Creativity*, ed. Sternberg (New York: Cambridge University Press, 1999), p. 300.

28. One of the most famous theorems in the history of mathematics, Fermat's last theorem, was stated by Pierre de Fermat in the 1630s. It states that there are no positive integers for which $x^n + y^n = z^n$ when n is greater than 2. Andrew Wiles announced a solution in 1993, but it had an error. After a year working on it with Richard Taylor, Wiles finally announced a refined proof, developed with ideas from Barry Mazur. Others who did work on which Wiles relied include Gerhard Frey, Jean-Pierre Serre, and Ken Ribet. See http://www.nsf.gov/discoveries/disc_summ.jsp?cntn_id=100029 (accessed May 18, 2007) and http://en.wikipedia.org/wiki/Fermat's_last_theorem (accessed May 18, 2007).

29. Collins and Amabile, "Motivation and Creativity," p. 300.

30. Amabile et al., "Work Preference Inventory," p. 950.

31. Collins and Amabile, "Motivation and Creativity," p. 297. "Although creativity can arise from a complex interplay of motivational forces, motivation that stems from the individual's personal involvement in the work—love if you will—is crucial for high levels of creativity in any domain."

32. Ibid. From Teresa M. Amabile, *Growing Up Creative* (Buffalo, NY: Creative Education Foundation, 1989), p. 56.

33. Amabile et al., "Work Preference Inventory," cited in Collins and Amabile, "Motivation and Creativity," p. 301.

34. Http://www.coe.uga.edu/coenews/2003/EPTorranceObit.html (accessed May 18, 2007). Also, Collins and Amabile, "Motivation and Creativity," p. 298.

35. Mihaly Csikszentmihalyi, *Finding Flow: The Psychology of Engagement in Everyday Life* (New York: Basic Books, 1997).

36. Csikszentmihalyi, *The Evolving Self: A Psychology for the Third Millennium* (New York: HarperCollins, 1993), pp. 193–94.

37. Csikszentmihalyi, *Creativity: Flow and the Psychology of Discovery and Invention* (New York: Harper Perennial, 1996), pp. 2–4, 157.

38. Richard M. Ryan and James P. Connell, "Perceived Locus of Causality and Internalization: Examining Reasons for Acting in Two Domains," *Journal of Personality and Social Psychology* 57, no. 5 (1989): 749–61.

39. James Paul Gee, "The Classroom of Popular Culture: What Video Games Can Teach Us about Making Students *Want* to Learn," *Harvard Education Letter* (November/December 2005): 6–8.

40. Richard M. Ryan, C. Scott Rigby, and Andrew Przybylski, "The Motivational Pull of Video Games: A Self-Determination Theory Approach," *Motivation and Emotion* 30, no. 4 (December 2006): 355.

41. Richard M. Ryan, e-mail message to Kathy Seal, May 19, 2007.

CHAPTER 6

1. Edward L. Deci, Robert E. Driver, Lucinda Hotchkiss, Robert J. Robbins, and Ilona Wilson, "The Relations of Mothers' Controlling Vocalizations to Children's Intrinsic Motivation," *Journal of Experimental Child Psychology* 55 (1993): 151–62.

2. Edward L. Deci, John Nezlek, and Louise Sheinman, "Characteristics of the Rewarder and Intrinsic Motivation of the Rewardee," *Journal of Personality and Social Psychology* 40, no. 1 (1981): 1–10.

3. Edward L. Deci, Allen J. Schwartz, Louise Sheinman, and Richard M. Ryan, "An Instrument to Assess Adults' Orientations to Control versus Autonomy with Children: Reflections on Intrinsic Motivation and Perceived Competence," *Journal of Edu-*

cational Psychology 73, no. 5 (1981): 642–50.

4. Wendy Grolnick and Richard M. Ryan, "Parent Styles Associated with Children's Self-regulation and Competence in School," *Journal of Educational Psychology* 81 (1989): 143–54.

5. Wendy S. Grolnick, Suzanne T. Gurland, Wendy DeCourcey, and Karen Jacob, "Antecedents and Consequences of Mothers' Autonomy Support: An Experimental Investigation," *Developmental Psychology* 38, no. 1 (2002): 143–55.

6. Suzanne T. Gurland and Wendy S. Grolnick, "Children's Expectancies and Perceptions of Adults: Effects on Rapport," *Child Development* 74 (2003): 1212–24.

7. Rachel R. Avery and Richard M. Ryan, "Object Relations and Ego Development: Comparison and Correlates in Middle Childhood," *Journal of Personality* 56, no. 3 (1988): 547–69.

8. L. H. Chiu, "Child Rearing Attitudes of Chinese, Chinese-American, and Anglo-American Mothers," *International Journal of Psychology* 22 (1987): 409–19. C. C. Lin and V. R. Fiu, "A Comparison of Child-Rearing Practices among Chinese, Immigrant Chinese, and Caucasian-American Parents," *Child Development* 61 (1990): 429–33.

9. Daniel Golden, *The Price of Admission: How America's Ruling Class Buys Its Way into Elite Colleges—and Who Gets Left outside the Gates* (New York: Crown Publishing Group, 2006). Cited by Timothy Egan, "Little Asia on the Hill," *New York Times,* January 7, 2007.

10. Ruth K. Chao, "Beyond Parental Control and Authoritarian Parenting Style: Understanding Chinese Parenting through the Cultural Notion of Training," *Child Development* 65 (1994): 1111–19.

11. Dorothy Chin and Velma A. Kameoka, "Sociocultural Influences of Adult Psychopathology," in *Comprehensive Handbook of Personality and Psychopathology*, vol. 2: *Adult Psychopathology*, ed. Frank Andrasik (New York: Wiley, 2006), p. 73.

12. Ronald P. Rohner and Sandra M. Pettengill, "Perceived Parental Acceptance-rejection and Parental Control among Korean Adolescents," *Child Development* 56 (1985): 524–28.

13. Dorothy Chin, e-mail message to Kathy Seal, April 4, 2007.

14. Xinyin Chen, Qi Dong, and Hong Zhou, "Authoritative and Authoritarian Parenting Practices and Social and School Performance in Chinese Children," *International Journal of Behavioral Development* 21 (1997): 855–73.

CHAPTER 7

1. Haim Ginott, *Between Parent and Child: New Solutions to Old Problems* (New York: Macmillan Company, 1965), pp. 21–22.

2. Ibid.

3. Patti Jones, "Seven Educators Come Clean about Their Own Kids' Homework," *Working Mother* magazine, September 2003, 49.

4. William B. Swann and Thane S. Pittman, "Initiating Play Activity of Children: The Moderating Influence of Verbal Cues on Intrinsic Motivation," *Child Development* 48 (1977): 1128–32.

5. Richard deCharms, *Enhancing Motivation: Change in the Classroom* (New York: Irvington Publishers, 1976).

6. Avi Assor, Haya Kaplan, and Guy Roth, "Choice Is Good But Relevance Is Excellent: Autonomy-enhancing and Suppressing Teacher Behaviours Predicting Students' Engagement in Schoolwork," *British Journal of Educational Psychology* 72 (2002): 261–78.

7. Idit Katz and Avi Assor, "Choice and the Need for Autonomy: A Cross-Cultural Investigation of Various Aspects of Autonomy Support," unpublished manuscript (Ben-Gurion University: Israel, 2005).

8. Richard Koestner, Richard M. Ryan, Frank J. Bernieri, and Katherine Holt, "Setting Limits on Children's Behavior: The Differential Effects of Controlling versus Informational Styles on Intrinsic Motivation and Creativity," *Journal of Personality* 52 (1984): 244–48.

9. Summer Sanders, *Champions Are Raised, Not Born: How My Parents Made Me a Success* (New York: Delacorte, 1999).

10. C. W. Nevius, "Soccer Players Get the Silent Treatment—and It's a Good Thing," *San Francisco Chronicle*, October 15, 2004, http://www.sfgate.com/cgi-bin/article.cgi?f=/c/a/2004/10/15/EBG6N959LP1.DTLandhw=SOCCER+PLAYERS+SILENT+TREATMENTandsn=001andsc=1000 (accessed May 15, 2007).

11. Jon C. Hellstedt, "Early Adolescent Perceptions of Parental Pressure in the Sport Environment," *Journal of Sports Behavior* 13 (1990): 135–44.

12. Ann K. Boggiano, Marty Barrett, Anne Weiher, Gary H. McClelland, and Cynthia M. Lusk, "Use of the Maximal-operant Principle to Motivate Children's Intrinsic Interest," *Journal of Personality and Social Psychology* 53 (1987): 866–79.

13. Edward L. Deci, "Effects of Externally Mediated Rewards on Intrinsic Motivation," *Journal of Personality and Social Psychology* 18 (1971): 105–15.

14. Mark R. Lepper, David Green, and Richard E. Nisbett, "Undermining Children's Intrinsic Motivation with Extrinsic Rewards: A Test of the 'Overjustification Hypothesis,'" *Journal of Personality and Social Psychology* 28 (1973): 129–37.

15. Kenneth O. McGraw and John C. McCullers, "Evidence of a Detrimental Effect of Extrinsic Incentives on Breaking a Mental Set," *Journal of Experimental Social Psychology* 15 (1979): 285–94.

16. Wendy S. Grolnick and Richard M. Ryan, "Autonomy in Children's Learning: An Experimental and Individual Difference Investigation," *Journal of Personality and Social Psychology* 52 (1987): 890–98.

17. Teresa M. Amabile, "Children's Artistic Creativity: Detrimental Effects of Competition in a Field Setting," *Personality and Social Psychology Bulletin* 8 (1982): 573–78; also Beth A. Hennessey, "The Social Psychology of Creativity," *Scandinavian Journal of Educational Research* 47, no. 3 (2003): 259–60.

18. Teresa M. Amabile, Beth A. Hennessey, and Barbara S. Grossman, "Social Influences on Creativity: the Effects of Contracted for Reward," *Journal of Personality and Social Psychology* 50 (1986): 14–23.

19. Mary Ann Collins and Teresa M. Amabile, "Motivation and Creativity," in *Handbook of Creativity*, ed. Robert J. Sternberg (New York: Cambridge University Press, 1999), p. 306.

20. Beth A. Hennessey and Susan M. Zbikowski, "Immunizing Children Against the Negative Effect of Reward: A Further Examination of Intrinsic Motivation Training Techniques," *Creativity Research Journal* 6, no. 3 (1993): 297–307. Also interview of Hennessey by Kathy Seal, November 12, 2007.

21. Audrey Kast and Kathleen Connor, "Sex and Age Differences in Response to Informational and Controlling Feedback," *Personality and Social Psychology Bulletin* 14 (1988): 514–23.

22. Ginott, *Between Parent and Child*, pp. 38–41.

23. Avi Assor, Guy Roth, and Edward L. Deci, "The Emotional Costs of Parents' Conditional Regard: A Self-Determination Theory Analysis," *Journal of Personality* 72 (2004): 47–88.

CHAPTER 8

1. Earvin "Magic" Johnson with William Novak, *My Life* (New York: Random House, 1992), pp. 3–21.

2. Steve Springer, "Could It Be Magic?" *Los Angeles Times*, June 5, 2002, p. D1.

3. Nancy Gibbs, "Parents Behaving Badly," *Time.com*, February 13, 2005, http://www.time.com/time/magazine/article/0,9171,1027485,00.html (accessed May 15, 2007).

4. Wendy S. Grolnick and Richard M. Ryan, "Parent Styles Associated with Children's School-Related Self-Regulation and Competence," *Journal of Educational Psychology* 81 (1989): 143–54.

5. Anne T. Henderson and Karen L. Mapp, *A New Wave of Evidence: The Impact of School, Family, and Community Connections on Student Achievement* (Austin, TX: Southwest Educational Development Laboratory, 2002), p. 112.

6. The federal No Child Left Behind Act requires parental involvement in all Title 1 schools, meaning those serving low-income children. Anne T. Henderson,

Karen L. Mapp, Vivian R. Johnson, and Don Davies, *Beyond the Bake Sale: The Essential Guide to Family-School Partnerships* (New York: New Press, 2007), pp. 9–11, 38–39.

7. Wendy S. Grolnick and Maria L. Slowiaczek, "Parents' Involvement in Children's Schooling: A Multidimensional Conceptualization and Motivational Model," *Child Development* 65 (1994): 237–52.

8. See http://nces.ed.gov/surveys/nels88/ (accessed May 15, 2007).

9. Esther Ho Sui-Chu and J. Douglas Willms, "Effects of Parental Involvement on Eighth-Grade Achievement," *Sociology of Education* 69 (April 1996): 126–41.

10. Laurence Steinberg, *Beyond the Classroom* (New York: Simon and Schuster, 1996), pp. 83–100. Key factors behind Asian students' achievement, Steinberg found, were parental expectations and peers who valued good grades. (When asked for the lowest grade they could get without their parents getting angry, Asian children said it was a B-plus.) Two beliefs—believing that hard work counts more than native ability and that doing well in school would help them lead a successful life—also played an important role.

11. Anne Henderson, interview by Kathy Seal, February 22, 2007.

12. For more information about parental involvement in children's schooling, see Henderson et al., *Beyond the Bake Sale.*

13. Rosalind Wiseman with Elizabeth Rapoport, *Queen Bee Moms and Kingpin Dads: Dealing with the Parents, Teachers, Coaches, and Counselors Who Can Make—or Break—Your Child's Future* (New York: Crown Publishers, 2006), pp. 41–42. "A Queen Bee Mom," writes Wiseman, "has to be in control" and that includes exerting her social power over other parents. "When she or her child include you or your child, you feel like you're special, you've made it."

14. Anne Henderson, interview by Kathy Seal, February 22, 2007.

15. Evie Frankl, interview by Kathy Seal, March 29, 2007.

16. Gabrielle Carpenter, interview by Kathy Seal, April 16, 2007.

17. Wendy S. Grolnick, Caroline O. Kurowski, Kelly G. Dunlap, and Cheryl Hevey, "Parental Resources and the Transition to Junior High," *Journal of Research on Adolescence* 10 (2000): 465–80.

18. Laura A. Weiss and Wendy S. Grolnick, "The Roles of Parental Involvement and Support for Autonomy in Adolescent Symptomatology," paper presented at the biennial meeting of the Society for Research in Child Development, Seattle, Washington, April 1991. Internal symptoms are those felt internally like depression and anxiety. They cause internal distress. External symptoms are those expressed outwardly—like disrupting others, aggressive behavior, stealing, lying, etc.—all kinds of acting out.

19. Laurence Steinberg, Susie Lamborn, Sanford Dornbusch, Nancy Darling, "Impact of Parenting Practices on Adolescent Achievement: Authoritative Parenting, School Involvement, and Encouragement to Succeed," *Child Development* 63 (1992): 1266–81.

20. Barbara A. Brown, Gail Frankel, and Marilyn P. Fennell, "Hugs or Shrugs: Parental and Peer Influence on Continuity of Involvement in Sport by Female Adolescents," *Sex Roles* 20, nos. 7–8 (1989): 397–412.

21. Heather Barber, Holly Sukhi, and Sally A. White, "The Influence of Parent-Coaches on Participant Motivation and Competitive Anxiety in Youth Sport Participants," *Journal of Sports Behavior* 22 (1999): 162–76.

22. Suzanne M. Bianchi, John P. Robinson, and Melissa A. Milkie, *Changing Rhythms of American Family Life* (New York: Russell Sage Foundation Publications, 2006). Robert Pear, "Married and Single Parents Spending More Time with Children, Study Finds," *New York Times*, October 17, 2006; D'vera Cohn, "Do Parents Spend Enough Time with Their Children?" Population Reference Bureau, http://www.prborg/Articles/2007/DoParentsSpendEnoughTimeWithTheirChildren.aspx (accessed May 15, 2007).

23. Suzanne Bianchi, interview by Kathy Seal, February 12, 2007.

24. Jane Magrath, interview by Kathy Seal, August 8, 2006.

25. Ingrid Clarfield, interview by Kathy Seal, September 3, 2006.

26. Laurence Steinberg, *10 Basic Principles of Good Parenting* (New York: Simon and Schuster, 2004), pp. 47–64.

27. Ibid., p. 52.

28. Ibid., pp. 57–60.

29. Anne Adams, interview by Kathy Seal, September 10, 2006.

30. Brenda Ueland, *Tell Me More* (Tucson: Kore Press, 1998).

31. Jim Thompson, interview by Kathy Seal, December 8, 2005.

32. http://www.positivecoach.org/subcontent.aspx?SecID=209 (accessed May 16, 2007).

33. Wiseman and Rapoport, *Queen Bee*, p. 115.

34. Joseph L. Mahoney, Angel L. Harris, and Jacquelynne S. Eccles, "Organized Activity Participation, Positive Youth Development, and the Overscheduling Hypothesis," *Social Policy Report, Society for Research in Child Development* 20, no. 4 (August 2006).

35. Lonnie Sherrod, ed., *Social Policy Report* of the Society for Research in Child Development in Mahoney et al., "Organized Activity," p. 2.

CHAPTER 9

1. Wendy Grolnick and Richard M. Ryan, "Parent Styles Associated with Children's Self-Regulation and Competence in School," *Journal of Educational Psychology* 81 (1989): 143–54.

2. Grazyna Kochanska, "Children's Interpersonal Influence with Mothers and Peers," *Developmental Psychology* 28, no. 3 (1992): 491–99.

3. Haim Ginott, *Between Parent and Child: New Solutions to Old Problems* (New York: Macmillan Company, 1965), pp. 102–103.

4. Robert J. Vallerand and Greg Reid, "On the Causal Effects of Perceived Competence on Intrinsic Motivation: A Test of Cognitive Evaluation Theory," *Journal of Sport Psychology* 6 (1984): 94–102.

5. Alfred L. Baldwin, Clara Baldwin, and Robert E. Cole, "Stress-Resistant Families and Stress-Resistant Children," in *Risk and Protective Factors in the Development of Psychopathology,* ed. Jon Rolf, Ann S. Masten, Dante Cicchetti, Keith H. Nüechterlein, and Sheldon Weintraub (New York: Cambridge University Press, 1990), pp. 257–80.

CHAPTER 10

1. Christine Padesky, interview by Kathy Seal, March 15, 2007. Padesky's popular cognitive therapy workbook with Dennis Greenberger, *Mind Over Mood* (New York: Guilford Press, 1995), helps readers combat problems including anxiety and depression. I am indebted to Padesky for helping me apply the ideas of cognitive therapy to the Pressured Parent Phenomenon in this chapter.

2. Http://www.bfnorth.com/relaxation_exercises.htm (accessed May 17, 2007).

3. Http://www.ukhypnosis.com/ProgRela.htm; and http://en.wikipedia.org/wiki/Jacobson%27s_Progressive_Muscle_Relaxation (accessed May 15, 2007).

4. Thanks to Christine Padesky for this example.

5. Dee Shepherd-Look, interview by Kathy Seal, January 12, 2006.

6. George Manderlink and Judith M. Harackiewicz, "Proximal vs. Distal Goal Setting and Intrinsic Motivation," *Journal of Personality and Social Psychology* 47 (1984): 918–28.

7. Lawrence J. Walker and John H. Taylor, "Family Interaction and the Development of Moral Reasoning," *Child Development* 62 (1991): 264–83.

8. "Honor the game" and "learn life lessons" are recommendations of the Positive Coaching Alliance. Jim Perry, Positive Coaching Alliance, speech at PCA workshop for parents, La Cienega Park, Los Angeles, December 15, 2005; and Jim Thompson, executive director of the PCA, interview by Kathy Seal, December 8, 2005. See also http://www.positivecoach.org.

9. Josephson Institute of Ethics, "Survey of High School Athletes" (February 20, 2007), http://www.josephsoninstitute.org/sports_survey/2006/ (accessed May 16, 2007).

10. Jim Thompson, interview by Kathy Seal.

11. Jim Perry speech at PCA workshop for parents, La Cienega Park, Los Angeles.

12. Society for Neuroscience, "The Musician in the Mirror: New Study Shows

Brain Rapidly Forms Link between Sounds and Actions that Produce Them," press release, January 12, 2007, http://www.sfn.org/?pagename=news_011207 (accessed May 16, 2007). Also, Sandra Blakeslee, "Cells That Read Minds," *New York Times*, January 10, 2006, http://select.nytimes.com/search/restricted/article?res=F60A12 F934540C738DDDA80894DE404482 (accessed May 16, 2007); and Daniel Goleman, "Friends for Life: An Emerging Biology of Emotional Healing," *New York Times*, October 10, 2006, http://www.nytimes.com/2006/10/10/health/psychology/10essa .html?ex=1179460800anden=c9c5c238a7936033andei=5070 (accessed May 16, 2007).

13. Andrew Meltzoff and Keith M. Moore, "Imitation in Newborn Infants: Exploring the Range of Gestures Imitated and the Underlying Mechanisms," *Developmental Psychology* 25 (1989): 954–62.

BIBLIOGRAPHY

Alsever, Jennifer. "A New Competitive Sport: Grooming the Child Athlete." *New York Times,* June 25, 2006.

Amabile, Teresa M. "Children's Artistic Creativity: Detrimental Effects of Competition in a Field Setting." *Personality and Social Psychology Bulletin* 8 (1982a): 573–78.

Amabile, Teresa M., Beth A. Hennessey, and Barbara S. Grossman. "Social Influences on Creativity: The Effects of Contracted for Reward." *Journal of Personality and Social Psychology* 50 (1986): 14–23.

Amabile, Teresa M., Karl G. Hill, Beth A. Hennessey, and Elizabeth M. Tighe. "The Work Preference Inventory: Assessing Intrinsic and Extrinsic Motivational Orientations." *Journal of Personality and Social Psychology* 66, no. 5 (1994): 950–67.

Ames, Carole, Russell Ames, and Donald W. Felker. "Effects of Competitive Reward Structure and Valence of Outcome on Children's Achievement Attributions." *Journal of Educational Psychology* 69 (1977): 1–8.

Assor, Avi, Guy Roth, and Edward L. Deci. "The Emotional Costs of Parents' Conditional Regard: A Self-determination Theory Analysis." *Journal of Personality* 72 (2004): 47–88.

Assor, Avi, Haya Kaplan, and Guy Roth. "Choice Is Good But Relevance Is Excellent: Autonomy-enhancing and Suppressing Teacher Behaviours Predicting Students' Engagement in Schoolwork." *British Journal of Educational Psychology* 72 (2002): 261–78.

Avery, Rachel R., and Richard M. Ryan. "Object Relations and Ego Development: Comparison and Correlates in Middle Childhood." *Journal of Personality* 56, no. 3 (1988): 547–69.

Baldwin, Alfred L., Clara Baldwin, and Robert E. Cole. "Stress-Resistant Families and Stress-Resistant Children." In *Risk and Protective Factors in the Development of Psychopathology*, edited by Jon Rolf, Ann S. Masten, Dante Cicchetti, Keith H. Nüechterlein, and Sheldon Weintraub. New York: Cambridge University Press, 1990.

Barber, Heather, Holly Sukhi, and Sally A. White. "The Influence of Parent-Coaches on Participant Motivation and Competitive Anxiety in Youth Sport Participants." *Journal of Sports Behavior* 22 (1999): 162–76.

———. "The Influence of Parent-Coaches on Participant Motivation and Competitive Anxiety in Youth Sport Participants." *Journal of Sport Behavior* 22 (1999): 162–76.

Barrett, Paul H., Peter J. Gautrey, Sandra Herbert, David Kohn, and Sydney Smith, ed., *Charles Darwin's Notebooks, 1836–1844*. Ithaca, New York: Cornell University Press, 1987.

Barron, Frank. "Putting Creativity to Work." In *The Nature of Creativity*, edited by Robert J. Sternberg. New York: Cambridge University Press, 1988.

Bartels, Andreas, and Semir Zeki. "The Neural Correlates of Maternal and Romantic Love." *NeuroImage* 21 (2004): 1155–66. Available online at http://www.science direct.com.

Bates, John E. "The Concept of Difficult Temperament." *Merrill-Palmer Quarterly* 26 (1980): 299–319.

Beiswenger, Krista L., and Wendy S. Grolnick. "Interpersonal and Intrapersonal Factors Associated with Adolescents' Autonomy in After-School Activities." Unpublished manuscript. Worcester, MA: Clark University, 2007.

Bianchi, Suzanne M., John P. Robinson, and Melissa A. Milkie. *Changing Rhythms of American Family Life*. New York: Russell Sage Foundation Publications, 2006.

Blakeslee, Sandra. "A Small Part of the Brain, and Its Profound Effects." *New York Times*, February 6, 2007. http://select.nytimes.com/search/restricted/article?res =F30612FB385B0C758CDDAB0894DF404482 (accessed May 11, 2007).

Boggiano, Ann K., Marty Barrett, Anne Weiher, Gary H. McClelland, and Cynthia M. Lusk. "Use of the Maximal-Operant Principle to Motivate Children's Intrinsic Interest." *Journal of Personality and Social Psychology* 53 (1987): 866–79.

Brown, Barbara A., Gail Frankel, and Marilyn P. Fennell. "Hugs or Shrugs: Parental and Peer Influence on Continuity of Involvement in Sport by Female Adolescents." *Sex Roles* 20, nos. 7–8 (1989): 397–412.

Chao, Ruth K. "Beyond Parental Control and Authoritarian Parenting Style: Understanding Chinese Parenting through the Cultural Notion of Training." *Child Development* 65 (1994): 1111–19.

Chen, Xinyen, Qi Dong, and Hong Zhou. "Authoritative and Authoritarian Parenting Practices and Social and School Performance in Chinese Children." *International Journal of Behavioral Development* 21 (1997): 855–73.

Chin, Dorothy, and Velma A. Kameoka. "Sociocultural Influences." In *Comprehensive Handbook of Personality and Psychopathology*," 2nd ed., edited by Frank Andrasik. Hoboken, NJ: Wiley, 2006.

Chiu, L. H. "Child Rearing Attitudes of Chinese, Chinese-American, and Anglo-American Mothers." *International Journal of Psychology* 22 (1987): 409–19.

Clifford, Margaret M. "Effect of Competition as a Motivational Technique in the Classroom." *American Educational Research Journal* 9 (1972): 123–37.

Cohen, Margaret W., Andrea M. Emrich, and Richard deCharms. "Training Teachers to Enhance Personal Causation in Students." *Interchange* 7, no. 1 (1976–1977).

Cohn, D'vera. "Do Parents Spend Enough Time with their Children?" Population Reference Bureau. http://www.prb.org/Articles/2007/DoParentsSpendEnoughTimeWithTheirChildren.aspx (accessed May 15, 2007).

Collins, Mary Ann, and Teresa M. Amabile, "Motivation and Creativity." In *Handbook of Creativity*, edited by Robert J. Sternberg. New York: Cambridge University Press, 1999.

Crocker, Jennifer, and Lora E. Park. "The Costly Pursuit of Self-esteem," *Psychological Bulletin* 130 (2004): 392–414.

Csikszentmihalyi, Mihaly. *Finding Flow: The Psychology of Engagement in Everyday Life.* New York: Basic Books, 1997.

———. *Creativity: Flow and the Psychology of Discovery and Invention.* New York: Harper Perennial, 1996.

———. *The Evolving Self.* New York: HarperCollins, 1993.

Dawber, Tess T., and Leon Kuczynski. "The Question of Ownness: The Influence of Relationship Context on Parental Socialization Strategies." *Journal of Social and Personal Relationships* 16 (1999): 475–93.

deCharms, Richard. "From Pawns to Origins: Toward Self-Motivation." In *Psychology and Educational Practice*, edited by G. Lesser. Glenview, IL: Scott, Foresman and Co., 1968.

———. *Enhancing Motivation: Change in the Classroom.* New York: Irvington Publishers, 1976.

Deci, Edward L. "Effects of Externally Mediated Rewards in Intrinsic Motivation." *Journal of Personality and Social Psychology* 18 (1971): 105–15.

———. *Intrinsic Motivation.* New York: Plenum, 1975.

Deci, Edward L., and R. M. Ryan. *Intrinsic Motivation and Self-Determination in Human Behavior.* New York: Plenum, 1985.

Deci, Edward L., Allen J. Schwartz, Louise Sheinman, and Richard M. Ryan. "An Instrument to Assess Adults' Orientations to Control versus Autonomy with Children: Reflections on Intrinsic Motivation and Perceived Competence." *Journal of Educational Psychology* 73, no. 5 (1981): 642–50.

Deci, Edward L., Gregory Betley, James Kahle, Linda Abrams, and Joseph Porac.

"When Trying to Win: Competition and Intrinsic Motivation." *Personality and Social Psychology Bulletin* 7 (1981): 79–83.

Deci, Edward L., John Nezlek, and Louise Sheinman. "Characteristics of the Rewarder and Intrinsic Motivation of the Rewardee." *Journal of Personality and Social Psychology* 40, no. 1 (1981): 1–10.

Deci, Edward L., Robert E. Driver, Lucinda Hotchkiss, Robert J. Robbins, and Ilona Wilson. "The Relations of Mothers' Controlling Vocalizations to Children's Intrinsic Motivation." *Journal of Experimental Child Psychology* 55 (1993): 151–62.

Dillon, Sam. "A Great Year for Ivy League Colleges, but Not So Good for Applicants to Them." *New York Times*, April 4, 2007.

Dreifus, Claudia. "He Turned His Nobel into a Prize for Women." Interview with Paul Greengard, Nobel winner in physiology or medicine. *New York Times*, September 26, 2006.

Dweck, Carol. *Self Theories: Their Role in Motivation, Personality, and Development.* New York: Psychology Press, 1999.

Egan, Timothy. "Little Asia on the Hill." *New York Times*, January 7, 2007.

Ewing, Martha E., and Vern Seefeldt. "Participation and Attrition Patterns in American Agency-Sponsored and Interscholastic Sports—An Executive Summary." Study funded by the Athletic Footwear Council, Sporting Goods Manufacturer's Association, 1988.

Gee, James Paul. "The Classroom of Popular Culture: What Video Games Can Teach Us about Making Students Want to Learn." *Harvard Education Letter* (November/December 2005): 6–8.

Gibbs, Nancy. "Parents Behaving Badly." *Time.com*, February 13, 2005. http://www.time.com/time/magazine/article/0,9171,1027485,00.html (accessed May 15, 2007).

Gibson, Eleanor J., and Richard D. Walk. "The 'Visual Cliff.'" *Scientific American* 202 (1960): 64–71.

Gill, D. L., J. Gross, and S. Huddleston. "Participation Motivation in Youth Sports." *International Journal of Sports Psychology* 14 (1983): 1–4.

Ginott, Haim. *Between Parent and Child: New Solutions to Old Problems.* New York: Macmillan Company, 1965.

Golden, Daniel. *The Price of Admission: How America's Ruling Class Buys Its Way into Elite Colleges—and Who Gets Left outside the Gates.* New York: Crown Publishing Group, 2006.

Gottfried, Adele E. "Academic Intrinsic Motivation in Elementary and Junior High School Students." *Journal of Educational Psychology* 77 (1985): 631–45.

Green, Jesse. "The Making of an Ice Princess." *New York Times Magazine*, December 18, 2005.

Grolnick, Wendy, and Richard M. Ryan. "Parent Styles Associated with Children's Self-Regulation and Competence in School." *Journal of Educational Psychology* 81 (1989): 143–54.

———. "Autonomy in Children's Learning: An Experimental and Individual Difference Investigation." *Journal of Personality and Social Psychology* 52 (1987): 890–98.

Grolnick, Wendy S., and Maria L. Slowiaczek. "Parents' Involvement in Children's Schooling: A Multidimensional Conceptualization and Motivational Model." *Child Development* 65 (1994): 237–52.

Grolnick, Wendy S., Ann Frodi, and Lisa J. Bridges. "Maternal Control Style and the Mastery Motivation of One-Year-Olds." *Infant Mental Health Journal* 5 (1985): 15–23.

Grolnick, Wendy S., Caroline O. Kurowski, Kelly G. Dunlap, and Cheryl Hevey. "Parental Resources and the Transition to Junior High." *Journal of Research on Adolescence* 10 (2000): 465–80.

Grolnick, Wendy S., Carrie E. Price, Krista L. Beiswenger, and Christine C. Sauck. "Evaluative Pressure in Parents: Effects of Situation, Maternal and Child Characteristics on Autonomy-Supportive versus Controlling Behavior." *Developmental Psychology* 43 (2007): 991–1002.

Grolnick, Wendy S., Laura Weiss, Lee McKenzie, and Jeffrey Wrightman. "Contextual, Cognitive, and Adolescent Factors Associated with Parenting in Adolescence." *Journal of Youth and Adolescence* 25 (1996): 33–54.

Grolnick, Wendy S., Suzanne T. Gurland, Wendy DeCourcey, and Karen Jacob. "Antecedents and Consequences of Mothers' Autonomy Support: An Experimental Investigation." *Developmental Psychology* 38 (2002): 143–55.

Gurland, Suzanne T., and Wendy S. Grolnick. "Children's Expectancies and Perceptions of Adults: Effects on Rapport." *Child Development* 74 (2003): 1212–24.

———. "Perceived Threat, Controlling Parenting, and Children's Achievement Orientations." *Motivation and Emotion* 29 (2003): 103–21.

Harlow, Harry F., Margaret K. Harlow, and Donald R. Meyer. "Learning Motivated by a Manipulation Drive." *Journal of Experimental Psychology* 40 (1950): 228–34.

Hellstedt, Jon C. "Early Adolescent Perceptions of Parental Pressure in the Sport Environment." *Journal of Sports Behavior* 13 (1990): 135–44.

Hellstedt, Jon C., Daniel S. Rooks, David G. Watson, and Virginia M. Kimball. *On the Sidelines: Decisions, Skills, and Training in Youth Sports.* Amherst, MA: Human Resource Development, 1988.

Helmreich, Robert L., William Beane, G. William Lucker, and Janet T. Spence. "Achievement Motivation and Scientific Attainment." *Personality and Social Psychology Bulletin* 4 (1978): 222–26.

Henderson, Anne T., and Karen L. Mapp. *A New Wave of Evidence: The Impact of School, Family, and Community Connections on Student Achievement.* Austin, TX: Southwest Educational Development Laboratory, 2002.

Henderson, Anne T., Karen L. Mapp, Vivian R. Johnson, and Don Davies. *Beyond the Bake Sale: The Essential Guide to Family-School Partnerships.* New York: New Press, 2007.

Hennessey, Beth A. "The Social Psychology of Creativity." *Scandinavian Journal of Educational Research* 47, no. 3 (2003): 259–60.

"Historical Income Tables—Families." US Census Bureau. http://www.census.gov/hhes/www/income/histinc/f09ar.html (accessed April 29, 2007).

Hull, Clark. *Principles of Behavior.* New York: Appleton-Century-Crofts, 1943.

Hunter, Jeremy P., and Mihalyi Csikszentmihalyi. "The Positive Psychology of Interested Adolescents." *Journal of Youth and Adolescence* 32, no. 1 (2003): 27–35.

James, William. *Principles of Psychology.* 1890. http://psychclassics.yorku.ca/James/Principles/index.htm (accessed May 14, 2007).

Johnson, David W., and Roger T. Johnson. "Toward a Cooperative Effort." *Educational Leadership* 46 (1989): 80–81.

Johnson, David, and Roger Johnson. "The Socialization and Achievement Crisis: Are Cooperative Learning Experiences the Solution?" In *Applied Social Psychology Annual 4*, edited by Leonard Bickman. Beverly Hills, CA: Sage, 1983.

Johnson, Earvin "Magic," with William Novak. *My Life.* New York: Random House, 1992.

Jones, Patti. "Seven Educators Come Clean about Their Own Kids' Homework." *Working Mother Magazine*, September 2003.

Kast, Audrey, and Kathleen Connor. "Sex and Age Differences in Response to Informational and Controlling Feedback." *Personality and Social Psychology Bulletin* 14 (1988): 514–23.

Katz, Idit, and Avi Assor. "Choice and the Need for Autonomy: A Cross-Cultural Investigation of Various Aspects of Autonomy Support." Unpublished manuscript. Ben-Gurion University: Israel, 2005.

Kochanska, Grazyna. "Children's Interpersonal Influence with Mothers and Peers." *Developmental Psychology* 28, no. 3 (1992): 491–99.

Koestner, Richard, Richard M. Ryan, Frank J. Bernieri, and Katherine Holt. "Setting Limits on Children's Behavior: The Differential Effects of Controlling versus Informational Styles on Intrinsic Motivation and Creativity." *Journal of Personality* 52 (1984): 244–48.

Kohn, Alfie. "Only for *My* Kid: How Privileged Parents Undermine School Reform." *Phi Delta Kappan*, April 1998, 569–77. http://www.alfiekohn.org/teaching/ofmk.htm.

———. *The Case against Competition.* New York: Houghton Mifflin, 1992.

Labaree, David F. *How to Succeed in School without Really Learning: The Credentials Race in American Education.* New Haven, CT: Yale University Press, 1997.

Lareau, Annette. *Unequal Childhoods: Class, Race, and Family Life.* Berkeley: University of California Press, 2003.

Lin, C. C., and V. R. Fiu. "A Comparison of Child-Rearing Practices among Chinese, Immigrant Chinese, and Caucasian-American Parents." *Child Development* 61 (1990): 429–33.

MacKinnon, Donald W. "The Nature and Nurture of Creative Talent." *American Psychologist* 17 (1962): 484–95.

Mahoney, Joseph L., Angel L. Harris, and Jacquelynne S. Eccles. "Organized Activity Participation, Positive Youth Development, and the Overscheduling Hypothesis." *Social Policy Report, Society for Research in Child Development* 20, no. 4 (August 2006).

Manderlink, George, and Judith M. Harackiewicz. "Proximal vs. Distal Goal Setting and Intrinsic Motivation." *Journal of Personality and Social Psychology* 47 (1984): 918–28.

Martens, Rainer. *Joy and Sadness in Children's Sports.* Champaign, IL: Human Kinetics Publishers, 1978.

McGraw, Kenneth O., and John C. McCullers. "Evidence of a Detrimental Effect of Extrinsic Incentives on Breaking a Mental Set." *Journal of Experimental Social Psychology* 15 (1979): 285–94.

Meltzoff, Andrew, and Keith M. Moore. "Imitation in Newborn Infants: Exploring the Range of Gestures Imitated and the Underlying Mechanisms." *Developmental Psychology* 25 (1989): 954–62.

Miller, Alice. *Prisoners of Childhood: The Drama of the Gifted Child and the Search for the True Self.* New York: Basic Books, 1981.

Minuchin, Salvador. *Families and Family Therapy.* Oxford, England: Harvard University Press, 1974.

"Mom Confessions: Baby Smarts, Bragging, and More." *Parenting* magazine, September 2006.

Nehring, Christine. Review of "Mating in Captivity: Reconciling the Erotic and the Domestic," by Esther Perel. "Of Sex and Marriage." *Atlantic Monthly,* December 2006. http://www.theatlantic.com/doc/200612/nehring-sex (accessed May 10, 2007).

Nesse, Randolph M. "The Smoke Detector Principle: Natural Selection and the Regulation of Defensive Responses." *Annals of the New York Academy of Sciences* 935 (2001): 75–85.

Nicholls, John G. "Achievement Motivation: Concepts of Ability, Subjective Experience, Task Choice, and Performance." *Psychological Review* 91 (1984): 328–46.

Nicholls, John, and Arlen Miller. "Reasoning about the Ability of Self and Others: A Developmental Study." *Child Development* 55 (1984): 1990–99.

Nicholls, John G., Michael Patashnick, and Susan B. Nolen. "Adolescents' Theories of Education." *Journal of Educational Psychology* 77 (1985): 683–92.

Nissen, Henry. "A Study of Exploratory Behavior in the White Rat by Means of the Obstruction Method." *Journal of Genetic Psychology* 37 (1930): 361–76.

Pear, Robert. "Married and Single Parents Spending More Time with Children, Study Finds." *New York Times,* October 17, 2006.

Pelletier, Luc G., Michelle Fortier, Robert J. Vallerand, Kim M. Tuson, Nathalie M. Brière, and Marc R. Blais. "Toward a New Measure of Intrinsic Motivation,

Extrinsic Motivation, and Amotivation in Sports: The Sport Motivation Sale (SMS)." *Journal of Sport and Exercise Psychology* 17 (1996): 35–54.

Reeve, Johnmarshall, and Edward L. Deci. "Elements of the Competitive Situation That Affect Intrinsic Motivation." *Personality and Social Psychology Bulletin* 22 (1996): 24–33.

Richtel, Matt. "School Cellphone Bans Topple (You Can't Suspend Everyone)." *New York Times*, September 29, 2004, p. 1.

Rivera, Carla. "Tutors Prepare Them—for Preschool and Kindergarten." *Los Angeles Times*, September 24, 2006.

Roan, Shari. "Narrowing the Field." *Los Angeles Times*, October 2, 2006.

Rohner, Ronald P., and Sandra M. Pettengill. "Perceived Parental Acceptance-Rejection and Parental Control among Korean Adolescents." *Child Development* 56 (1985): 524–28.

Rosten, Leo. *The Joys of Yiddish.* New York: McGraw-Hill, 1968.

Ruble, Diane, Ann Boggiano, Nina S. Feldman, and Judith H. Loebl. "Developmental Analysis of the Role of Social Comparison in Self-Evaluation." *Developmental Psychology* 16, no. 2 (March 1980): 105–15.

Ryan, Richard M., James P. Connell, and Robert W. Plant. "Emotions in Nondirected Text Learning." *Learning and Individual Differences* 2 (1990): 1–17.

Ryan, Richard M., and James P. Connell. "Perceived Locus of Causality and Internalization: Examining Reasons for Acting in Two Domains." *Journal of Personality and Social Psychology* 57, no. 5 (1989): 749–61.

Ryan, Richard M., C. Scott Rigby, and Andrew Przybylski. "The Motivational Pull of Video Games: A Self-Determination Theory Approach." *Motivation and Emotion* 30, no. 4 (2006): 355.

Samuelson, Robert J. "Prestige Panic: Too Many Parents Are Pushing Kids to Get an Elite Degree Even Though It's No Guarantee of Success in Later Life." *Newsweek*, August 21–28, 2006. http://www.msnbc.msn.com/id/14325089/site/newsweek/ (accessed April 27, 2007).

Sanders, Summer. *Champions Are Raised, Not Born: How My Parents Made Me a Success.* New York: Delacorte, 1999.

Saulny, Susan. "In Baby Boomlet, Preschool Derby Is the Fiercest Yet." *New York Times*, March 3, 2006.

Sherrod, Lonnie, ed. *Social Policy Report* of the Society for Research in Child Development. In Mahoney et al., "Organized Activity," p. 2.

Silverstein, Stuart. "Seniors Hedge College Bets, but Now It's Time to Choose." *Los Angeles Times*, April 24, 2005.

Sorce, James F., Robert M. Emde, Joseph J. Campos, and Mary D. Klinnert. "Maternal Emotional Signaling: Its Effects on the Visual Cliff Behavior of One-Year-Olds." *Developmental Psychology* 21 (1985): 195–200.

Springer, Steve. "Could It Be Magic?" *Los Angeles Times,* June 5, 2002, p. D1.

Steinberg, Laurence. *10 Basic Principles of Good Parenting.* New York: Simon and Schuster, 2004.

———. *Beyond the Classroom.* New York: Simon and Schuster, 1996.

Steinberg, Laurence, Susie Lamborn, Sanford Dornbusch, and Nancy Darling. "Impact of Parenting Practices on Adolescent Achievement: Authoritative Parenting, School Involvement, and Encouragement to Succeed." *Child Development* 63 (1992): 1266–81.

Stipek, Deborah. *Motivation to Learn: From Theory to Practice.* 3rd ed. Needham Heights, MA: Allyn and Bacon, 1998.

Sui-Chu, Esther Ho, and J. Douglas Willms. "Effects of Parental Involvement on Eighth-Grade Achievement." *Sociology of Education* 69 (April 1996): 126–41.

Swann, William B., and Thane S. Pittman. "Initiating Play Activity of Children: The Moderating Influence of Verbal Cues on Intrinsic Motivation." *Child Development* 48 (1977): 1128–32.

Talbot, Margaret. "A Stepford for Our Times." *Atlantic Monthly,* December 2003. http://www.theatlantic.com/doc/200312/talbot (accessed May 10, 2007).

Tavris, Carol. "Deconstructing Harry." *American Scientist Online* (March–April 2003). http://www.americanscientist.org/template/BookReviewTypeDetail/assetid/17 181;jsessionid=baa9 (accessed May 11, 2007). Review of Deborah Blum's *Love at Goon Park: Harry Harlow and the Science of Affection,* a biography of Harlow (New York: Perseus Publishing, 2002).

Trivers, Robert. "Parental Investment and Sexual Selection." In *Sexual Selection and the Descent of Man,* edited by Bernard Campbell. Chicago: Aldine de Gruyter, 1972.

Ueland, Brenda. *Tell Me More.* Tucson: Kore Press, 1998.

USA Today/NBC poll as reported in Mike Dodd, "Children Say Having Fun Is No. 1." *USA Today,* September 13, 1990.

Vallerand, Robert J., and Greg Reid. "On the Causal Effects of Perceived Competence on Intrinsic Motivation: A Test of Cognitive Evaluation Theory." *Journal of Sport Psychology* 6 (1984): 94–102.

Walker, Lawrence J., and John H. Taylor. "Family Interaction and the Development of Moral Reasoning." *Child Development* 62 (1991): 264–83.

Walker-Andrews, Arlene, and Wendy S. Grolnick. "Discrimination of Vocal Expressions by Young Infants." *Infant Behavior and Development* 61 (1983): 491–98.

Wankel, Leonard M., and Philip Kreisel. "An Investigation of Factors Influencing Sport Enjoyment across Sport and Age Groups." Paper presented at the North American Society for the Psychology of Sport and Physical Activity conference. College Park, MD: April 1982.

Warner, Judith. "The Nation: Kids Gone Wild." *New York Times,* November 27, 2005.

Weisfeld, Glenn. "The Benefits of Nausea." Letter to the *New York Times,* October 31, 2006, p. D4.

Weiss, Laura A., and Wendy S. Grolnick. "The Roles of Parental Involvement and Support for Autonomy in Adolescent Symptomatology." Paper presented at the biennial meeting of the Society for Research in Child Development. Seattle, WA: April 1991.

White, Robert. "Motivation Reconsidered: The Concept of Competence." *Psychological Review* 66 (1959): 297–333.

Whybrow, Peter C. *American Mania.* New York: W. W. Norton and Co., 2005.

Williams, Kipling D., and Steven J. Karau. "Social Loafing and Social Compensation: The Effects of Expectation of Co-Worker Performance." *Journal of Personality and Social Psychology* 61 (1991): 570–81.

Wilson, Edward O. "Problems without Borders." *Vanity Fair,* May 2007, 164.

———. *Naturalist.* Washington, DC: Island Press, 1994.

———. *Sociobiology: The New Synthesis,* 25th anniversary ed. Cambridge, MA: Belknap Press of Harvard University Press, 2000.

Wiseman, Rosalind, with Elizabeth Rapoport. *Queen Bee Moms and Kingpin Dads: Dealing with the Parents, Teachers, Coaches, and Counselors Who Can Make—or Break—Your Child's Future.* New York: Crown Publishers, 2006.

Wolff, Rick. *Good Sports.* Champaign, IL: Sports Publishing, 1997.

Wright, Robert. *The Moral Animal: Evolutionary Psychology and Everyday Life.* New York: Vintage Books, 1994.

INDEX

Page numbers in *italic* indicate boxed and shaded materials.

"ability grouping," 182note

"About Me" questionnaires, 99–100, 104

academics. *See* schools

achievements, *173*

and autonomy, 135–38

and inner passion, 111–12

linking love to, 171–72

acknowledging child's feelings, 141, 146, 147, 149–53, 192, 207, *230*

ACTH, 74

"acting out," 260n18

Adams, Anne, 121–22, 168

adversity, gaining from, 226–27

African American families, *183*, 186note

Aguilar family (Susan, Bill, and Sam), 143–46, 147

allopaternal care, 252n11

Allport, Gordon W., 102

Amabile, Teresa, 117–19, 120, 126, 140, 166–67, *168*

Amateur Athletic Union, 41

American Idol (TV show), 42, 122

American Psychological Association, 15

American Youth Soccer Organization (AYSO), 39, 50

Ames, Carole and Russell, 59–60

anger, *179*

in children, 92, 130, 133, *142*, 151, 207, 212

parental, 13, 26, 38, 215, 227, 260n10

turning into rage, 35–36

Annenberg Institute for School Reform, Community Involvement Program, 180

anxiety, 18, 26–27, 176, 185, 260n18, 262n1

avoiding looking for disasters, 223–29

benefits of sharing with others, 222

channeling into rules and guidelines, 203–18

and competition, 27, 57, 238–41

contagiousness of, 36–37, 239–40, 241–42

and parents, 33–35, 37–40

physical feelings, 30–31, 219–22

separation anxiety, 80–82

value of, 84–86
ways to calm, 122, 219–44
See also Pressured Parent Phenome-
    non; stress; worry
Araton, Harvey, 115–16
Armstrong, Michael, 248n15
Aronson, Elliott, 68
arts, 121
    competition in, 55–56, 193–94
    research projects, 155–56, 158–60, 164,
        166–67
    See also creativity; music; theater pro-
        grams, competition in
Ashburn, Virginia, *183*
Asian cultures, 114note, 260n10
    and parenting, 30, 34, *145–46*, 179–80
Assor, Avi, 156–57, 172
AT&T, 49, 248n15
attachment theory, 11
Attention Deficit Hyperactivity Dis-
    order, 143
authority, 132, 135, 197, 204, 210
autonomy, 12, *94*, 100, 103, 126–28,
        129–47, 184–85, *201*, 243
    child's need for, 92
    vs. control, 132–35. *See also* control
    impact on relations with child, 141–43
    importance of language, 158–60
    importance of relevance, 156–57, 207
    need for, 110
    research projects on, 141–42
    in sports, 160–62
    and structure, 206–207. *See also* structure
    and video games, *127*
    ways to encourage, 138–39, 149–73,
        208–10
    See also choices, allowing child to have
Averbuch family (Gloria and Yael),
    115–16

Avery, Rachel Robb, 141
avoidance of pain, 108
awards, parents' need for child to
    receive, 71–72
AYSO. *See* American Youth Soccer Orga-
    nization

Baby Milestone Game, 45
baby talk, 80
Baldwin, Alfred and Clara, 217–18
Barber, Heather, 187–88
Bard College, 237–38
Bartels, Andreas, 80
Bates, John E., 98
behavioral problems, 185, 260n18
behaviorism, 108
Beledius spectabilis, 83–84
Bianchi, Suzanne, *188–89*
biological needs, 108
Boggiana, Ann, 163–64
bonding with children, 80
bragging, role of love in, *82–83*
Branch family (Felecia and Alanna), *154*
breathing and calmness, 221
Breitweiser family (David and Josh), 72,
    73
Brenner family (Rachel, Tom, and
    Noah), 227–29, 242
Brown, Barbara A., 187
burnout, 161, 189–91
Burrows family (Steve, Joan, Mark, Jed),
    243–44

calmness, creating, 219–44
Campbell, Kelly, 96
Carpenter, Gabrielle D., *183*
Carson, Loretta, 50
cartoons
    autonomy, *94*

competition to get into best preschool, *46*

cell phones, 81, 252n19

challenges, 70, 113, 119, 120, *121*, *127*, 137

   in applying Three-Part Framework, 219–43

   "optimal challenge," 156

change, *225*, *231*

Chao, Ruth, *145–46*

character development, 233–36

cheating, 65–66, 70, 124–25, 235, 250n41

Chen, Xinyin, *146*

Child and Family Development Laboratory (Clark University), 14

child prodigies, *121*

Chin, Dorothy, *146*

Chinese culture, 114note

   and parenting, *145–46*

choices

   allowing child to have, 146, 147, 155–58, 208–10

   having limits, 213

   "illusion" of choice, 155–56

   importance of relevance, *157*, 157–58, 207

   meaningful choices, 156–57

   misusing of, 157–58

   reasonable choices, 157

   See also autonomy; decisions, allowing child to participate in

Citigroup, 49, 248n15

Clarfield, Ingrid, 67, 171–72, 195

Clark University, Child and Family Development Laboratory, 14

Clifford, Margaret M., 59

Club 2012, *183*

coaches and coaching, 26, 35, 38–40, 51, 52, 53, 63, 65, 69, 161, 187–88, 190, 235

coerced motivation, 123–24, 125, 126

cognitive therapy, 221, 262n1

collective vs. individual, 30

college

   anxiety about child getting into, 163, 181, *200*, 223, 224, 236–38, 240, 241–42

   rejections, 31–32, 237–38

Collins, Mary Ann, 120

Community Involvement Program (Annenberg Institute for School Reform), 180

comparing self to others, 47–48

competence, 110, 126, 128, 167, 204, 209, 216

   children choosing competence boosters, 156

   incompetence, 60

   restrictive parents and kids' competence, 217–18

   and video games, *127*

competition, 59–60, 122

   alternative to, 67–69

   and anxiety, 27, 57, 238–41

   and elementary school children, 47–48

   getting into right school, 45, 50, 163, 181, *200*, 223, 224, 236–38, 241–42, *243–44*

   hypercompetition, 53–54

   kids feelings about, 41–70

   national and international competitions, 55, 69–70, 195

   negative effects of, 58–60, 64–66

   and parents, 99–100, 102–104, 231–36

   parents feeling competitive, 13–14, 30–31, 32–35, 55, 71–72, 193–94

positive effects of, 66–67
pressure and, 61–63
thrill of, 32
"concerted cultivation," 43
conditional love, 172
connection, 126, 128
and video games, *127*
consequences, 96, 128, 144, 147, 204, 205,
    206, 209, 210, 211–12, 215, 216, 218
See also rules, children's need for
contagiousness of anxiety. *See* anxiety
control
    vs. autonomy, 132–35. *See also*
        autonomy
    vs. in control, 134–35
    in dangerous neighborhoods, 217–18
    parents helping vs. taking over, 10–11,
        91–105, 110, 153–54, *154*, 242–43.
        See also ego involvement of par-
        ents
        causes of parents taking control,
            28–30
        control through misuse of choice,
            157–58
        impact on relations with child,
            141–43, *142*
        language and control, 158–60
        praise as a control of child, 170–71
        research projects on, 9, 12, 92–93,
            135–36, 137–38
        science fairs, 191–93
        when to intervene, 227–29
    perception of in Asian cultures,
        145–46
    Queen Bee mothers, 181, 260n13
    vs. structure, 206–207. *See also* struc-
        ture
cooperation as alternative to competi-
    tion, 67–69

coping with setbacks, 225–26
Cortez, Eliane, 52
corticotophin, 74
creativity, 117–22, *121*, 140
    impact of controlling language on,
        159
    and love, 120, 256n31
    research projects on, 118–19, 120
    spoiled by rewards, 166–67
    See also inner passion
Crocker, Jennifer, 102
Csikszentmihalyi, Mihaly, 117, *121*, *123*
curiosity, 107, 108–10, 118

Damasio, Antonio, 115
Dancing With the Stars (TV show), 32
dangerous neighborhoods, 217–18
Dansville (New York) study, 93, 137,
    139, 177, 178, 205
Darrah, Chuck, 43
Dart, Greta and Jim, 175–76
Darwin, Charles, 75, 78
Davidson family (Stewart, Joyce, and
    Matt), 189–91
Dawber, Tess, 77
deadlines, meeting, 126
deCharms, Richard, 114–15, 156
Deci, Ed, 11–12, 58, 59, 61–62, 110, 136,
    164
decisions, allowing child to participate
    in, 129–47
    See also choices, allowing child to have;
        problem solving
defense mechanism, 85
demographics and sports competition, 54
Dennis family (Leslie and Maya), 54, 71,
    111–12, *142*, *179*, 222, 226–27, 241
depression, 117, 185, 260n18, 262n1
depth perception of babies, 10

Diamond, Jared, 229

difficult children, parental response to, 98

disagreements, empathy during, 152

Docter family (Bill, Marie, and Devon), 55

Doman, Glen, 35

dopamine, 80

drama. *See* theater programs, competition in

Drama of the Gifted Child, The (Miller), 15, 29

Dreamgirls (movie), 122

"drives," biological, 108

drop outs, 60

Dweck, Carol, 113

Eagle Ridge Middle School (Ashburn, Virginia), *183*

Edison, Thomas, 170

Effort, Learning, and Mistakes are OK. *See* ELM tree method

ego involvement of parents, 100–105, 135–36, 234, 246n3

   impact of modern urban life on, 105

elementary schools

   competition in, 47–48

   parent involvement with, 184

ELM tree method, 236

emotions

   emotional health, 125

   enhancing rational thought, 115

   See also feelings

empathy, 141, 146, 147, 149–53, 192, 207, *230*

encouraging vs. pushing kids, 19–20

enjoyment, 116–17

   and children's inner passion, 111–15

   vs. competition, 58–59

flow, 120, *121*

   and intrinsic motivation, 111–15, *157*, 195, 232

   as motivation for learning, 112–13

enmeshment, 29–30

ethics. *See* cheating

evolutionary aspects of parenting, 74–78, 87, 252–53n26

   fathers, 78–79

   genetic basis of, 83–87

   role of love in, 79–83, *82–83*

examples

   Aguilar family (Susan, Bill, and Sam), 143–46, 147

   Averbuch family (Gloria and Yael), 115–16

   Branch family (Felecia and Alanna), *154*

   Breitweiser family (David and Josh), 72, 73

   Brenner family (Rachel, Tom, and Noah), 227–29, 242

   Burrows family (Steve, Joan, Mark, Jed), *243–44*

   Cortez, Eliane, 52

   Davidson family (Stewart, Joyce, and Matt), 189–91

   Dennis family (Leslie and Maya), 54, 71, 111–12, *142*, *179*, 222, 226–27, 241

   Docter family (Bill, Marie, and Devon), 55

   Garfield family (Ellen, Steve, and Jack), 81, 86, 87–88

   Grolnick family (Allison and Rebecca)

      Allison, 13, 66, 162–63

      Rebecca, 13, *82*, 133

   Hoffman family (Marcia and Mark), 225

   Hughes family (John, Emily, and Sarah), 101

Janet and Kristin, 52

Kelly family (Gina, Danielle, Brandon, and Nicole)
Brandon, 41–42
Danielle, 41, 57, 82
Nicole, 30, 42, 74, 82

Miller family (Beth, Mike, and Jennifer), 13, 129–31

Notley family (Cynthia, Kevin, and Lauren)
Kevin, 233–34
Lauren, 194

Pollard family (Lucy, Rich and Travis), 37–40

Seal family (Jeff and Zach)
Jeff, 17–18, 37, 84
Zach, 17–18, 71, 84, 91–92, 110, 149, 153–54, 192–93, 210

Shellenberger family (Laurie and Oliver), 86–87

Weiler family (Michelle and Megan), 132–33

Wexler, Erin, 237–38, 242

Willie and Sophie, 95

excessive defense mechanism, 85

exercise and calmness, 220–21

expectations, 19, 135, 139, 180, 182, 185, 191, 203–18, 260n10

exploration, 107

extrinsic motivation, 121, 168

failures turned into successes, 37–40

fathers, 78–79, 252n11
Club 2012, *183*
father-blaming, 72
guilt about lack of involvement, *189*
narcissistic fathers, 28–29
See also involvement, parental; parent-child interaction

Federal Department of Education, 44

feedback, 140, 209, 213–14, 235–36

feelings
acknowledging child's feelings, 141, 146, 147, 149–53, 192, 207, *230*
emotional health, 125
enhancing rational thought, 115

Fermat, Pierre de, 119, 255n28

FIRST Robotics Competion, 69

flexibility, 166, 226
flexible thinking, 165
in structure, 210–11

"flight-or-fight," 30, 73–74, 92

flow, 120, *121*

"fostered relevance," 156–57

FPSP. *See* Future Problem Solving Program

Frankl, Evie, 182

free play, *200*

Frey, Gerhard, 255n28

Frodi, Ann, 11

Future Problem Solving Program, 69, 120

Garfield family (Ellen, Steve, and Jack), 81, 86, 87–88

Gee, James Paul, *127*

"genius" grants, *168*

Gibson, Eleanore "Jackie," 9–10

Ginott, Haim, 151, 171, 212

goals
long-term, *231*, 232–33
short-term, 232–33

Golden, Daniel, *145*

Gottfried, Adele Eskeles, 113

grades in school
getting good grades, 113–15
grade grubbers, 48

Grease (musical), 194

Grey's Anatomy (TV show), 94–97

Grolnick family (Allison and Rebecca)
  Allison, 13, 66, 162–63
  Rebecca, 13, *82*, 133
Grubman, Jack B., 49, 248n15
grudges, parents feeling, 31
guilt about parental involvement, 178–
  79, *188–89*
"guilty" motivation. *See* introjected
  motivation
Guns, Germs, and Steel (Diamond), 229
"gun to the head." *See* coerced motivation

"habituation paradigm," 10
Hall, G. Stanley, 15
"hands on" vs. "hands off" parenting, 16,
  132, 135
happiness and intrinsic motivation,
  116–17. *See also* enjoyment
"Happy Cube" puzzles, 61
Harackiewicz, Judith, 232
hardwiring of parents, 71–89, 92, 93, 99,
  101, 105, 110, 122, 191, 220, 223
Harlow, Harry, 107–10, 112
"helicopter parents," 177
helping
  vs. taking over, 10–11, 91–105, 110,
    153–54, *154. See also* ego involve-
    ment of parents
  causes of parents taking control,
    28–30
  control through misuse of choice,
    157–58
  fighting desire to take over, 242–43
  impact on relations with child, 141–
    43, *142*
  language and control, 158–60
  praise as a control of child, 170–71
  research projects on, 9, 12, 92–93,
    135–36, 137–38

science fairs, 191–93
when to intervene, 227–29
ways to help, 139–41
Helreich, Robert L., 69–70
Hemiptera insects, 75, 251n2
Henderson, Anne T., 180–81
Hennessey, Beth, 168–69
high expectations, 19, 180, 182, 260n10
"high investment parenting," 76–77
high schools
  competition in, 48–49
  high school graduates, statistics on, 43,
    44, 247n3
  parent involvement with, 185–86
  Report Card on Ethics of American
    Youth (Josephson Institute), 65,
    250n41
Hoffman family (Marcia and Mark), 225
Holloway, Wanda, 36
homework assignments, 150, 163, 185,
  186
  child's reasons for doing, 124, 125, 216
  parents involvement, 13, 132, 137,
    143–46, 178, 179, *183*, 197–98,
    215–16, 221
  temptation to take over, 92, *154*
  ways to help, 139–41
  stress caused by, 35, 86
  timing of, 138–39, 144, 147, 151, 157,
    160, 205, 209
honoring the game, 234–35
"hovering" over children, 177
Hudson, Jennifer, 122
Hughes family (John, Emily, and Sarah),
  101
"Hugs or Shrugs" study, 187
hunger, 108
Hunter, J. P., 117
hypercompetition, 53–54

identified ("I agree") motivation, 123–26

"illusion" of choice, 155–56

immunizing child against positive poisons, 168–69

inborn talents, 113–15, 114note

incentives, disadvantages of rewards as, 162–69

incompetence, 60

independence, 132, *146*, 185

individuals

children as, 28–29

collective vs. individual, 30

inner passion, 12, 107–28

discovering, *123*

learning for its own sake, 113–15

spoiled by rewards, 164

See also enjoyment; intrinsic motivation

intellectual involvement, 178

intelligence, growth of, 113–15, 114note

"intensive parenting," *189*

interdependence, *146*

internal distress, 260n18

internalization, 123–28

and structure, 216–17

internal reward system, 80–83

intervention, 227–29

intrinsic motivation, 11–12, 61–62, 111, *123*, 129–47, 242

and creativity, 117–22

and enjoyment, 111–15, *157*, 195, 232

and flow, 120, *121*

and happiness, 116–17

learning behavior of primates, 108–10

stifling of, 92–93, 133

and structure, 216

ways to encourage, 126, 136, 209

See also inner passion

introjected motivation, 124, 125, 126

investment in parenting, 76

involvement, parental, 127, 128, 178, 260n18

ego involvement of parents, 100–105

false danger of "overinvolvement," 177–78

maximizing parental involvement, 175–201

with older children, 183–85

schools, 178–79, *179*, 180–87, 196

Asian parents and, 179–80, 260n10

science fairs, 191–93

sports, 187–88

coaching of teams, 187–88

ways to be more involved, 199

time parents spend, *188–89*

ways to increase parental involvement, 195–99

Iowa Test of Basic Skills, 115

Irving, John, 120

"It takes a village," *183*

Jabobson, Edmund, 221

Jack London Youth Soccer Club, 161–62

James, Lebron, 53

James, William, 9–10, 102

Japanese culture, 114note

and parenting, 34

"jigsaw method" of teaching, 68

Johnson, David, 67

Johnson, Earvin, Sr., 175

Johnson, Magic (Earvin, Jr.), 175–76

Jordan, Michael, 64

Josephson Institiue of Ethics

Report Card on Ethics of American Youth, 65, 250n41

Josephson Institute of Ethics, 65, 235

junior high schools. *See* middle school/junior high

Kast, Audrey, 171
Kelly family (Gina, Danielle, Brandon,
    and Nicole)
  Brandon, 41–42
  Danielle, 41, 57, 82
  Nicole, 30, 42, 74, 82
kindergarten
  competition, 47
  empathy in, 150
  "red-shirting," 37, 246–47n9
Koestner, Richard, 158
Kohn, Alfie, 64, 92
Korean culture and parenting, *146*
"K-selected" parenting patterns, 76
Kumon programs, 36, 47

Labaree, David, 50
Lang Lang, 171–72
language, 229
  babies learning, 80, 252n16
  of control, 158–60
  noncontrolling language, 160
  ways to explain limits, 212
Lareau, Annette, 43
laughter, importance of, 222
Laureyssens, Dirk, 61
learning for its own sake. *See* inner
    passion
Learning Gap, The (Stigler and
    Stevenson), 114note
Lepper, Mark, 164
life's lessons learned through sports, 234,
    236
limits, 212–13
listening, 131, 199
Little Shop of Horrors (musical), 56
long-term goals, *231*, 232–33
love, 79–83
  importance of in creativity, 120, 256n31

price of, *173*
and pride, *82–83*
unconditional love, 171–73
of work, 120
Luczynski, Leon, 77

MacArthur, Robert, 75–76
MacArthur Foundation, *168*
Magrath, Jane, 195
Mahoney, Joseph L., *200–201*
Manderlink, George, 232
Mang, Rosita, 56, 59, *134*, *173*
manipulation, 162–64, 167–69, *168*
  through misuse of choice, 157–58
Maslow, Abraham, 102
Mazur, Barry, 255n28
McCullers, John, 165
MCEF. *See* Montgomery County Educa-
    tion Forum
McGraw, Kenneth, 165
meaningful choices, 156–57
middle school/junior high, 184–85
  competition in, 48–49
Miller, Alice, 15, 29
Miller family (Beth, Mike, and Jennifer),
    13, 129–31
misbehavior in children, 77
Monday Night Football (TV show), 144,
    147
monkeys, learning behavior of, 108–10
Montgomery County Education Forum,
    182
moral values, 233–36
mothers
  mother-blaming, 14–15, 72
  narcissistic mothers, 15, 28–29
  single mothers, *188–89*
  See also involvement, parental; parent-
    child interaction

motivation, 123–28, 204, 215–17, 256n31
of behavior, 108
dampened by competition, 58–59
impact of autonomy on, 135–38
See also coerced motivation; extrinsic
motivation; identified ("I agree")
motivation; intrinsic motivation;
introjected motivation; rewards
motivational psychology, 210
mountains into molehills, *230*
muscle relaxation, 221–22
music, 171–72
being pushed too hard, *134*
competition in, 55–56, 66–67, 69–70,
173, 195
examples, 59
intrinsic motivation in, 121–22
parents getting involved, 198–99
Music Teachers National Association,
62
My Man Godfrey (movie), 205, 212

NAACP, 182
naches, 105
narcissistic parents, 15, 28–29
national and international competitions,
55, 69–70, 195
National Education Longitudinal Study,
179
natural selection, 85
needs, biological, 108
negative feedback, 213–14
negotiation, 209, 210–11
NELS. *See* National Education Longitudinal Study
Nesse, Randolph, 84–85
Newsweek (magazine), 27
New York Times (newspaper), *83*
Nicholls, John, 47

noncontrolling language, 160
Notley family (Cynthia, Kevin, and
Lauren), 56
Kevin, 233–34
Lauren, 194
nurturing, 141–42

"optimal challenge," 156
Origin of Species (Darwin), 75
Orlick, Terry, 51
overachievers, 48
"overinvolvement," 177–78
overreaction, 83–87
overscheduling, *200–201*

Padesky, Christine A., 221, 226, 262n1
Pajama Game, The (musical), 194
panic, parental, 37–40
parental investment, 76
parental involvement, 127, 128, 260n18
ego involvement of parents, 100–105,
135–36
false danger of "overinvolvement,"
177–78
intellectual involvement, 178
maximizing parental involvement,
175–201
with older children, 183–85
personal involvement, 178
schools, 178–79, *179*, 180–87, 196
and Asian parents, 179–80, 260n10
science fairs, 191–93
sports, 187–88
coaching of teams, 187–88
ways to be more involved, 199
time parents spend, *188–89*
ways to increase parental involvement,
195–99
parent-blaming, 72

parent-child interaction, 11
  allopaternal care, 252n11
  children internalizing parents' values,
    123–28
  hardwiring of parents, 71–89, 92, 93,
    99, 101, 105, 110, 122, 191, 220,
    223
  misbehavior in children, 77
  parents helping vs. taking over, 10–11,
    91–105, 110, 153–54, *154*, 242–43
    causes of parents taking control,
      28–30
    control through misuse of choice,
      157–58
    impact on relations with child,
      141–43, *142*
    language and control, 158–60
    praise as a control of child, 170–71
    research projects on, 9, 12, 92–93,
      135–36, 137–38
    science fairs, 191–93
    when to intervene, 227–29
  parent using child to gain satisfaction,
    246n3
  protecting children, 81–82
Parenting (magazine), *82*
parenting styles
  "concerted cultivation," 43
  evolutionary aspects of parenting,
    74–78
    fathers, 78–79
    genetic basis of, 83–87
    role of love in, 79–83, *82–83*
  "hands on" vs. "hands off," 16
  "intensive parenting," *189*
  "K-selected" parenting patterns, 76
  in other cultures, 30, 34, *145–46*, 179–80
  "r-selected" parenting patterns, 76,
    251n2

Structured and unstructured, 205–206
  using different style for different chil-
    dren, 97–98
parent-teacher conferences, 28, 178
  anxiety caused by, 87–88
Park, Lora E., 102
parochial schools. *See* private and
    parochial schools
patience, 96, 122
PCA. *See* Positive Coaching Alliance
peer influence, 186note
Pelletier, Luc, 116
*People's History of the United States: 1492 to
    Present, A* (Zinn), 229
performing arts. *See* music; theater
    programs
Perry, Jim, 53, 60, 63–64
persistence, 48, 110, 114, 129, 136, 170,
    212, 236
personal involvement, 178
physical exercise and calmness, 220–21
Poch, Bruce, 65
point of view, recognizing child's, 141,
    146, 147, 149–53, 192, 207, *230*
Pollard family (Lucy, Rich and Travis),
    37–40
Positive Coaching Alliance, 53, 63, 199,
    235, 236
positive feedback, 213–14, 235–36
positive poisons, 162–69
potty training, 162–63
Power of Negative Thinking, The, 222
PPP. *See* Pressured Parent Phenomenon
praise, use of, 48, 88, 149, 162, 169–71, 236
preschools
  competition to get into best, 33, 49,
    248n15
  feeling need to put child into, 72, 73
pressure

and competition, 61–63
pressure point, 104
pressuring children, 110
reducing, 161
and short-term goals, 232–33
Pressured Parent Phenomenon, 26–27,
    153–54, 176
antidotes to
    intrinsic motivation as, 111, 122
    ways for parents to be, 241–42
challenges to overcome, 219–44
channeling into structure, 208–10
contagiousness of, 36–37
    ways to fight, 240
hardwiring of parents, 71–89
physical feelings, 30–31, 219–22
roots of, 74–78
stress and, 28
See also anxiety; control; Three-Part
    Framework
*Price of Admission: How America's Ruling
    Class Buys Its Way Into Elite Colleges—
    And Who Gets Left Outside the Gates,
    The* (Golden), *145*
pride, *173*
    and love, *82–83*
Principles of Psychology (James), 102
private and parochial schools, competi-
    tion to get into best, 45, 50, *243–44*
problem solving, 243
    children doing, 122, 146, 147
    undermined by rewards, 165–66
    using to get child to do homework,
        143–46
    ways to encourage, 153–54
protecting children, 81–82
Przybylski, Andrew, *127*
purpose, sense of, *183*
pushiness, 14, 28, 34–35, 159, 160

pushing vs. encouraging kids, 19–20
puzzles and competition, research pro-
    jects on, 11–12, 58, 60, 61–62, 164

"quality time," *188*
*Queen Bee Moms and Kingpin Dads: Dealing
    with the Parents, Teachers, Coaches, and
    Counselors Who Can Make—or
    Break—Your Child's Future*
    (Wiseman), 181
Queen Bee mothers, 181, 260n13

rage, crimes of, 35–36
reasonable choices, 157
"red-shirting" in kindergarten, 37,
    246–47n9
Reed, John, 248n15
Reeve, Johnmarshall, 61
relaxation
    and long-term goals, 232–33
    relaxed breathing and calmness, 221
relevance, importance of, 156–57, *157*, 207
Report Card on Ethics of American
    Youth (Josephson Institute), 250n41
research projects
    "About Me" questionnaires, 99–100, 104
    Asian cultures and control, *146*
    on autonomy, 141–42
    children choosing competence
        boosters, 156
    on creativity, 118–19, 120
    Dansville (New York) study, 93, 137,
        139, 177, 178, 205
    ego involvement of parents, 102–103
    enjoyment as motivation for learning,
        112–13
    on explaining relevance, 156–57
    Grolnick's on babies and mothers, 9,
        12, 92–93, 135–36

"Hugs or Shrugs" study, 187
impact of controlling language, 158–60
impact of short-term goals, 232
on importance of feedback, 213–14
on kinds of motivation, 125–26
learning behavior of primates, 108–10
on moral reasoning, 233
on multinational research and development, 247n7
National Education Longitudinal Study, 179
on parent involvement, 184, 186, 187, 187–88, *188–89*
parents helping vs. taking over, 9, 12, 92–93, 135–36, 137–38
puzzles and competition, 11–12, 58, 60, 61–62, 164
restrictive parents and kids' competence, 217–18
on rewards, 163–64, 165–67, 168–69
studying intrinsic motivation, 117
survey of afterschool activities, *200–201*
on use of praise, 171
on value of video games, *127*
"visual cliff" experiment, 10, 11
resentment, 111, 133, 159, 179
resilience, 125, 126, 225–26
responsibility, child developing sense of, 94–95, 131, 135, 138–39, 147, *154*, 178, 210, 216, 218, 231–32, 234
rewards
distracting rather than motivating, 12, 18, 109–10, 162–69, *168*
internal reward system, 80–83
research projects on use of, 163–64, 165–66, 168–69
spoiling creativity, 166–67
use of praise, 169–71

when to use, 167–68
positive uses, *168*
Ribet, Ken, 255n28
Rigby, Scott, *127*
Rogers, Carl, 102
Rohner, Ronald P., *146*
Rorty, Richard, 227–29
Rosenbaum, Linda, 150–51
rove beetles, parenting of, 83–84
"r-selected" parenting patterns, 76, 251n2
Rubin, Vera, *123*
rules, children's need for, 135, 203–18, 211–12
dangerous neighborhoods requiring more parental control, 217–18
providing reasons for, 207
See also consequences
runaway train, 223, *230*
Ryan, Rich, 11–12, 92, 112, 125, *127*, 165–66

Sanders, Summer, 116
Sapolsky, Robert, 74
schools, 179–80
banning cell phones, 81, 252n19
college
high stress of choosing, 236–38
rejections, 31–32, 237–38
competition, 46–49
children competing in academics, 42
to get into the best schools, 45, 50, 237–38, *243–44*
parents feeling competitive, 32–33
elementary schools
competition in, 47–48
parent involvement with, 184
helping children find programs, 132–33
high schools

competition in, 48–49
  high school graduates, statistics on,
    43, 44
  parent involvement with, 185–86
"jigsaw method" of teaching, 68
middle school/junior high, 184–85
  competition in, 48–49
parent involvement with, 178–79, *179*,
    180–87, 196
  Asian parents, 179–80, 260n10
  science fairs, 191–93
private and parochial schools, 50, *243–
  44*
special programs, 181–82
  competition to get into the best, 86–
    87
structure in, 218
See also homework assignments; sports
science fairs, 191–93
Seal family (Jeff and Zach)
  Jeff, 17–18, 37, 84
  Zach, 17–18, 71, 84, 91–92, 110, 149,
    153–54, 192–93, 210
self-confidence, 82, 113–15, 232
Self-Determination Theory, 19
self-esteem, 27, 54, 67, 102, 117, 170,
    177, 184–85, 242
  of parents, 29, 101, 104, 239, 240. *See
    also* ego involvement of parents
self-image, 129, *183*
self-worth, 137, 171, *183*, 185
separation anxiety, 80–82
Serre, Jean-Pierre, 255n28
sex, 108
shame
  kids feeling, 172
  parents feeling, 33–35, 72
Shellenberger family (Laurie and
  Oliver), 86–87

Shepherd-Look, Dee, 65, *230–31*
Shors, Tracey, 78
short-term goals, 232–33
Show Biz Moms and Dads (TV show), 35
Silent Saturdays Movement, 161–62
silver linings, *230*
skills learned through sports, 234,
    235–36
"smoke detector principle," 84–85
social dilemmas, 100
Sociobiology: The New Synthesis (Wilson),
    75
Spitzer, Eliot, 248n15
sports
  building skills, 234, 235–36
  burnout, 189–91
  competition
    children dropping out of sports, 60
    children's competitive standing in,
      41–42, 50–51
    demographics and sports competi-
      tion, 54
    making children anxious, 57
    parents feeling stress, 74, 84
  failures turned into successes, 37–40
  honoring the game, 234–35
  intrinsic motivation and, 115–16
  kids having fun before there was com-
    petition, 63
  learning life's lessons, 234, 236
  parent involvement with, 187–88
    coaching of teams, 187–88
    parental competitive feelings, 52
    ways to be more involved, 199
  professionalization of youth sports,
    53–54
  Silent Saturdays Movement, 161–62
  supporting autonomy, 160–62
Sports Illustrated (magazine), 235

Sports Moms and Dads (TV show), 35

stage. *See* theater programs, competition in

Star Wars civilization, 87, 252–53n26

Steinberg, Laurence, 179, 186, 196

Stevenson, Harold, 114note

Stigler, James W., 114note

stress, 28, 74, 84

    learning to deal with, 236–38

    and parents taking over for kids, 94–97

    response to, 73

    See also anxiety; Pressured Parent

        Phenomenon; worry

structure, 19, 127, 128, 203–18

    with autonomy, 207

    vs. control, 206–207

    flexibility in, 210–11

    includes consequences, 211–12

    kids reactions to, 215–17

    limits, 212–13

    ways to set up, 207, 208–10

    See also expectations

Stump, Linda, 62

successes, failures turned into, 37–40

Sui-Chu, Esther Ho, 179

Suite Life of Zack and Cody, The (TV

    show), 144

Swann, William B., 155

taking over, parents, 10–11, 91–105, 110,

    153–54, *154*, 242–43

    causes of, 28–30

    control through misuse of choice,

        157–58

    impact on relations with child, 141–

        43, *142*

    language and control, 158–60

    praise as a control of child, 170–71

    research projects on, 9, 12, 92–93,

        135–36, 137–38

science fairs, 191–93

    when to intervene, 227–29

    See also ego involvement of parents

Tale of Two Cities, A (Dickens), 131

Taylor, Richard, 255n28

teenagers, 60, 65, 98, 117, *121*

    parent involvement with, *146*, 185–86,

        186note

"Tell-Me-More" attitude, 199

"Tell Me More: On the Fine Art of Lis-

    tening" (Ueland), 199

theater programs, competition in, 56,

    193–94

thirst, 108

Thompson, Jim, 53, 199, 235

Thompson, Michael, 81

Three-Part Framework, 98, 107–10, 127,

    131, 173, 176, 204

    ways to apply, 219–44

    See also autonomy; intrinsic motiva-

        tion; involvement, parental;

        structure

Time (magazine), 177

Torrance, E. Paul, 120

"tracking," 182, 182note

Trivers, Robert, 76

trust, 218

TV reality shows and competition

    American Idol, 42, 122

    Dancing With the Stars, 32

    Show Biz Moms and Dads, 35

    Sports Moms and Dads, 35

Ueland, Brenda, 199

unconditional love, 171–73

underachievers, 48

unspoken expectations, 17, 214–15

Vallerand, Robert J., 213–14

video games, *127*
  parents getting involved, 196–97
  ways to encourage children to do
    homework instead, 143–46
"visual cliff" experiment, 10, 11
volition. *See* autonomy

Walker, Lawrence J., 233
Walker-Andrews, Arlene, 10
Wall Street Journal (newspaper), 35, 49
Watson, John, 170
Weiler family (Michelle and Megan),
    132–33
Weill, Sanford I, 49, 248n15
West, Mike, 55
Wexler, Erin, 237–38, 242
"What Teachers Hate about Parents"
    (*Time*), 177
White, Robert, 107, 110
Whybrow, Peter C., 44
Wiles, Andrew, 255n28
Willie and Sophie, 95
Wilson, Edward O., 75–76, 87
winning, 47, 59, 168, *173*

importance of, 27, 64
making winning less important, 52, 60,
    66, 198, 234
positive feedback of, 58
pressure to win, 61–63, 64, 65, 70, 121,
    188, 235
Wiseman, Rosalind, 181
Wolff, Rick, 51
workplace, future of for children, 44,
    247n7
worry
  contagiousness of, 241–42
  managing, 223–29
  See also anxiety; Pressured Parent Phe-
    nomenon; stress
worst case scenario, fear of, 223–29

Yee, Juliet, *145–46*
Young Artists Piano Competition, 195

Zeki, Semir, 80
Zhang, Raymond, 195
Zinn, Howard, 229